STŪPA AND ITS TECHNOLOGY:
A TIBETO-BUDDHIST PERSPECTIVE

A unique structure of Stūpa located below the Hemis monastery.
Probably, a Khang bu brtegs pa for storing tsha tsha.

STŪPA AND ITS TECHNOLOGY:
A Tibeto-Buddhist Perspective

By
PEMA DORJEE

Foreword by
M.C. Joshi

INDIRA GANDHI NATIONAL CENTRE FOR THE ARTS
NEW DELHI
AND
MOTILAL BANARSIDASS PUBLISHERS PRIVATE L
DELHI

First Edition: Delhi, 1996
Reprint: Delhi, 2001

Published by
INDIRA GANDHI NATIONAL CENTRE FOR THE ARTS
Central Vista, Janpath, New Delhi-110 001
in association with
MOTILAL BANARSIDASS PUBLISHERS PRIVATE LIMITED
Bungalow Road, Jawahar Nagar, Delhi-110 007

ISBN: 81-208-1301-4
Price: Rs. 550

Printed in India
at Shri Jainendra Press
A-45, Naraina Industrial Area, Phase-I,
New Delhi-110 028

Dedicated
to
Our Beloved Leader
His Holiness The 14th Dalai Lama
Ngawang Lobsang Tenzin Gyatso

Now a days this doctrine of Lord Śākya-muni, diminishes day by day like a pond whose tributary streams have dried up. The brilliant ones should understand this plight and those who desire liberation must strive [for its preservation].

Śākya Paṇḍita

The Indira Gandhi National Centre for the Arts is deeply grateful to Venerable Doboom Tulku, Director, Tibet House, New Delhi, the Cultural Institution by H.H. the Dalai Lama, for graciously agreeing to allow the Centre to publish Mr. Pema Dorjee's thesis entitled STŪPA AND ITS TECHNOLOGY: A TIBETO-BUDDHIST PERSPECTIVE. The research was undertaken by the author when he was the first awardee of Thonmi Sambhota Research Fellow (Instituted by) Tibet House.

Foreword

Generally associated with Buddhism, stūpa had a pre-Buddhist origin. According to ancient tradition its other synonyms are *caitya* and *dhātugarbha* in Sanskrit or *dāgobā* in Sinhalese. Literally stūpa denotes a made up heap of earth or of any other materials to serve a specific purpose. In the *Ṛgveda*, a collection of flames of fire has been styled as stūpa (VII. 2. 11). It seems that the stūpa has its origin in the form of an altar (*citi*) or a tumulus piled at site of a funeral pyre (*citā*) as some kind of memorial with a tree or a wooden post planted in its centre, and on this account it was also called a *caitya*, the tree on it as *caitya-vṛkṣa* and the post as *caitya-yūpa*. The *Śatapatha-brāhmaṇa* speaks about circular (*parimaṇḍala*) and quadrangular (*catusśrakti*) *caityas* which were perhaps being raised traditionally as the memorials for departed personages of significant status. The same test also mentions that the circular variety of the *caityas* was popular with the easterner *prācyas* or the people of eastern India. Regarding the tradition of non-Buddhist stūpa, an interesting example is seen in a Sanchi relief depicting *Jaṭila* ascetics engaged in fire-sacrifies with stūpas (without any crowning member) in the background suggesting their connection with *Jaṭila* cult of Brahmanical origin.

The term *dhātugarbha* refers to a construction serving as a repository of *dhātus* or corporeal relics. The ancient practice of erecting the *caityas* for the dead is also confirmed by a statement attributed to Buddha following an enquiry by Ānanda, his favourite disciple, in connection with the disposal of his own body after his passing away as indicated in *Mahāparinibbāna-sutta*. According to this reference Buddha told Ānanda that following the cremation of his body a stūpa should be constructed on his mortal remains at the meeting points of four roads (*catuṣpatha*) in the same manner in which the *cakravartins* or the great rulers of yore (a *catummahepatharāñño cakkavattissa thūpaṁ karonti*) had been honoured by raising a memorial stūpa. After his *parinibbāna* (decease), Buddha's bodily relics were divided into eight parts amongst various ruling clans, viz., the Mallas of Kuśīnagara and Pāvā, Licchavīs of Vaiśālī, Śākyas of Kapilavastu, Koliyas of Rāmagrāma, Bulīs of Allakappa and Brāhmaṇas of Veṭṭhadvīpa and Ajātaśatru, the king of Magadha; all of whom erected stūpas over their share of relics in their respective localities according to Pali traditions.

It is also recorded in the same source that Brāhmaṇa Droṇa, who was also a devotee of Buddha, built a stūpa enshrining the jar in which relics were kept before their division, and Mauryas of Pipplivana erected a stūpa on charcoal remains collected from the site of Buddha's cremation. The available archaeological evidence reveals that the early Buddhist stūpas, which were made of earth had a circular plan, possibly with a peaked elevation but other details about them cannot be clearly ascertained.

On the basis of data available, it has been suggested that the stūpas were constructed by the Buddhists not only over the bodily relics of Buddha and Buddhist saints but also as commemorative monuments connected with a particular event or over the objects of religious significance associated with Buddha. With the passage of time, the practice of erecting stūpas with or without relics or even drawing just their outline on a wall or elsewhere was considered to be an act of great piety, and numerous votive stūpas of various sizes were thus brought into existence as sacred offerings at the centres of pilgrimage.

Interestingly, one of the epigraphs of Emperor Aśoka mentions that during his fourteenth regnal year, he doubled (enlarged) the stūpa of Kanakamuni, the fifth human (*mānuṣī*) Buddha before Śākyamuni, the seventh one in the line. According to northern Buddhist tradition, Aśoka is said to have constructed 84,000 stūpas over the fragments of the *dhātus* (relics) of Buddha after unearthing them from the earlier stūpas, redistributing and re-enshrining them in different parts of the country. The tradition attributing to Aśoka the erection of 84,000 stūpas on the *dhātus* of Buddha seems to be somewhat exaggerated but not totally devoid of truth. There is indirect evidence to show that

Dharmarājikā stūpas at Sarnath and Taxila and original stūpa at Sanchi and elsewhere were certainly built by Aśoka.

The idea to preserve the mortal remains of a person fully or partially in a structural memorial was most likely based on the age-old concept of sympathetic magic conditioned by the belief of inseparability of connections between an organism and its constituents, even after the former had become lifeless or detached from its original form. The bodily relics of Buddha and his living personality thus had an inseparable relation to each other, suggesting that every bit of his bone represented the eternal presence of the Master through each stūpa raised on his remains. Aśoka's attempts to establish more stūpas with fragments of Buddha's original *dhātus* seems to have been solely guided by the belief that every Buddhist intending to worship the stūpa in his locality must feel the living presence of the Master therein.

Architecturally, early standardized form of a stūpa consisted of a solid dome (*aṇḍa*) placed on a raised base (*medhi*) in one or two stages and topped by a railed enclosure (*harmikā*) containing centrally a rod or post (*yaṣṭi*) supporting umbrellas (*chatrāvali*). Very often it was surrounded by one or two railed circumambulatories (*pradakṣiṇāpathas*), as offering salutations with folded hands and going round the stūpa (*pradakṣiṇā*) was a part of its ritual worship. It was also propitiated with offerings of *gandha* (scented paste), fragrant flower-garlands, and various other presents, (cf. *Aśokāvadāna*: '*......sugandhi-puṣpa-mālyagandhalepaiḥ sarvopahāraiḥ sthaviro-paguptam abhyarcya.....*')

With the growth of Buddhism in the course of time, the early structural model of stūpa or *caitya* underwent gradual architectural transformation in various regions of India and elsewhere. Penetration of Buddhism in Sri Lanka, Central Asian, South-East Asian and East Asian countries besides Nepal and Tibet was followed by the transmission of the religio-cultural traditions, concepts, and forms of Buddhist architecture including the stūpa from their birth place to these foreign lands, where these were preserved, adapted and developed in accordance with local requirements, beliefs and taste.

The present work by a young researcher Shri Pema Dorjee *"Stūpa and its Technology : A Tibeto-Buddhist Perspective,"* which is being brought out under the Kalāsamālocana Series by the Indira Gandhi National Centre for the Arts (IGNCA) is a significant contribution to Buddhist studies. It brings to light interesting facets of stūpa construction and some of its hitherto little known aspects including associated rituals and traditions. Buddhism with its evolved Mahāyāno-Vajrayānic form reached Tibet or Bhoṭa mainly from eastern India around the seventh century A.D. With the introduction of Buddhism in Bhoṭa (Tibet), a cultural communication commenced between Tibet and India which continued for several centuries.

Tibetan Buddhist monks and successive generations of disciples took special care to preserve the basic tenets and characteristics of Buddhism. However, it was adapted to local needs within Tibet's own colourful cultural aesthetic norms sustained through political patronage and socio-religious institutions. As in the case of many other countries of Asia, the religious order founded by Buddha, continues till today as a living faith amongst Tibetans.

Tibeto-Buddhist traditions carry a special significance in the context of ancient Indian culture, as much of that, which has been forgotten or lost in the terms of Buddhist traditions and Sanskritic Buddhist literature in India, is preserved by Tibetans in the form of texts, sacred hymns, thought and religious practices.

Shri Dorjee studies and discusses the Tibetan Vinaya text and commentaries on them pertaining to the stūpas and their varieties and rituals and concepts associated with their construction besides surviving stūpas in upper Indus Valley in Ladakh region of India. He presents important data on the Buddhist structural tradition treating stūpa as the *dharmakāya* (cosmic body) of Buddha.

The contents of Pema Dorjee's work acquire great significance if these are assessed in the light of the tradition and history of Buddhist stūpa in India as known to us. According to the Tibetan texts, as recorded by the present author, stūpas in India were built during the life-time of Buddha by Anāthapiṇḍika, the famous merchant prince of Śrāvastī, the capital of Kośala country. He specially cites the example of the stūpa raised on the relics of Śāriputra, one of the principal disciples of Buddha, containing a stepped-base, a *kumbha*-shaped (pitcher-like) elevation topped with a *yaṣṭi* (rod) and *chatra*. This tradition is also confirmed by Pali texts relating to Thervāda Buddhism. On the basis of Tibetan texts, e.g., *Dul ba lung rnam'byed (Vinaya-kṣudraka vastu)*; *Li yul lung bstan pa* (*Kaṁśadiśavyākaraṇa*); *Mchod rten gyi cha dbye ba'dul pa las byung ba' imdo (Caitya-vibhaṅga Vinayoddhṛta Sūtra)*; and *Byababsdus Pa* (*Kriyāsaṁgraha*); and stūpa construction manuals of Desid and Kongtul, Dorjee refers to other varieties of stūpas viz., associated variously with Tathāgata (Buddha), Pratyeka Buddha, Buddhist devotees classed as *Śrotāpanna, Sakṛdāgāmin, Anāgāmin* and *Arhat* (in accordance with their stages of mental elevation) and *Śrāvakas* (monastic followers), each with its own distinguishing features. Several other structural types of stūpa with specific religious associations are also mentioned in the Tibetan tradition like the one resembling a heap of grains, an alms bowl, a vase, victory-banner or a pillar besides a form called *gandhakuṭī* which appears to be a structure containing a stūpa within.

In the present context, it is relevant to cite an interesting reference, to an Indian rock-cut cave styled as *gandhakuṭī,* in an inscription at Ajanta (Cave 17), which mainly records the construction of a *vihāra,* i.e. Cave 17 itself. In this case the term *gandhakuṭi* seems to refer to the adjoining *caitya* hall (Cave 19) with a tallish stūpa inside.

In the Tibetan Buddhist tradition three varieties of stūpa classed under Mahāyāna type, according to Nāgārjuna, as recorded by Dorjee, are stated to be of the form of an inverted bowl, a tiny-house and group of eight-stūpas. Some of these types can still be seen in Tibet and its neighbouring areas including Ladakh.

In the Tibetan Buddhist tradition, however, the names of the sites wherein original stūpas were built on mortal relics of Buddha are different than those found in the Pali texts as already mentioned above.

Shri Dorjee also makes a reference to two more interesting varieties of stūpa: one simulating a raised post or column and the other a structure with multiple auspicious doors. We do not have any example of the former type extant in India but Minār-i-Cakrī in Afghanistan, which is known as a pre-Islamic Buddhist monument (*minār*), may represent a post like stūpa recorded in the Tibetan tradition. It is possible that the origin of such a structure could have links with Vedic concept of *skambha* (a pillar like structure) which was perhaps adapted by the Buddhists. The other variety stated to have multiple doors, with some surviving specimens in Ladakh, appears to have had its origin in the terraced stūpas of India, of which a fine example could be observed in the ancient structure at Sarnath called Caukhaṇḍi stūpa. This type travelled to South East Asia and culminated in Borobudur with additions and modifications. A noteworthy feature found in the elevational treatment of some of the stūpas of Ladakh area is their striking similarity with the *pīḍhā* type of spires containing a pyramidal body of receding stepped-mouldings of the Orissan temples suggesting some close cultural links between Orissan and Indo-Tibetan structural tradition.

The author of the present monograph also gives some details of rituals associated with the construction and consecration of the stūpas as prescribed in the Tibetan versions of two main texts, *Vimaloṣṇīṣa* and *Raśmivimala*, originally Sanskrit works written in India but now lost. Most of the rites and rituals are closely interlinked with Buddhist Tāntricism, and these are to be conducted by a highly qualified *Vajrācārya* (priest) having an expert knowledge of *mantras, mudrās* and principles of renunciation, Bodhicitta and *śūnyatā* (emptiness). The process of stūpa construction begins with the selection of site and ends with final consecration. To sanctify a stūpa, besides relics, scrolls and tablets containing *mantras/dhāriṇīs* written on them are also enshrined within it. Many features of these rituals including selection of the site etc., are comparable with the Āgamic tradition associated with temple building in India.

The author of the monograph visualizes the stūpa (*Mchod rten*) not in isolation as a structural entity but as a living phenomenon within a perspective of Tibeto-Buddhist tradition. Reflecting the temporal and supratemporal propensities of Buddhist devotees, the sacred presence of a *Mchod rten* or stūpa in a locality opens before us an integrated vision binding together, its concept, symbolism, philosophy, rituals combining the *mantra, mudrā, maṇḍala* and *upacāras* with the actual artistic form and guiding the worshipper from the earthly plane to the domain of eternal bliss. The idea is basically Indian but never applied to the Buddhist monuments of India so far. What is essential is now to assess and study the Buddhist architecture of Sanchi, Nagarjunakonda, Amarāvati etc., or some of the notable rock-cut caves with a multi-dimensional approach. In this context the Buddhist traditions extant in Sri Lanka, Nepal and South East-Asian and East-Asian Buddhist countries may provide us significant clues.

Shri Dorjee also throws light on various aspects of Buddhist stūpas of Tibetan structural affiliation like their proportions, forms, associated rites, rituals and various symbolic concepts. On structural symbolism of stūpa the writer brings to our notice different but interesting interpretations recorded in the Tibetan traditions (appendix 'D'), which are meaningful from the standpoint of Buddhist art and thought.

To carry out this research work on the stūpa architecture of Tibet as a doctoral dissertation, Shri Pema Dorjee was awarded the prestigious Thonmi Sambhota Fellowship by Tibet House. Ven. Duboom Tulku, the Director of Tibet House, New Delhi was mainly responsible for encouraging this research. Pema Dorjee worked under the able guidance and scholarly support from Ven. Prof. S. Rinpoche of the Central Institute of Higher Tibetan Studies, Sarnath. IGNCA expresses its deep gratitude to both of them.

Under the guidance of Dr. Kapila Vatsyayan, Academic Director of the Institution, IGNCA has initiated multi-dimensional studies in the arts. Monuments like the other arts are viewed as cultural symbols within a living tradition. Architecture is no longer seen merely as archaeological evidence of historical value. Instead, all its aspects are studied together. The two major projects, viz. the Bṛhadiśvara temple in Thanjavur in the south and Govindadeva shrine at Vrindavana in the north, have been launched with a multi-disciplinary approach. Soon the results of these studies will be published. Also IGNCA has published monographs solely devoted to architecture such as A.K. Coomaraswamy's *Essays in Early Indian Architecture*; Vasundhara Filliozat's *The Temple of Mukteśvara at Cauḍādānapura*, and Adam Hardy's *Indian Temple Architecture: Form and Transformation.*

IGNCA is naturally also interested in Buddhist art. It has already published the English translation of a Chinese book in the form of an illustrated volume on the art of the Buddhist caves at Dunhuang (China) entitled *Dunhuang Art from the Eyes of Duan Wengie.* IGNCA also proposes now to launch a new sub-series (under Kalāsamālocana Series) on the Buddhist stūpas which would not be restricted to India alone. Shortly, IGNCA will bring out Paul Mus' famous work on the Buddhist Stūpa at Burobudur which has been translated into English from original French. This was published several decades ago. In fact, IGNCA intends to bring out other works on the subject, particularly on the stūpas in different parts of Asia, so that interested art-historians and archaeologists can understand this important structural form in totality in relation to its wide geographical spread and the distinctive features of particular developments in different countries.

IGNCA is happy to publish the present monograph containing original Tibetan material properly edited, illustrated and commented upon by a young and promising researcher, Pema Dorjee.

We thank him, as also Ven. D. Tulku and Rev. S. Rinpoche. We are grateful to Dr. L.M. Gujral of IGNCA without whose help it may not have been possible to bring out this monograph.

M.C. Joshi
Member Secretary
Indira Gandhi National Centre for the Arts

New Delhi
8th August, 1995

Preface

Among all the religious monuments of the world, the stūpa has the longest uninterrupted historical development spanning more than 3 millenniums. The stūpa as a religious object was adopted and sanctified by the Buddha himself as his Truth Body (*Dharmakāya*). Even Lord proclaimed that Arhats, Bodhisattvas, and Tathāgatas are worthy of Stūpas, and that whoever may pay respects and understand this significance will experience furtherance in their minds. The stūpa then changed from a monument for the dead into a monument for the living. Over the course of time, more and more religious and spiritual values were added to it, so that it eventually was considered as a miniature of the entire cosmos. Stūpa architecutre went wherever Buddhism flourished, but it acquired various architectural shapes in different countries.

Most of the Asian Buddhist countries modelled their stūpas after the Indian prototype constructed at different stages of its development. Over time, the structural shape of the stūpa underwent significant modifications in India and abroad. The major factors responsible for the successive modification, embellishment and elaboration of the architecture of the diverse forms of stūpas all over the Buddhist countries were the characteristics of the particular prototype adopted and the architectonic skill of the inhabitants. In addition, the change in the socio-economic milieu and dominant religious outlook must have had something to do with this developmental trend.

Among the Buddhist countries, Tibet was the last country to be converted into and accept Buddhism as its state religion. In Tibet, the stūpa as an object of veneration was placed on equal footing with scriptures and images. The twilight of Buddhist culture in India was at the same time the dawning phase of Tibeto-Buddhist culture. The earnestness and the zeal of our predecessors made Tibet, the treasure-house and citadel of Buddhist culture and literature. The hallmark of Tibeto-Buddhist culture is that it preserved the Indian Buddhist culture in its purest form to the maximum possible extent, while later showing genius by developing it and giving it a specific salient feature. The same fact applies to the Tibeto-Buddhist stūpa architecture and its related literature. Generally, all the scholars unanimously believe that the Tibeto-Buddhist stūpa architecture developed from the stūpa of the Pala period. Similarly, text dealing with stūpa architecture, such as the Vimaloṣṇīṣa, which are no longer extant in India were translated into Tibetan, and later commentaries were written by Tibetan scholars to highlight the stūpa's religious significance. This practice stemmed from the need to avoid deformities in craftsmanship, and to maintain the architectural purity of the stūpa as a primary object of veneration.

The stūpa is one of the most important religious objects, especially in Vajrayāna. It has different levels of meanings in different fields. The literal meaning of the Tibetan word for stūpa or *caitya*, is *mchod rten*, which means "the receptacle of offerings." In fact, in Tibet, images, scriptures and stūpas were integrated into the religious trilogy of *sku* (physical body), *gsungs* (speech) and *thugs* (heart), respectively. But on deepest level, the stūpa symbolises the essence of the Tathāgata's Dharmakāya. Thus the structural components of the stūpa in ascending order were closely connected to the sequences of the Essence of Tathāgata's Dharmakāya.

The first chapter of this monograph was the subject of a paper presented under the title "Literary Background of the Architecture and Architectonic Principles of the Buddhist Stūpa," at the international seminar on "Buddhist Architecture and National Cultures in Asia," held in Varanasi in 1989. It deals with the literary sources of the architecture and architectonic principles of the Buddhist stūpa of which primary and secondary Buddhist literature is replete. In general, the chapter highlights important texts covering stūpa architecture, and is more comprehensive than the paper presented in the said seminar.

The second chapter deals with various ritual activities associated with the construction of the stūpa at three different stages—rites prior to the commencement of the construction, during the actual construction, and after the completion of the construction—under the title "The Ritualistic Way of Constructing the Tibeto-Buddhist Stūpa".

The third chapter deals with the eight fundamental types of Tibeto-Buddhist stūpas and their main structural components. Additionally, it includes the proportional differences as elucidated in various literary sources. A table has also been included to analyse the differences in data more easily.

The fourth chapter is a survey of stūpas found in the Upper Indus Valley which was once culturally akin to the Tibeto-Buddhist tradition. The leading archaeological specimens of various Tibeto-Buddhist stūpas as found in the Leh region, particularly between the Spituk and Hemis monasteries, are more viably investigated. The illustrations displayed in appropriate order are intended to document the monuments, and closely analyse their styles and conditions. The standing monuments in Ladakh, which are hitherto surviving precariously have not received much attention in the field of research and conservation as well.

The appendix contains the English translations of four important short Tibetan texts preceded by transliterations of their texts. The first two translation works, i.e. *Caitya vibhaṅga vinayoddhṛta sūtra* of Śāntigarbha and *Samanta mukha praveśa raśmi vimaloṣṇīṣa prabhāsa sarva tathāgata hṛdaya samaya vilokita nāma dhāraṇīvṛtti* of Sahajavilāsa, are respectively substantiated as primary sources for studying the various symbolic meanings and the proportional manual of the different parts of the Stūpa. Both translations are based on the Tibetan version of the lost Sanskrit originals available in the Tangyur Testament. The remaining two translated texts, originally composed by Buston Rinchendup and Desid Sangyas Gyatso, deal with the proportional manual of the Tibeto-Buddhist Stūpa architecture in minutest detail.

There has been worldwide interest in the study of the stūpa and its religious significances and technological aspects. This is due to the great role that the architectural developments of stūpa have played in Buddhist world throughout the course of history. The contribution of Tibetans to the above field has not received adequate attention in past researches. It was in this context that a few years back, Prof. S. Rinpoche, the Director of Central Institute of Higher Tibetan Studies and supervisor of this project advised me, to undertake the study of the Tibeto-Buddhist stūpa and its technology. Fortunately, the first Thonmi Sambhota Fellowship at the nick of time gave me the right impetus and sufficient means to fulfil this long cherished dream.

The area of this field is so vast and intricate that the study itself was an arduous task, and difficulties have been many. The work required a multi-disciplinary approach involving the fields of Archaeology, Tibetology, Architecture, and Religious Studies. Likewise, any Buddhist stūpa irrespective of its size and material is rather not considered with sanctity without enshrining relics inside the stūpa. Thus, relics virtually inherent to the stūpa is irrefutable, however, deliberately untouched here, because the theme required an indepth independent research—because of involvement of more religious and philosophical significances, values, etc. than the architectural standpoint.

It has been my experience that many important texts both of the primary and secondary nature referred to in the works of several later authors are rarely accessible even if extant. Insofar as the stūpa architecture is concerned, I have been vexed to find the appropriate words for some of the old archaic and symbolic meanings with their correct orthographical connotation.

There is a growing interest in Tibetan Buddhism and its cultural heritage, which is gradually tending to become an integral part of the all-inclusive world culture. It is my earnest hope that the present work will illuminate this previously untouched field eliminating the gap, and stimulate further interest and inquiry into the Tibeto-Buddhist Stūpa architecture as enshrined in the vast treasures of Tibetology and Buddhology.

PEMA DORJEE

New Delhi
April 1995

Acknowledgements

I take full responsibility for the outcome of this monograph, yet it is with a sense of gratitude that I acknowledge the following persons and institutions to whom I am particularly indebted. My contribution to this drop into the ocean of Tibetology would not have been possible without their valuable help and guidance.

Firstly, my inexpressible thanks are due to Ven. Duboom Tulku, Director of Tibet House, a Cultural Institute of H.H. The Dalai Lama, New Delhi for awarding me the first prestigious Thonmi Sambhota Fellowship under the auspices of Thonmi Sambhota Fellowship Scheme.

I owe a very special debt of gratitude to the Advisory Committee Members of this project (in alphabetical order): Dr. Lokesh Chandra, Prof. Deshpandey, Prof. S. Rinpoche, Ven. Duboom Tulku and Dr. (Mrs) Kapila Vatsyayan for going through the manuscript and offering much invaluable advice and suggestions for improving the manuscript.

I am deeply beholden to my Supervisor, Prof. S. Rinpoche for his unflagging attention, kind help and encouragement, right from the outset of this project.

To those scholars, academicians and authorities of the Central Institute of Higher Tibetan Studies (Deemed University), Sarnath, Varanasi, with an interest in Tibetology, who have helped and encouraged me, I express my deepest gratitude, especially to the Librarians of CIHTS and Tibet House, and to their colleagues for always providing ready reference and for other such allied assistance.

Thanks are also due to Ven. Migmar Tsering, Principal of Sakya College, and Ms. Gayle Zilber for their pains in improving my English. Finally, I am deeply indebted to my family members for their moral support, encouragement and patience.

Contents

Scheme of Transliteration

The following are the points to the noted in the scheme of transliteration followed in this work:

ི	i	ུ	u	ེ	e	ོ	o
ཀ	ka	ཁ	kha	ག	ga	ང	nga
ཅ	ca	ཆ	cha	ཇ	ja	ཉ	nya
ཏ	ta	ཐ	tha	ད	da	ན	na
པ	pa	ཕ	pha	བ	ba	མ	ma
ཙ	tsa	ཚ	tsha	ཛ	dza	ཝ	va
ཞ	zha	ཟ	za	འ	'a	ཡ	ya
ར	ra	ལ	la	ཤ	sha	ས	sa
ཧ	ha	ཨ	a				

Abbreviations

IAIC = International Academy of Indian Culture

LTWA = Library of Tibetan Works and Archives

MCHOD = *Mchod rten gyi cha dbye ba 'dul ba las 'byung ba'i mdo (Caitya vibhaṅga vinayoddhṛta sūtra)* text of Śāntigarbha

Toh. = Tohoku Catalogue

VIM = *Vimaloṣṇīṣa* text of Sahajavilāsa

Xyl. = Xylograph

List of Figures

List of Plates

1

Literary Background of the Architecture and Architectonic Principles of the Buddhist Stūpa

While the literature on the symbolism, origin and ritual significance of the Buddhist stūpa is considerably enormous, the architectural aspect has been comparatively neglected till date.

To begin with the Vinaya sources, there are four categories of *Vinayasūtra (catvārī Vinayāgamasūtra)*, viz., *Vinayavastu ('dul ba lung bzhi), Vinayavibhaṅga ('dul ba lung rnam 'byed), Vinaya-kṣudraka Vastu ('dul ba lung phran tshegs)*, and *Vinaya Uttaragrantha ('dul ba bzhung dam pa)*. Among them, the latter two throw valuable light upon the architecture of the Buddhist stūpa. Both these texts are the Tibetan versions of the lost Sanskrit originals, found in the Kagyur Testament.

Vinaya-kṣudraka Vastu

A Tibetan version of the *Vinaya-kṣudraka Vastu* of the *Mūlasarvāstivādins* text is in fact a supplementary work containing fiftynine chapters and seventeen thousand seven hundred (17,700) *ślokas* (stanzas). A detailed structural illustration of the Buddhist stūpa is well described in the 21st chapter of this text which relates the construction of a stūpa over the corporeal relics of Śāriputra.[1] In this source, we come across the Buddha's own instructions which are as follows:

> Much earlier, the relics of Ārya Śāriputra were carried away by the householder *(gṛhapati)* Anāthapiṇḍaka and placed in a prominent

1. Kagyur, Vinaya, Derge, Vol. THA, (Toh. 6), fol. 244b3-247a4.

place of his house to enable the people to come there and pay homage. On a certain occasion, he locked the door of his house and went to a hilly site for a minor work. When people came to show their veneration, they found that there was no place for them to worship, and the people accused him of interfering with their obtaining of merits. He heard this upon his return, and raised the matter before the Buddha whom he asked to give his consent for constructing a stūpa over the corporeal relics of Śāriputra at a spot visible or readily accessible to all for making offerings. After the Buddha granted his permission to have a stūpa built for the venerable Śāriputra's relics—Anāthapiṇḍaka asked how to build the stūpa. The Buddha instructed: "One should build a gradual flight of four steps *(catāśro-vedyaḥ)* and then a vase-support or vase-base *(kuṁbha sandhī).* Upon these, a vase *(kuṁbha)* or stūpa dome, a *bre*[2] *(droṇa),* an axle-pole *(yaṣṭi),* one umbrella or two or three or four, up to thirteen umbrellas should be made, and the rain-cloak *(varṣā sthālī)* should be placed." The Buddha said that the stūpa should be built like this.

The text further informs us of the structural distinctions among the stūpas for the different classes of the Buddhist saints. The text runs as follows:

> When Anāthapiṇḍaka was unaware of whether such a stūpa should be built for Ārya Śāriputra alone or for all Āryas, the *Bhikṣus* conveyed the matter to the Buddha. The Buddha said to *gṛhapati* that the stūpa for the Tathāgata should be built in a complete form, consisting of at least thirteen umbrellas. For the stūpa of a Pratyekabuddha, the cover of the umbrella should not be placed, although the other parts are like that of the Tathāgata's stūpa. The stūpa for *Arhats* should have four umbrellas, for the never-returners *(Anāgāmin)* only three, for the once-returners *(Sakṛḍagāmin)* two, and only one for the stream-enterers *(Śrotāpanna).* The stūpa for virtuous laymen *(Kuśala pṛthagjana)*

2. *Bre* is an artefact having a quadrangular shape (like a *harmikā),* and used to measure grains in Tibet. One *bre* is equal to a sixth part of a *Phul.*

is to be constructed without any elevation of the umbrellas.[3] The Buddha said that these were the types of stūpas for the *Arhats* and the virtuous laymen. However, as it was unknown as to in which place Śāriputra's stūpa should be constructed, the Buddha said that it should be constructed in accordance with the rank or order of seats which both Śāriputra and Maudgalyānaputra occupied in the *Saṃgha* in relation to the seat of the Tathāgata. Respectively, the stūpas of other Elder members have likewise to be arranged in due order of their rank *(vṛdhanta).* Stūpas of the Virtuous laymen, however, have to be constructed outside the *Saṃgha*-compound *(Saṃghārāma).*

Thus, these passages precisely illustrate that the main structures of the Buddhist stūpa including the structural distinctions for the different classes of the Buddhist saints, are indicated by the number of umbrellas entitled to them. This narration is, perhaps, one of the oldest stūpa references in the Buddhist Testament.

Vinaya-Uttaragrantha

The *Vinaya-Uttaragrantha* deals with the problematic issues of the first two sources of the *Vinayasūtra* in the form of an answer to a petition. It has a total of sixtyfive chapters in two divisions. The first twelve chapters deal with the unfinished petition and the remaining fortythree chapters deal with the finished petition.

Details of a Buddhist stūpa is illustrated in the thirtyfifth chapter of this source, recording the tradition of the construction of a stūpa over the Buddha's hair and nails.[4] This text abides by the same structural distinctions with regard to the number of umbrellas for the different classes of the Buddhist saints. For each of the different classes of Buddhist saints, there is a different type of stūpa. The text does not precisely inform us of the specific shape of the stūpa. However, the structural shape of the stūpa of the Pratyekabuddha is described here differently from what is in all other sources as it is stated: "The stūpa of the Pratyekabuddha is to be built without any fold on the vase (stūpa

3. It implicitly signifies the absence of the axle-pole as well.
4. Kagyur, Vinaya, Derge, Vol. PA, (Toh. 7), fol. 264b4-7.

dome)".[5] Thus, this implies that the stūpas of the other Buddhist classes might have folds on their vases.

In addition, we come across a long list of additional structural components and ornamental parts which, if circumstances require, can be added successively to the stūpa constructed over the Buddha's hair and nails by Anāthapiṇḍaka during his life time. The purposes and reasons behind the presentation of each of those additional structural components and ornamental parts are explicated elaborately in the four sections of the above mentioned Kagyur Testament. In the seventh, eighth, ninth and tenth stanzas of the *sūtra* from the third section of the prologue, we find a very extensive description of this in the traditional verbose style of presentation. The author does not see the need to repeat this elaborate style here, and would like to emphasise the categorical specifications rather than the stylistic formulation of these.

The following account is mentioned in the seventh stanza of the *sūtra* from the third section of the prologue.[6] Anāthapiṇḍaka prostrated before Lord Buddha and asked for his permission and consent to erect a stūpa over the Buddha's hair and nails. The Buddha permitted him to erect the stūpa as proposed by him. However, Anāthapiṇḍaka realised that until the stūpa was coated with white-wash, it would appear unattractive. He thought of building a stūpa, which would look fascinating to every body and the matter was again placed before the Buddha, to have his consent for applying the white-wash. After obtaining his permission, Anāthapiṇḍaka applied white-wash to the stūpa, followed by offerings of incense, scent, and flowers. After the stūpa was coated with white-wash, he noticed that the stūpa did not look nice due to lack of illumination in the evening. So, he brought the matter before the Buddha, and asked for permission to offer a circle of butter-lamps. The Buddha's instructions for installing the ensemble of lamps were tested in three ways: by putting the lamps on the upper-part of the stūpa, from where the oil drippings from the lamps tarnished the white colour of the stūpa; this made the architect to place the lamps in the lower part, from where the lamps were easily accessible to dogs who consumed the oil from the vessels and which caused the architect to provide niches for holding the lamps.

5. *Rang sangs rgyas kyi ni bum pa sul can med par bya'o,* op. cit., fol. 264b6.
6. *Vinaya-uttaragrantha,* op. cit., fol. 114a2-115b1.

Similar problems came to attention with regard to cows and other such animals, who polluted the environment of the stūpa by strewing their dung indiscriminately. From that as well, the Buddha assured respite to Anāthapiṇḍaka by permitting him to erect railings all around the stūpa, to prevent its despoilment by the animals. Finding the above arrangements to be still insufficient for keeping the stūpa in a perfect condition, it was advised that the gateways *(toraṇa)* be constructed. The materials needed for the accessories were brought by Anāthapiṇḍaka, his relatives and friends, who honoured the stūpa in deep reverence after seeing it completed. The stūpa evoked great joy and happiness among the devotees, who were enthralled by the very presence of the Tathāgata's corporeal relics.

In the eighth stanza of the *sūtra* from the third section of the prologue,[7] it is mentioned that Anāthapiṇḍaka sought permission from the Buddha to allow him to raise *Gandhakuṭi* all around the stūpa along with the construction of gateways. Thereafter, he asked for the Buddha's approval to make a dome for the stūpa and this was granted. Again, he sought permission to encircle the stūpa with a dome, and this too was granted. Further, he proposed the necessity of painting the pillars with vermilion *(mtshal)* and making drawings on the walls with lac-dye *(rgya skyes)*. The Buddha agreed to all these proposals made by Anāthapiṇḍaka.

Moreover, the ninth stanza of the *sūtra* from the third section of the prologue[8] informs us about the following interesting incidents. In order to make offerings, the *Bhikṣus* fixed a peg on the stūpa and hung flower garlands on it. Such an act was witnessed by the *Brahmins* and householders, who accused the *Bhikṣus* and demanded to know why had they fixed the peg on the stūpa which had no peg earlier. The Buddha said that the accusation was correct and one should only place a small peg like a cow's tooth. However, when the *Bhikṣus* were busy with the implanting of the peg through digging a niche in the stūpa, the Buddha instead advised them to set the peg during the construction of the stūpa, and not drill a hole after the completion of the construction. Thus, in order to make offerings, the *Bhikṣus* hung flower garlands

7. *Vinaya-Uttaragrantha* fol. 119a7-b6.
8. Ibid., fol. 119b6-120b7.

from the *harmikā's* neck by climbing up on to the stūpa. This latter action was also condemned by the *Brahmins* and householders who now accused the *Bhikṣus* of treading over the stūpa in an offensive manner. The matter was brought before the Buddha who agreed that the condemnation was just, and that the *Bhikṣus* should not walk or tread over the stūpa of the Buddha. For the purpose of making offerings, only a layman should climb over the stūpa, but first he had to wash his feet and anoint them with perfumes or wrap them with cloth. If a layman was not available to do the job, a novice should be asked to do it. If a novice was also not available, then the *Bhikṣus* could ascend the stūpa after making the same preparations, all the time visualizing the stūpa as the Buddha, and when thinking that it was the appropriate time they had to draw upon it with scent. When a stūpa was found to be too large to climb up, the Buddha instructed that they might climb it with the help of a rope.

Thereafter, Anāthapiṇḍaka noticed that the stūpa looked unattractive when the flower garlands offered to it faded out. And he placed the matter before the Buddha, who gave consent to his request that garlands made of precious substances could be offered. Moreover, it was found that birds, such as the crows were resting on the stūpa and making it dirty with their excrements. Therefore, Anāthapiṇḍaka sought permission for a cover to be made for the stūpa. The Buddha consented as proposed, and the cover was made. However, the cover of the stūpa decayed in the summer rains and left the stūpa dark and blurred. The Buddha's permission to make a *chab sgo*[9] was sought, who gave his consent accordingly.

Lastly, the tenth stanza of the *sūtra* from the third section of the prologue[10] informs us of the following incidents. Anāthapiṇḍaka laid a proposal for making stūpas of bronze and gold. The Buddha, agreeing to the proposal, added that one should make stūpas out of as precious material as possible, such as silver, *lapis-lazuli* and crystal etc. Thereafter, Anāthapiṇḍaka proposed to offer victory-banners *(dhvaja)* for the stūpas and the Buddha gave his consent. However, when Anāthapiṇḍaka was unaware of what type of victory-banner should be offered, the

9. Door for water exit.
10. *Ibid.,* fol. 120b7-121b1.

Buddha answered that there were four types of victory-banners: the crocodile, bull, nāga, and lion victory-banners.

Subsequently, Anāthapiṇḍaka requested that the Buddha should allow him to anoint the stūpa with oil and red arsenic *(ldong ros);* the Buddha, accepting the proposal added that in the same way one should also anoint the stūpa with sandal perfume.

Commentarial Works on Vinaya

We have a very limited number of commentarial works in the Vinaya which throw some light on the architecture of the Buddhist stūpa. These are the *Vinayasūtra* text *('dul ba mdo rtsa ba)*[11] and the *Vinayasūtravṛtti* text *('dul ba mdo' i rgya cher 'grel pa)*[12] of Guṇaprabha,[13] the *Vinayasūtraṭīkā* text *('dul ba mdo'i rgya cher 'grel pa)*[14] of Dharmamitra[15] and the *Vinayasūtravyākhyāna* text *('dul ba mdo'i rnam bshad)*[16] of Prajñākara.[17] However, these texts only provide us with a very limited amount of information, and all these sources are in conformity with the architectural structures and ornamental aspects mentioned in the *Vinaya-Uttaragrantha* of the Kagyur Testament. The only difference is that the above texts increase the number of umbrellas by one for all those stūpas according to the classes of the Buddhist saints, excluding the stūpas of the Tathāgata and the Pratyekabuddha.

In all the above mentioned sources, one can find two types of stūpas designated for the virtuous novice monk *(pravrajita),* but their structural shapes do not tally with one another. According to Guṇaprabha's text,[18] the two types of stūpas are termed as a *Gandhakuṭi (gtsang khang)* type of stūpa and a pillar type of stūpa. However, it is the opinion of Dharmamitra[19] that the *Gandhakuṭi* type of stūpa is so called, because it has projectional *Gandhakuṭis* towards the vase, and

11. Tangyur, Dodrel, Narthang, Vol. ZU, fol. 449a4-452a3.
12. *Ibid.,* Vol. SU, fol. 382b6-384b7.
13. Yontan Yod.
14. Tangyur, Dodrel, Narthang, Vol. LU, fol. 449a4-452a3.
15. Chos kyi bshes gnyen.
16. Tangyur, Dodrel, Narthang, Vol. SHU, fol. 299b5-301a4.
17. Shes rab byed pa.
18. *Vinayasūtra,* op. cit., fol. 101b6.
19. *Vinayasūtraṭīkā,* op. cit., fol. 449a4-5.

the pillar type of stūpa is so called because of its pillar like erection without the *Gandhakuṭi.* In Prajñākara's text,[20] we find a nutmeg *(sbubs can*[21]) shape of stūpa instead of a *Gandhakuṭi* type, while the other is same as mentioned above.

Twin Commentarial Works on *Vimaloṣṇīṣa*

In addition to the Vinaya sources, the Tantric section of the Tangyur Testament contains twin works on *Vimaloṣṇīṣa* but with different titles. The authorship of the first is attributed to Sahajavilāsa[22] and the other to the anonymous. Even the usual Sanskrit title is missing from the latter.[23] Both works turn out to be constructional manuals of the Buddhist stūpas dealing specifically with the proportions of the stūpa 'of Enlightenment'. The number of umbrellas cited therein for the stūpas of different classes of Buddhist saints is congruent with the above-mentioned texts.

Moreover, they provide us with a very comprehensive account of the places, where the stūpa should be erected and the substances upon which one should engrave or erect the stūpa. In this regard, Sahajavilāsa says: "One should erect the stūpa over the corporeal relics of Lord Buddha at an attractive place (avoiding a cemetery etc.) on a hill, or plain or valley."[24] He further mentions that not only a stūpa should be erected, "but should be engraved on earth or rock in accordance with the rules of experienced craftsmen, or it can be erected by collecting earth, stone or wood."[25] Regarding this matter, we have a fair amount of archaeological evidence in India to confirm our literary sources.

---

20. *Vinayasūtravyākhyāna,* op. cit., fol. 299b5.
21. Syn. *sbubs skyes* and *shubs 'bras.*
22. *Kun nas sgor 'jug pa'i 'od zer gtsug tor dri ma med par snang ba de bzhin gshegs pa thams cad kyi snying po dang dam tshig la rnam par lta ba zhes bya ba'i gzungs kyi rnam par bshad pa (Samanta mukha praveśa raśmivimaloṣṇīṣa prabhāsa sarva tathāgatahṛdayasamaya vilokita nāma dhāranivṛtti),* Tangyur, Gyud drel, Derge, Vol. THU, (Toh. 2688), fol. 313a2-314a5.
23. *Mchod rten gyi cha rnam par dbye ba,* Tangyur, Gyud drel, Peking, Vol. TU, fol. 192a1-194a2.
24. *Ri'am thang ngam ljongs gang dag / dur khrod la sogs spangs pa yi / yid 'ong gnas su rgyal ba yi / sku gdung mchod rten brtsig par bya // Vimaloṣṇīṣa,* op. cit., fol. 313a4-5.
25. *yang na sa' am rdo dag la / mkhas pas tshul bzhin brko bar bya / sa' am rdo 'am shing dag gam / yang na tshogs pas brtsig par bya //,* Ibid., fol. 313a5.

The text precisely indicates the various structural components of the stūpa and their proportions to be kept in mind during construction.[26] Finally, just at the end of the texts, there is a vivid description of the colours to be put to the various structural components of the stūpa.[27]

Another fragmentary work on the *Vimaloṣṇīṣa* is supposed to exist, but the authorship of that is controversial, and is a matter of special inquiry which requires systematic investigation. Regarding this issue, Buston (1290-1363 A.D.) had stated that his work of the 'Proportional Manual of the Stūpa of Enlightenment',[28] was based on a commentary of the *Vimaloṣṇīṣa* but unfortunately, he neither mentioned the names of its author and translator, nor quoted its complete title anywhere in his entire work. Buston had another work entitled, *Dpal dus kyi khor lo' i gshin po rjes su 'dzin pa' i cho ga ngan 'gro rnams 'joms,*[29] in which he stated at the very end of the text that the work was a compilation of various sources and references, such as a commentary by Jayadeva on the *Vimaloṣṇīṣa, Caityavibhaṅga-vinayoddhṛta sūtra* of Śāntigarbha, and various other allied works. In support of Buston's statement, it was the view of Chenga Lodos Gyaltsen (1390-1448 A.D.) that the *Vimaloṣṇīṣa's* quotations cited by Buston appeared to have been taken from Jayadeva's commentary on the *Vimaloṣṇīṣa.*

Thus, it is evident that the quotations extracted by Buston are found in their exact and complete forms in the twin Tantric works of the Tangyur Testament mentioned earlier. Moreover, none of the Tangyur editions assign the authorship of any of these commentaries to Jayadeva; these texts only mention that he (Jayadeva) was attributed as the translator of the commentary of *Vimaloṣṇīṣa,* the author of which was known to be Sahajavilāsa. It is worth noticing that neither of Buston's texts (mentioned earlier) throw any light on the commentary of Sahajavilāsa.

Therefore, these controversial statements and their complexities coupled with the lack of biographical information lead us to the

26. *Ibid.,* fol. 313b4-314a4. See in Section B (Translation) IV for details.
27. *Ibid.,* fol. 314a4-5.
28. *Byang chub chen po' i mchod rten gyi tshad bzhugs so,* Collected Works, Vol. PHA (14), pp. 554-58.
29. Collected Works, Vol. CA (5), p. 612.

conclusion that the very originality of the works of the unknown authorship is questionable as the texts do not give us any indication of their sources, authors or translators, and that it is doubtful whether or not Jayadeva ever wrote any commentary on the *Vimaloṣṇīṣa.* Most probably, Buston might have mistakenly quoted the translator of Sahajavilāsa's commentary as its author.

Caitya-Vibhaṅga-Vinayoddhṛta-Sūtra

The text *Caitya-Vibhaṅga-Vinayoddhṛta-Sūtra* is the lost Sanskrit original manuscript available in a Tibetan version entitled, *Mchod rten gyi cha dbye ba 'dul ba las byung ba' i mdo,* which is referred in the Tantric section of the Tangyur Testament.[30] In the text itself, there is no indication of any attribution to its authorship as well as its translation. However, Buston, one of the chief editors of the Kagyur and Tangyur Testaments, does not fail to fill this gap. In one of his works known as *Dpal dus kyi khor lo gshin po rjes su 'dzin pa' i cho ga,*[31] the authorship of the said text is attributed to Śāntigarbha.

The text strictly deals with the symbolical meanings of main structures of the stūpa together with additional structural parts and ornaments in due order of their sequences with the essence of the Tathāgata's *Dharmakāya.* The essence of the Tathāgata's *Dharmakāya* are the four close mindfulnesses, the four perfect abandonments, the four miracle powers, the five faculties, the five forces, the seven factors of enlightenment, the eight-fold noble paths, the ten types of consciousness, the ten mystical powers, and the three absolute unshared mindfulness, and the great compassion that are closely connected with the structures of stūpa by the following references: "The reflected image of these sets of dogmatic notions (mentioned above) is called as the reflected image of the *Dharmakāya.*"[32] This view holds the conception of the stūpa as the resemblance of the Truth body *(Dharmakāya)* of the Tathāgata. Besides, it continues to enumerate the

30. Narthang, Vol. TU, fol. 174a3-5; Derge, Vol. PU (Text 3078), fol. 173b3-175b1; and Peking, Vol. TU, fol. 187b4-189b7.
31. Collected Works of Buston, op. cit., fol. 612.
32. *Mchod rten gyi cha dbye ba 'dul ba las 'byung ba'i mdo (Caitya Vibhaṅga Vinayoddhṛta Sūtra),* Gyud, Derge, Vol. PU, (Toh. 30780, fol. 178b3-175b2) Narthang, Vol. TU.

additional structural parts and ornaments, along with their symbolical meanings. The text does not fail to retain the main structures of the stūpa, although its additional structural parts and ornaments are somewhat different from those of the *Vinaya Uttaragrantha* text mentioned earlier.

Kaṁsadeśavyākaraṇa

The *Kaṁsadeśavyākaraṇa (Li yul lung bstan pa)* text of the Tangyur Testament[33] provides us with two out of eight kinds of great stūpas viz., the eight great stūpas of the Tathāgata and the eight great stūpas of the Buddha's relics divided into eight parts. These two divisions can also be called respectively as eight great stūpas of the non-relics and the eight great stūpas of the relics. They are also called respectively as eight great stūpas of the eight sacred places and the eight great stūpas of the eight major cities.

The former eight, i.e. the eight great stūpas of the Tathāgata are commemorative of the eight great events of the Buddha's life and the stūpas were constructed by the inhabitants of their respective places, where the events had taken place. The latter eight, i.e. the eight great stūpas of the relics came into existence as a consequence of distribution of the Buddha's relics among the eight claimants by Brahmin Droṇa. This view was unanimously accepted in all the Buddhist canonical and non-canonical literatures as well as in the works of the modern scholars that after the *Mahāparinirvāṇa* of Lord Buddha his relics were distributed among the eight claimants of the eight major cities, who constructed stūpas in each of their respective places in order to preserve and pay homage to their share of relics. However, the scholars differ in their views in regard to the builders, localities and names of some of the stūpas in both the groups of the eight stūpas. Detailed lists of both the groups of the eight great stūpas enumerated by the different scholars are as follows:

The eight great stūpas of the Tathāgata according to *Kaṁsadeśavyākaraṇa* text[34] are:

---

33. Tangyur, Lekha-Parikathā, Derge, Vol. NGE, (Toh. 4202), fol. 172b4-173a2.
34. Ibid., fol. 172b5.

Name of stūpa	*Locality*
Birth	Lumbini garden in Kapilavastu
Enlightenment	On the banks of the Narañjanā river near Vajrāsana in the Rājagṛha city of Magadha
Vanquishing Eighteen Lakhs of Evil Forces	Rājagṛha in the city of Magadha
. . . .	On the spot where Brahmā had requested the Buddha for turning the Wheel of Law
Turning the Wheel of Law	Mṛgdāva in the city of Kāśi
Great Miracle	Śrāvastī in the city of Koṣala
Descent from Heaven	Sāṁkāśya[35]
Nirvāṇa	Kuśinagara of Malla country.

The eight great stūpas of the relics illustrated in the *Kaṁsadeśavyākaraṇa* are: one each at the place of Rāmagrāma, Pava, Malla country of [Kuśinagara], Vaiśālī, Canyacākalpa, Viśnudrīva, Kapilavastu and Rājagṛha.

The eight stūpas of Tathāgata according to the Chinese *Pata-ling-t'a-ming-hao-ching (Hachi-dai-ryō-tō-myō-gō-kyō,* lit., "the Sūtra that describes the names of the Eight Spiritual Stūpas") (Taisho, No. 1685, Vol. 32, p. 773)[36] are:

1. The first stūpa was constructed in the Lumbini garden of Kapilavastu where the Buddha was born.
2. The second stūpa was on the shore of the Narañjanā river in the kingdom of Magadha, where the Buddha had attained enlightenment.
3. The third stūpa was constructed in the Varanasi city of Kāśi where he turned the great Dharmacakra.
4. The fourth stūpa was constructed in the Jetavana of Śrāvastī where he performed the great miracles.

---

35. In the text written as Sāṅkāśya.
36. Hajime Nakamura, cf. The *Aṣṭamahāsthānacaityastotra* and the similar Tibetan versions of a text *Indianisme Et Bouddhisme, Me'langes* offers a 'Mgr E'tienne Lamotte, Universite Catholique De Louvan Institut Orientaliste, Louvain-La-Neuve, 1980; English translation of Indo-Tibetica I, p. 23.

5. The fifth stūpa was constructed in the Kānyakubja city of Sāṅkāśya where the Buddha descended from the Trāyastriṃśāḥ (the palace of thirty-three gods).
6. The sixth stūpa was constructed at Rājagṛha where he reconciled the schism in Saṅgha *(saṅghabheda)*.
7. The seventh stūpa was constructed in the city of Vaiśālī where he prolongated his life span *(āyuḥpramāṇa).*
8. The eighth stūpa was constructed in the city of Kuśinagara where he entered Nirvāṇa.

The eight great stūpas of the Tathāgata according to Nāgārjuna *(circa* 1st-2nd century A.D.)[37] are:

Name	*Locality*
Sugāta *(Bde gshegs)*	In the Lumbini of Kapilavastu
Enlightenment	On the banks of Narañjanā river in Magadha
Divine Wisdom *(Ye shes)*	Varanasi in the Kāśi kingdom
Conquest of Tīrthikas (heretics)	In the Jetavana of Śrāvastī
Descent from Trāyastriṃśāḥ	In the Sāṅkāśya
Maitreya *(Byams ngos)*	In the Veṇuvana of Rājagṛha
Blessing *(Byin brlabs)*	In the Vaiśālī
Nirvāṇa	In the Kuśinagara

The eight great stūpas of the Tathāgata according to Buston,[38] Phreng Kha ba,[39] Bodong,[40] Chenga[41] and Lodos Sangpo[42] are:

37. *Gnas chen po brgyad kyi mchod rten la bstod pa (Aṣṭamahāsthānacaitya stotra), Śtotragana,* Derge, Vol. KA (Toh. 1133); Narthang, Vol. KA; Hajime Nakamura, op. cit., 262-65.
38. Buston Rinchendup, *Byang chub chen po'i mchod rten gyi tshad bzhugs so, Collected Works of Buston,* Vol. PHA (14), Ed. by Dr. Lokesh Chandra, IAIC, New Delhi, 1969.
39. Phreng Khapa Lodos Pal Sangpo, See Gega Lama, *Principles of Tibetan Arts,* p. 76.
40. Bodong Panchen Choglas Namgyal, *Rten gsum bzheng tshul bstan bcos lugs bshad pa bzhugs so, Collected Works of Bodong,* Vol. KHA (2), Ed. S.T. Kazi, Repd., Tibet House, New Delhi, 1969.
41. Chenga Lodos Gyaltsen Pal Sangpo, *Mchod rten gyi tshad ston pa legs bshad gser gyi phreng ba,* Vol. CA.
42. *Bde bar gshegs pa'i sku gzugs kyi tshad kyi rab tu byed pa yid bzhin nor bu,* See English Translation of Tucci's Indo-Tibetica I, pp. 113-7.

Name of stūpa	*Locality*
Heaped Lotuses	Kapilavastu
Enlightenment or Conquest of Māra	Vajrāsana in the Magadha
Multiple Auspicious Doors	Sārnāth near Vārānasī
Descent from Heaven	Sāṅkāśya[43]
Miracle or Vanquishing of heretics	Śrāvastī
Reconciliation	Veṇuvana
Victory or Blessing	Vaiśālī
Nirvāṇa	Kuśinagara

The eight great stūpas of the Tathāgata according to Jamyang[44] (*'jam dbyangs)* are:

Name of stūpa	*Builder*	*Locality*
Heaped Lotuses	Śuddhodana	Kapilavastu
Enlightenment	Śuncata	Magadha
Multiple Auspicious Doors	Sharnaser	Brahmadatta
Descent from Heaven	Indravami	Gsal ldan
Miracles	Prasenajit	Śrāvastī
Reconciliation	Mallas	Veṇuvana
Victory	Licchavi	Vaiśālī
Nirvāṇa	Ajātaśatru	Kuśinagara

The eight great stūpas of the Tathāgata according to Desid Sangyas Gyatso[45] are:

Heaped Lotuses	Śuddhodana	Kapilavastu
Enlightenment	Bimbisāra, etc.	Rājagṛha

43. Mentioned as gsal ldan (which stands for Kāśi) instead of *Sāṅkāśya.*

44. Jamyang Zhaypa Ngawang Dorjee, *Mchod rten gyi thig rtsa mdor bdus, Collected Works of Jamyang Zhaypa,* Vol. 1, New Delhi, 1974.

45. Desid Sangyas Gyatso, *Vaidurya dkar po las 'phro pa'i snyen sgron dang dri len g.ya' sel bzhugs so,* Vol. 2, Repd. from original texts from the Collection of Tsepon W.D. Shakapa by T. Tsepal Taikhang, New Delhi, 1971.

Name of stūpa	*Builder*	*Locality*
Multiple Auspicious Doors	Five Disciples[46]	Vārānasi
Descent from Heaven	Inhabitants	Saṅkāśya
Miracles	Licchavi	Jetavana
Reconciliation	Jeta	Rājagṛha
Victory	Inhabitants	Vaiśālī
Nirvāṇa	Malla	Kuśinagara

The eight great stūpas of the Tathāgata according to Sahajavilāsa[47] are:

Name of stūpa	*Builder*	*Locality*
Descent from Heaven	Śuddhodana	Kapilavastu
Enlightenment	Ajātaśatru	Magadha
Great Miracle	Mallas	Kuśinagara
Turning the Wheel of Law	Brahmadatta	Vārānasi
Multiple Auspicious Doors	Prasenajit	Śrāvastī
Luminous	'dun 'dzin ta la[48]	Tshad ge
Kanika	Licchavi prince	Vaiśālī
Lotus-shaped	Indravarma	Ti ka sta shi[49]

The eight great stūpas of the relics according to *Dīgha Nikāya*[50] are:

---

46. The names of five disciples (*pañca bhādrapariḷadya)* are:
    1. Ajñātakauṇḍinya (Kun gzhi ko'u di na ya),
    2. Aśvajit (rta thul),
    3. Vāṣpa (rlang pa),
    4. Mahānāma (ming chen), and
    5. Bhadrika (bzang ldan), Tsepak Rigzin, op. cit., cf. *'khor lnga sde bzang po.*
47. Sahajavilāsa, *op. cit.,* fol. 313a7-b3.
48. Śuncidala has been interpreted by Dr. Lokesh Chandra in his introduction note of the English translation of Tucci's Indo-Tibetica I text, p. vi.
49. Tikacaśi, *Ibid.,* p. vi.
50. Ten Suttas from Dīgha Nikāya, pp. 301-02, Bibliotheca Indo-Tibetica Series No. XII, Rpt., of Burma Pitaka Association Publication, published by Central Institute of Higher Tibetan Studies, Varanasi, 1989.

Builder	*Locality*
Ajātaśatru	Rājagṛha at Magadha
Licchavi prince	Vaiśālī
Śākya prince	Kapilavastu
Buli prince	Allakappa
Koliya prince	Rāmagrāma
Brāhmaṇa	Vaṭṭhadvīpa
Malla prince	Pāvā
Malla prince	Kuśinagara

The eight great stūpas of the relics according to *Vinaya Kṣudraka Vastu*[51] and Buston[52] are:

Mallas	Kuśinagara
Kṣatriya Buluka	Allakappa *(Yul rtogs pa gyo ba)*
Kṣatriya Krodtya or Koliyas	Ravana *(sgra sgrogs)*
Brāhmaṇas	Viśnudvīpa *(khyab 'jug gling)*
Kṣatriya Śākyas	Kapilavastu
Kṣatriya Licchavis	Vaiśālī
Vaisdehiputra Ajātaśatru	Magadha
Mallas	Pāvā

The names of the great stūpas of the relics enumerated in the Sahajavilāsa text are somewhat doubtful as rest of the lists do not provide us the names of the eight great stūpas of the relics. On the other hand, the list itself is contradictory in respect of some of their localities and builders compared with the rest of the lists. Even in the lists of the eight great stūpas of the Tathāgata mentioned above, one can notice all kinds of divergences with regard to their names, localities and builders as well as the events which they had commemorated. Thus, it deserves

51. Kagyur, Vinaya, Derge, Vol. THA, fol. 245; Narthang, Vol. DA, 452b.
52. *Byang chub chen po'i mchod rten gyi tshad bzhugs so,* Vol. 14 (PHA), p. 552.

a special attention and a systematic study in order to achieve uniformity in all these lists.

Tibeto-Buddhist Architectonic Literature

Apart from the two great Testaments, we come across a very large number of stūpa construction manuals written by the Tibetan scholars. Among them are the construction manuals of Desid[53] and Kongtul,[54] which classify the Buddhist stūpa into three categories on the basis of the three vehicles, i.e. the stūpa of Śrāvakas, of Pratyekabuddhas, and of Mahāyāna orders (Figure 1).

(1) The Śrāvaka stūpa looks like a mendicant's staff *(mkhar gsil,* Skt: *Khakkhara)* resting on an alms-bowl upside down placed upon a religious robe folded four times.

(2) The Pratyekabuddha stūpa has a quadrangular foundation upon which is a square block with twelve circular steps and eight spokes of wheel.

(3) The Mahāyāna stūpa category, according to Nāgārjuna,[55] is further divided into three sub-divisions, i.e. (*a*) a stūpa like an inverted alms-bowl, which is circular like a *Bimba*,[56] (*b*) a stūpa which is like a little house, and (*c*) a group of eight stūpas similar to victory-banners.

A full discussion of all aspects of Buddhist stūpas belonging to the three vehicles is far beyond the scope of this book and, moreover, the texts do not furnish us with the structural details of these stūpas, except in the case of the eight stūpas similar to victory-banners. Regarding the stūpas like victory-banners, the last chapter of the *Kriyāsaṁgraha (Bya ba bsdus pa)*[57] of the Tangyur Testament explains that this sub-division is further classified into two: the vase-shaped and the bell-shaped types. This clearly indicates that the "victory-banner stūpas refer to the

53. *Vaiḍūrya dkar po las 'phros pa'i snyan sgron dang dri lan gya' sel,* Collected Works, Vol. 2, fol. 290a5-6.
54. *Shes bya kun khyab mdzod,* Vol. 2, pp. 281-82.
55. It seems that Nāgārjuna has one work to his credit entitled, *Mchod rten gyi rtog pa,* which is referred in the work of Chenga Lodos Gyaltsen. However, the text has not been found yet.
56. *Bimba* is a kind of red fruit having a round shape.
57. Tangyur, Gyud drel, Derge, Vol. KU (57), fol. 352a7-b1.

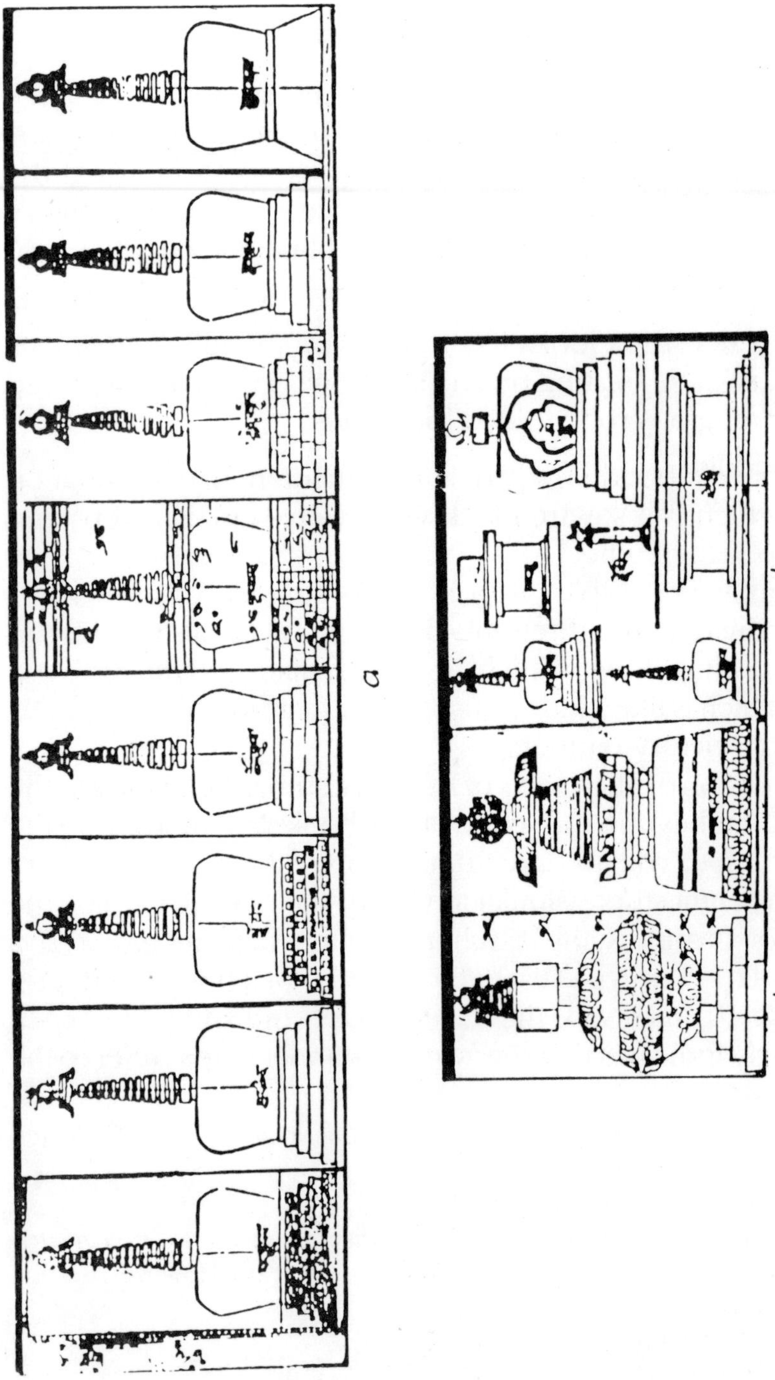

Figure 1. Stūpas of Different Members of the Buddhist Order (Extracted from Sumpa Khenpo text)
(a) Eight types of Tibeto-Buddhist Stūpa.
(b) Kalacakra Stūpa.
(c) Kadam Chorten (Stūpa).
(d) Stūpas of Pratyekabuddha, of Śrāvaka and of Virtuous Layman.

popular eight great stūpas of the Tathāgata" because the latter are all shaped either like a vase or a bell. We do have a fairly good number of secondary sources which furnish the structural details of these stūpas.

In most of the construction manuals of Buston Rinchen Dup,[58] Phreng Khapa,[59] Desid Sangyas Gyatso,[60] Chenga Lodos Gyalsten (Spyen lnga blo gros rgyal mtshan),[61] Jamyang Zhapay Dorjee ('jam dbyangs bzhad pa'i rdo rje),[62] Kontul Yontan Gyatso (Kong sprul yon tan rgya mtsho),[63] Rongtha Lobsang Damchos Gyatso (Rong tha blo bzang dam chos rgya mtsho),[64] Kunkhen Pema Karpo (Kun mkhyen pad ma dkar po)[65] etc., the eight basic types of the Tibeto-Buddhist stūpa architecture can be found. They conform to the types of the vase-shaped dome or the bell-shaped dome. It is evident that, principally, the structural components and proportions of Tibeto-Buddhist stūpas are identical with the patterns found in the commentary on *Vimaloṣṇīṣa,* excluding the modifications imposed upon the formation of the steps and the metre as well. Basically, each type of the Tibeto-Buddhist stūpa has the same architectural form with the vase-base and above, and the base of ten-virtues and below. The exceptions are found in the case of the steps (which are in between the base of ten-virtues and the vase-base), where one can notice distinct characteristics in each of the eight types of stūpas (excluding the stūpa of Nirvāṇa). The steps are generally square, circular, octagonal, or projectional in shape. However, in the case of the stūpa of Nirvāṇa, there are no steps and the bell-

---

58. *Collected Works of Buston,* op. cit., pp. 551-57.
59. See *Principle of Tibetan Arts,* pp. 76-96.
60. *Vaiḍurya dkar po las 'phros pa'i snyan sgron dang dri lan gy.a' sel,* op. cit., fol. 289b2-293b1.
61. *Mchod rten gyi tshad ston pa legs bshad gser gyi phreng ba,* op. cit., pp. 419-57.
62. *Mchod rten brgyad kyi thig rtsa mdor bsdus, Collected Works of Jamyang Zhaypa,* Vol. 1 (KA), pp. 439-46, New Delhi, 1974.
63. *Shes bya kun khyab mdzod,* op. cit., pp. 280-89.
64. *Thig gi lag len du ma gsal bar bshad par bzo rig mdzes pa'i kha rgyen zhes bya ba bzhugs so,* fol. 74a2-77a7.
65. *Mchod rten brgyad kyi thig rtsa bzhugs so,* Vol. 1, Rpd. from the *Gnam 'brug se ba byang chub gling* blocks by Kargyud Sungrab Nyamso Khang, Darjeeling, W. B., 1973.

shaped dome rests directly upon the base of ten-virtues. The remaining parts are similar to those of the other seven stūpas with vase-shaped domes.

Conclusion

The ancient Indian literature is replete with stūpa construction manuals which provide sources for the study of the Buddhist stūpa. The Tibeto-Buddhist stūpas, as seen today all over Tibet, Mongolia, Bhutan, parts of China, India and Nepal, in various sizes (ranging from a few centimetres as in *tsha tsha* to a multi-storeyed stūpa) are all invariably built in accordance with the specifications laid down in the literature. Surprisingly, there are hardly any major cases of variation from the structures and measurements prescribed in the treatises.

It is quite certain that the stūpa construction manuals are not later works nor of Tibetan origin. Then, why is the uniformity presented in the Tibeto-Buddhist stūpa architecture alone? This is a matter of special inquiry before us.

I presume that it was only over the course of time that the necessity of additional structural shapes arose leading to the modifications, embellishments and elaborations of the structures in diverse manners/permutations. The change in the socio-economic milieu and dominant religious outlook must have had something to do with this developmental trend. With the birth of the Mahāyāna, the architectural structure underwent a significant change. There was more emphasis on an upward movement, exemplifying the Mahāyānist approach, as shown in the addition of more tiers of umbrellas—thirteen instead of four, three and so on, and in the additional adornment of the sun, the moon, and the spherical pinnacle decorations. In the Buddhist tradition, the honorific umbrella with the sun and moon symbolised the supremacy of the higher teachings of the Vajrayāna.

The adaptations in stūpa construction were the result of the architectonic works of Tibetan scholars like Buston, Tagtsang Lotsawa, Tulku Phreng Khapa, etc., who wrote treatises on the construction manuals of the Tibeto-Buddhist stūpa architecture based on the renowned commentary on *Vimaloṣṇīṣa,* an Indian Buddhist text, under the supervision of other eminent scholars. They felt that it was indispensable to have a set law for the construction of stūpas in order to maintain uniform proportions and to prevent any deformities in workmanship. Their establishment of a norm does not mean that proportions were not at all set previously. However, some irregularity in proportions must have arisen, thus resulting in the need for firmly established rules. These rules could prevent any misproportions and maintain uniformity of the stūpa's components.

Therefore, in Tibet, an established norm for uniform proportions in the construction of the stūpa came into vogue in the first quarter of the 14th century A.D.

2

Ritualistic Way of Constructing the Tibeto-Buddhist Stūpa Architecture

Traditionally, in the construction of Tibeto-Buddhist monuments, whether stūpas, temples, monasteries, or others which serve as places for worship and the study of Dharma, it is necessary to perform specific rituals in accordance with the specifications laid down in the treatises.[1]

It is generally accepted that a stūpa made of stone or clay material, irrespective of its size is most efficacious and significant, if it is constructed by following the ritual instructions prescribed in the *Raśmivimala* and *Vimaloṣṇīṣa.* Otherwise, even a stūpa made from gold or other precious materials would remain an ordinary shrine, if not constructed by performing the proper rituals.[2] Likewise, the Kagyur

1. *Samantamukha praveśa raśmivimaloṣṇīṣa prabhāsa sarvatathāgata hṛdaya samayavilokita nāma dhāraṇī,* Gyudbum, Derge, Vol. PHA, (Toh. 599); Zungdus, Vol. WAM, (Toh. 983); *Sarvaprajñāntapāramitāsiddha caitya nāma dhāraṇī,* Gyudbum, Kagyur, Narthang, Vol. NA and Derge, Vol. PHA, (Toh. 601); Zungdus, Derge, Vol. E, (Toh. 884); *Ārya Raśmivimalaviśuddhaprabhā nāma dhāraṇī,* Kagyur, Gyud, Derge, Vol. NA, (Toh. 510); Sahajavilāsa, *Samantamukha praveśa raśmivimaloṣṇīṣa prabhāsa sarvatathāgata hṛdaya samayavilokita nāma dhāranīvṛtti,* Tangyur, Gyud drel, Derge, Vol. THU, (Toh. 2688); Minling Lochen Dharmaśri, *Dri med rnam gnyis kyi gzungs la brten te mchod rten bzhengs pa la nye bar mkho ba'i cho ga bklags pas 'grub pa,* Collected Works of Minling, Vol. PA (XIII); *Snga 'gyur bka' ma,* Vol. KHA.
2. *Snga 'gyur bka' ma,* op. cit., fol. 1b3-2a1.

Testament's tantric section informs us of the advantages of stūpas which have been blessed by certain *mantras,* irrespective of their size and material.[3]

Before defining the ritual procedures, it is important to note that the ritual activities should be performed by a fully qualified *Vajrācārya (rdo rje slob dpon)* who must possess at least the following qualities:[4] he must have the complete knowledge of the rituals, the *mantras* and the *mudrās*; he must be proficient in all the necessary ritual activities; he should be firm, calm and wise; he should also be patient, honest and without pretensions; he should have a firm understanding of the Three Principles of the Path, i.e. Renunciation, Bodhicitta, and Realization of Emptiness; and above all, he must have completed the *mantra*-recitation retreat which enables or qualifies him to preside over the ritual activities. It would be efficacious if the monk who assists the *Vajrācārya* has also completed the qualifying retreat.

The performances of the ritual activities can be broadly classified into three divisions on the basis of their performance at three different stages, i.e. (1) Performing ritual activities prior to the commencement of the construction, (2) Performing ritual activities during the actual construction, and (3) Performing ritual activities after the completion of the construction.

I. RITES PRIOR TO THE COMMENCEMENT OF THE CONSTRUCTION

Whosoever wishes to build a stūpa should initially find a suitable place either on a hill, or in a plain or valley which possesses good signs and characteristics. But first, in order to achieve the final purpose at the place where one intends to build a sacred stūpa, one should undertake the following indispensable ritual activities and examinations, before the commencement of the actual construction.

Recital Retreat

Before commencing the *mantra*-recitation retreat, the performer should be clean bathed who must remain serene, and only rely upon the three

3. Kagyur, (Toh. 510), *op. cit.,* fol. 12a4-b1.
4. Sharpa Tulku and Michael Perrott (Tr. & Prep.), *The Ritual of Consecration,* Tibet Journal, Library of Tibetan Works and Archives, Vol. X, 1985, p. 35.

white foods, i.e. milk, curd and butter, throughout the ritual activities and also while doing the recitation retreat.

According to the *sNga 'gyur bka' ma* text, "First of all, the *mantra*-recitation retreat, or reciting a committed number of *mantras (smakhya asevita)*, ought to be done by a fully qualified *Vajrācārya*, by reciting forty thousand *mūla-mantras* and four lakh *hṛdaya-mantras*."[5] If this is not accomplished, it would suffice for one to recite at least one thousand *mūla-mantras* and one lakh *hṛdaya-mantras*. One has to search out the exact name of the *mantras*, for they are not enumerated in the text. Those unspecified *mantras* are most probably the *mantras* of both the *vimalas*, i.e. *Vimaloṣṇīṣa* and *Raśmivimala*, as the text itself proclaims to be a stūpa construction manual in accordance with the ritualistic system of both the *vimalas*.

On an auspicious juncture, burning incense is offered, and the Earth-lord[6] is confined in a box. After the completion of Ritual illustrations, the *Vajrācārya* and his assistants read any *Prajñāpāramitāsūtra* like the *Sūtrasāma*, *Prajñāpāramitā-hṛdayasūtra* and *Aṣṭasāhasrikā* during the interlude of each session. After these preliminary rites, a site examination is made.

Examination of the Building Site

This process involves three aspects: (a) Examining the directions of the site, (b) Examining the characteristics of the earth, and (c) Examining whether the earth has any defects. In this manner, one identifies whether the proposed site is suitable or not for the construction of the stūpa.

(a) Examining the directions of the site

Traditionally, it is widely accepted that the site which is elevated at the centre and depressed in the east and north is a suitable place for constructing religious buildings. On the other hand, the site which is completely opposite in formation, that is, depressed in the centre and elevated in the east and north directions is considered, to be defective and not suitable as a base for religious constructions.

---

5. *Rnying ma bka' ma rgyas pa*, op. cit., 551.
6. Called *Bhūpati* in Sanskrit.

Apropos the above, in the tantric section of the *Śrī-vajraḍāka-nāma-mahā-tantrarāja (rgyud kyi rgyal po chen po dpal rdo rje mkha' 'gro zhes bya ba)* the consequences of building sacred monuments on auspicious and inauspicious land are mentioned. The text reads:

> The land which is depressed in the east and the north directions endows *siddhis* (spiritual accomplishments) to the mystic practitioner (*tantrika*). If it is elevated in the centre, it leads to the obtaining of both the kingdom and the abode of *Vidyādhara.* If elevated in the north, it either causes death, brings loss of property, or disease. If elevated in the east, it causes a rapid extinction of races. The land which is depressed in the centre is detrimental to the life of the practitioner.[7]
> *Shar dang byang du gzhol ba ni / sngags pa rnams kyi dngos grub 'gyur / dbus su mtho bas 'chi ' gyur ram nor rnams brlag par 'gyur ba ste / yang na nad kyis 'debs par 'gyur / ji skad bshad pa' shar mtho bas / myur du rigs rnams zad par 'gyur / dbus su dma' ba' rang bzhin sa / sgrub ba po ni 'joms dang ldan //*

In addition, the tantric section of the *Vajrāvali-nāma-maṇḍala-vidhi (dkyil 'khor gyi cho ga rdo rje phreng ba zhes bya ba)* in the Tangyur Testament elucidates the detrimental results of building religious monuments on defective lands. It explains as follows:

> The land which closely resembles a tortoise back causes either death or impoverishment. Being elevated in the north, it brings in a fear of an extinction of races, and being elevated in the east and depressed in the centre brings in a fear of extinction to the practitioner. Thus, one should completely abandon these sites.[8]
> *Sa shin tu rus sbal gyi rgyab lta bu ni / 'chi ba'am nor nyams pa' rgyu yin pa dang / byang mtho ba ni rigs chad pas 'jigs pa dang/ shar mtho ba dang dbus dma' ba ni / sgrub pa po nyams pas 'jigs pas yongs su dor te //*

(b) Examining the characteristics of the earth

Having ascertained the status of the directions of the site, and choosing

---

7. Kagyur, Tantra, Derge, Vol. KHA, (Toh. 370), fol. 99b7.
8. Abhyakaragupta, Tangyur, Derge, Gyud, Vol. PHU, (Toh. 3140), fol. 2b6.

that land which possess auspicious signs, one should carry out a digging test. First dig a knee-deep hole or pit. Then, refill the pit with the same soil. If there is more than sufficient soil to refill the hole, it is considered to be a good sign. If there is not enough soil to refill the hole, it is considered to be an inauspicious sign. As it is stated in the *Sarvamaṇḍala-sāmānya-vidhīnām-gūhya-tantra (dkyil 'khor thams cad kyi spyi'i cho ga gsang ba'i rgyud)* of the Tangyur Testament:

> Firstly, one should dig out the land about knee-deep and refill the pit with the same earth. If there is more than enough earth, it is said to endow *siddhis*. If the opposite occurs, then the performer should not undertake the construction. If undertaken, one may experience suffering and also not obtain the good.[9]
> *Dang por spus mo nub tsam brkos la / sa de nyid kyis dgang bar bya / gal te lhag par gyur na ni / dngos grub dag ni yod par shad/ de las bzlog par gyur na ni / sgrub pa pos ni las mi brtsam / brtsams na sdug bsngal myong 'gyur bzhing / legs pa dag kyang mi 'thob bo //*

The third chapter of the *Ārya Vajrapāṇi-Abhiṣeka-Mahā-Tantra ('phags pa lag na rdo rje dbang bskur ba' rgyud chen po)* in the Kagyur Testament also refers to the digging test. However, it differs slightly from the former one in respect to the measurement of the pit depth of the hole and the categorization of the characteristics of the earth. In this regard, the text explains as follows:

> At any place, an expert should dig out a cubit size pit (an arm's-length). That hole dug out by the *Tantric* practitioner (*Vajrācārya*) should be refilled with the same earth. If the soil is more than enough to refill the hole, the site is considered excellent. If the hole fills up to the rim only, the site should be considered an average spot. Avoid that place which does not become full; the expert must not undertake construction in that place.[10]
> *Gang yang rung ba' sa der ni / mkhas pas khru gang tsam brkos nas / sngags pa yis ni brkos pa de / sa de nyid kyi gang bar*

9. Kagyur, Gyud, Derge, Vol. WA, (Toh. 806), fol. 141b1.
10. Kagyur, Gyud, Derge, Vol. DA, (Toh. 496), fol. 32a1.

> *bya / lhag na rnam pa kun tu mchog / kha da chad na bring du brjod / gang bar ma gyur sa de spang / mkhas pas der ni brtsam mi bya //*

Thereafter, in order to further examine the characteristics, dig a pit about a span[11] in measurement and finally pat its interior firmly. Then, fill up the hole with water and walk a hundred paces facing east. Come back and examine the hole carefully. If the water level has not gone down and the hole remains full, it is an excellent site. If the water has been thoroughly absorbed, it is a bad sign. If the water makes a sound, then the place will be menaced by Nāgas, as mentioned in the *Dpal dus kyi khor lo'i cho ga yon tan kun 'byung* text of Buston.[12]

(c) Examining whether the earth has any defects

A final process of this examination is to determine, whether the site's soil contains any defects. If there are defects in the earth, such as steeply inclining slopes, thorny-brambles, potsherds, deep ravines, bones, tree-stumps, ant-hills, ashes, alkaline soil, stones, hairs and insects like ants, etc., it is inauspicious, and one must not undertake any construction work on that land. If these defects are absent, then one must keep that land for construction.

Normally, it is very difficult to find all of the aforementioned good signs and characteristics in one place, as well as a complete absence of the defects. Nonetheless, one should opt for that land which contains the minimum defects. As stated in the *Sarva-maṇḍala-sāmānya-vidhīnām-gūhya-tantra:*

> Possessing Absolute perfection is hard to find. In brief, [one should, thus accept] a well levelled place of fine texture, depressed in the east; a land possessing water resources, and adorned with trees of good qualities; attractive to one's eyes and mind, free from the defects of earth, and harmless in general features [should prefer].[13]

---

11. The measurement of a span is equal to the stretched length between the tip of the thumb to the tip of the middle finger, *Bod rgya tshig mdzod chen mo* and *A Tibetan-English Dictionary,* cf. *mtho.*
12. *Collected Works of Buston*, op. cit., fol. 2a4 (p. 172).
13. Kagyur, op. cit., fol. 142a4-5.

Phun sum tshogs pa kun bzang ba'i / tshogs pa dag ni rnyed par bka' / mdor na sa bzhi mnyam pa dang / mdangs snum shar du bzhol ba bzhed / chu mang ldan pa'i gnas dang ni / ljon shing bzang pos brgyan pa dang / bdag gi mig yid mgu ba dang / 'tse med zug rngu spangs pa ni //

Taking Possession of the Building Site

A plot of land that possess good signs and characteristics is not only advantageous from a religious point of view, but from an architectural angle as well. Therefore, whosoever intends to build a stūpa on such a spot should at first obtain that land from its landowner either through a verbal or legal agreement or through purchase. After use of the land has been granted by its landlords, consent from the local spirits is sought. Subsequently, one sets up the ritual articles such as the three-fold ritual offering cakes (*cha gsum btor ma)*, the five kinds of essential offerings,[14] the white mustard seeds, the *gu-gul*[15] and other requisite articles. Then, the *Vajrācārya* performs the recitation of the self-generating *(bdag bskyed bzlas pa,* Skt: *ātmotpāda japa).* He invites the *kṣetrapālas* (field protectors), offers the cake (*gtor ma,* Skt: *bali)* and outer and inner offerings. After the permission to use the site has been requested, the *kṣetrapālas* are sent back to their own abodes. Then, the invisible Earth-goddess is invited, offerings are made to her and her permission is also sought for the use of this site. Thus, the use of the site is requested both from the *kṣetrapālas* and the Earth-goddess.

Eliminating the Interfering Adversities from the Site

In order to eliminate all interferences and hindrances from the site, the performer should command the evil spirits and demons etc., who cause hindrances and behave mischievously in that very place, to satisfy themselves with the ritual cake and go back to their own abodes or somewhere else. Then the ritual offering cake is thrown near the

14. They are termed as *Nyer spyod lnga (upacāra),* which consist of flowers, incense, lamps, perfume and food, *Bod rgya tshig mdzod chen mo,* and Sarat Chandra Das, *A Tibetan-English Dictionary,* cf., *Nyer spyod lnga.*
15. *Gu gul* is a corrupt Sanskrit word *guggul.* It is one of the costly incense consisting of two kinds, i.e. one kind of which is white and another is black. They are used in medicine and their smell drives away the evil spirits. Sarat Chandra Das, op. cit., cf., *gu gul.*

entrance to the site accompanied by violent playing of the ritual musical instruments and reciting of the wrathful *mantras*. After this, the site is fumigated by the incense of *gugul*, white mustard seeds are scattered, scented water is sprinkled, and the ashes of the previous Fire Offering Rituals (*sbyin bsregs*) are spread all around the ground to eliminate all interfering evil spirits. By the power of these ritual acts, all residual hindrances are removed, and interferences are eliminated.

Preparation of the *Tsha Tsha*[16]

Before preparing the *tsha tsha,* one must first complete the preceding ritual activities. (Examining the site, taking possession of the site, and eliminating the interferences are the necessary prerequisites to be performed before proceeding to extract clay from the site.) Only after these preliminaries have been completed, may clay be extracted for making the *tsha tsha* preceded by fixing of five wooden pegs (one on each of the four cardinal directions and the fifth one in the centre of the proposed site). The practitioner must recite the *mantra* known as *"Oṁ vajra kili kili kilya sarva duṣṭān huṁ phaṭ"* seven times while fixing the pegs. The pegs have to remain fixed until the completion of extraction of clay. The clay should be refined and well-lavigated, so that it may have the qualities of smoothness, uniform texture, and be easily mouldable and capable of being baked well. The clay is mixed with clean water (sometimes even mixed with the powder of precious substances or with the ashes of the deceased priests or high lamas).

Apropos this, Sahajavilāsa says: "Ashes of the deceased person should be ground into powder, then mixed with clay, and the *tsha tsha* prepared from it. The prepared *tsha tsha* are then deposited within the stūpa or placed near a big river."[17]

The clay mixed with water and other substances has to be well-kneaded until it reaches its forging point. The well-kneaded clay has to be then moulded in a manner similar to the open-casting technique. First the mould is coated with oil, so that a clearer impression results, and the clay separates from the mould more easily. The mould is usually

16. *Tsha tsha* are the miniature images of the Buddhist pantheons or of stūpas, made of moulded clay which is either baked in the sun or fired in the kiln.
17. Sahajavilāsa, op. cit., fol. 312a2.

made of bronze material, attached with a wooden handle. After being separated from the mould, a hole should be made in the bottom centre of each *tsha tsha,* which has to be dried in the sun or fired in the kiln. Then a scroll of *mantras,* written either in gold or vermilion and rolled on a tiny stick (sometimes rolled without the stick) has to be inserted within the hole of each *tsha tsha.*

It seems that different schools have varying methods of rolling the scrolls. In this connection, Zuchen Tsultim Rinchen, a scholar of the present century adds:

> According to our [Śākyapa] tradition, we place the letters facing inwards and roll the mantra scroll starting with the heading, and ending with Supplication Prayers. The order of placing [various mantras]: The names of the priests and their mantras are to be placed in between the [thirteenth] wheel and the *harmika;* the mantras of the higher tantras *(rgyud sde gong ma,* Skt: *Anuttaryogatantra)* are to be placed above the shoulder of vase; the mantras of three lower tantras[18] *(rgyud sde 'og ma)* are to be placed in between the waist of vase and the steps; a set of five great *dhāranis*[19] *(gsungs chen sde lnga)* should be placed in all the upper and lower sections; the mantras of sūtra are to be placed above the steps; and the mantras of dharma-protectors *(dharmapāla)* and wealth-deities along with various auspicious wishing-prayers and so on should be placed inside the Throne section.[20]

Apropos the above, Khenchen Ngawang Chodak of the same school explains:

> Most of the Tantricians (Tantric practitioners) of the various schools (the Buston, Zongpa, and so forth, but excluding the

18. They are comprised of *Kriyātantra, Caryātantra* and *Yogatantra.*
19. They consist of *Gtsug tor rnam rgyal (Uṣṇīṣavijayā), Gtsug tor dri med (Vimaloṣṇīṣa), Gsang ba ring bsrel (Guyhadhātu), Bya ba rgyen 'bum* and *Rten 'brel snying po (Pratīyasamutpādahṛdaya), Bod rgya tshig mdzod chen mo,* cf., *Gzungs lnga.*
20. *Gzungs 'bul gyi lag len nyung gsal bzhugs so, Collected Writings of Zuchen Tsultim Rinchen,* Vol. CA (3), p. 318.

Ngorpa) roll the mantra scroll from the bottom end. This practice is not acceptable and may have adverse effects such as the migration of the border people towards the central region and misunderstanding between the ruler and subjects. Because of this practice, the heading mantra will be at the outside and the ending mantra will be in the centre. But rolling from the heading first is excellent, for this [the mantra] will have its heading in the centre.[21]

A tradition has also arisen of inserting three barley grains, *'bru gsum,* inside the *tsha-tsha.* Although there is no clear indication of this practice in the texts, it is possible that the custom grew out of a textually-based tradition in connection with the three syllables *"Oṁ āh huṁ,"*[22] which are referred to in the texts as *"yig 'bru gsum"* or in abbreviated form *'bru gsum.* These three syllables should be inscribed upon all religious objects immediately upon their completion, in order

21. Khenchen Ngawang Chodak, *Sdom gsum kha skong gi rnam par bshad pa legs shad rgyan gyi me tog,* Ven. T. G. Dhongthog Rinpoche (Ed. and Pub.), New Delhi, 1978, fol. 67b3-4 (p. 228).
22. The essence meaning of three syllables, i.e. *"Oṁ āh huṁ",* corresponds to religious trilogy: *sku (kāyā), gsung (vāk), thugs (citta)* respectively. In this connection, the English translation of Tucci's Indo-Tibetica I, footnote 1, p. 25, gives us a vivid description of the said formula as follows: "This threefold division, having such an important part in Tibetan mysticism, is also derived from India. The school which started to give an esoteric meaning to the three syllables *Oṁ āh huṁ*—symbols as they are of the adamantine Body, Word and Spirit, namely the indefectible emanations of the Supreme Being—is the school connected with the *Guhyasamāja.* This one, since the beginning of the two Tibetan sects of the *Bka' dam pa* and of the *Bka' rgyud pa,* was considered as the fundamental guide for mystical realizations and experience. The eleventh chapter *(paṭala)* of this text, wholly dedicated to the esoteric interpretation of the three syllables, among other things says:

    oṁkāraṁ jñānahṛdayaṁ kāyavajrasamāvahaṁ
    āḥkāraṁ bodhinairātmyaṁ vākyavajrasamāvahaṁ
    hūṁkāraṁ kāyavākcittaṁ trivajrābhedyamāvaham.

"The letter *oṁ* beginning of the mystic science is vehicle of the adamantine essence of the Body; the letter *āḥ* (symbol of the) impersonality of all things is the vehicle of the adamantine essence of the Word; the letter *huṁ* is (symbol) of the Body, of the Word and of the Spirit and is indestructible vehicle of the threefold adamantine essence."

to ward off interferences before performing the Ritual of Consecration. Given the similarity in spelling, it is possible that the latter practice of three barleys grew out of the former practice of three syllables—perhaps due to a misreading of the abbreviated form of *'gru gsum* as three barley grains or as a form of symbolizing the three syllables.

Finally, the *tsha tsha* should be painted with gold if affordable; otherwise, it would suffice to paint them in red or yellow or white. They can also be left without any paint. Finally, the hole should be closed by clay or with sealing-wax.

It is stated in the *Dri med rnam gnyis kyi mchod rten bzhengs bskabs nyer mkho'i zin bris gzhan phan zla snang* text that:

> 99 number yellow *tsha tsha* of *Raśmivimala* and 108 number white *tsha tsha* of *Vimaloṣṇīṣa* are to be manufactured in conformity with the ceremonial rites and inserted with their *mūla-mantras.* However, if the *mūla-mantra* does not fit well into the small *tsha tsha,* a provision is made for allowing insertion of the *hṛdya-mantra* instead. It is excellent if one produces as many *tsha tsha* as possible.[23]

Mahāyāna texts of both the Kagyur and Tangyur Testaments detail the ceremonial rites for preparing *tsha tsha,* accompanied with their appropriate *mantras.*[24] There are specific *mantras* for each

---

The Chinese translation (Taisho 18.479a) reads rather in a different way: "The *oṁ* is the foundation of the mystic science and is synonymous with the adamantine essence of the Body; the letter *āḥ* indicates the impersonality of things and is synonymous with the adamantine essence of Word; the letter *hūṁ* (stands for) the indestructible and is synonymous of the adamantine essence of the Spirit."

23. *Rnying ma bka' ma rgyas pa,* op. cit., pp. 551-52.
24. *Sarvaprajñāntapāramita-siddhacaitya-nāma-dhāraṇī,* Kagyur, Derge, Vol. PHA, Toh. 601, fol. 260a3-266b4; and Kagyur, Zungdus, Derge, Vol. E, Toh. 884, fol. 129a3-135b3; *Caityasādhanavidhi* of Śāntigarbha, Tangyur, Gyud, Derge, Vol. JU, Toh. 2652, fol. 302a2-306b5; and Narthang, Vol. GU, fol. 314b1-320b1; *Mchod rten gcig btab na bye ba btab pa 'gyur ba'i gzungs,* Kagyur, Zungdus, Derge, Vol. E, Toh. 921, fol. 265a1-7; *Mchod rten gcig btab na bye ba btab par 'gyur ba'i sngags dang choga,* Kagyur, Kontseg, Derge, Vol. PHA, Toh. 602, fol. 266b4-276a3; and Narthang, Vol. NA, fol. 319a4-b6; *Mchod rten dgu gdab pa'i cho,* Tangyur, Gyud, Derge, Vol. PU, Toh. 3075, fol. 171b6-7; *Mchod rten lnga gdab pa'i cho ga,* Ibid., fol. 171b3-6; *Mchod rten gsum gdab pa'i cho ga,* Ibid., fol. 171b1-3.

preparatory action, such as digging, kneading, forging, moulding, etc. For instance, the *mantra* for digging is: *"Oṁ vajra khan khan phaṭ svāhā*'', which could be rendered in English, *''Oṁ vajra dig dig phaṭ svāhā.*'' *Mantras* are sacred invocation, incantations or prayers and thus during the translation of Sanskrit texts into Tibetan, the original Sanskrit *mantras* were left untranslated in order to honour and preserve the sanctity and efficacy of the *mantras.*

Examination of the Serpent-bellied Earth-Lord

In order to examine the Earth-Lord, the constructional site is mapped out in a perfect square and then each of its four sides are divided into ten large units of equal size. Then each of those large units should be further divided into nine equal parts, so that every side of the square will have ninety small units equalling the number of days in three months of the lunar calendar.

Inside the square is drawn the Serpent-Bellied Earth-Lord. He has a hood of snakes above his head, the torso of a man, and from the navel and below, a serpent's body. In his right hand he holds a *maṇi* (jewel) over his right hip, while the left hand covers his left ear. Concerning the measurement of his body, his torso is five spans in length, and similarly, his snake tail measures five spans. In some illustrations, he is shown with horns;[25] in others, without horns (Figure 2).[26]

Way of Residing and the Movement of the Earth-Lord

In the first month of autumn, the Earth-Lord's head should reside at the north-east junction and the tip of his tail at the south-west with his mouth facing towards the south. Then, with the passing of each day, both his head as well as the tip of his tail should be moved one small unit each in a clockwise movement towards the south and west directions, respectively. In this way, he is moved through the ninety small units of each side in three months, and through the four groups of ninety small units in one year of the lunar calendar, that is, three hundred and sixty days.

---

25. See Thupten Legshay Gyatso, *Gateway to the Temple*, p. 31, figure 5.
26. Extracted from *Sumpa Khenpo* text.

Figure 2. Serpent-bellied Earth-Lord (Extracted from *Sumpa Khenpo* text).

Where to Dig First

The point to first strike the earth is decided upon the basis of the serpent's position. For instance, if his head is facing east, and the tip of his tail pointing west, then from the eastern edge, count twenty-seven small units to west (crossing the area of his hood, face and chest). Then count thirteen and half small units from the vertical axis towards the north, which is to the rear, and one then reaches the point to first strike the earth. Here one must first dig out the site from front of the

Earth- Lord's right armpit measuring nine small units to the west of that eastern edge and four and half small units to the south from the northern edge.

Regarding this, Tsong Khapa quoted a stanza from *Vibhūti* text, supposedly based on the *Maṇḍalavidhi,* which is not accessible. The stanza reads:

> Pass over twentyseven small units from the East and thirteen and a half from the North. Dig out first, from the front of the armpit, nine small units from the eastern edge to the West and four and a half small units to the South from the northern edge.[27]
> *Shar nas cha ni nyi shu rtsa bdun dor / byang nas phyed dang bcu bzhi cha dor bas / shar nub cha dgu lho byang phyed dang lnga/ 'di ni mchan gyi mdun du thog mar brko //*

Tsong Khapa further adds: "If one digs out the spot in conformity with the prescribed methods, one will fulfil all the wishes of oneself and others. If, however, one digs from any spot other than that prescribed, disadvantageous or adverse effects such as death, loss of wealth, and separation from dear ones may occur."[28]

In addition, there seems to be a tradition of digging first from the navel of the Earth-Lord. However, Buston does not agree with this view and asserts that it would be a mistake to start the digging from the navel.[29]

At this juncture, the digger should generate himself in the form of the wrathful deity known as *bgegs mthar byed.*[30] Subsequently, the

27. *Lam gyi rim pa gsang ba kun gyi gnad rnam par phye ba sngags rim chen mo,* Collected Works of Je Tsong Khapa Lobsang Dakpa alais Gyalwa Khabdag Dorjee Chenpo, Vol. GA, fol. 140a4. It is a critical exposition of the system of the Esoteric Buddhism (Mantrayāna or Vajrayāna Buddhism) in general. This is one of the most important works in the Gelukpa school and constitutes a fundamental introduction to the whole system of Buddhism of the Gelukpa school and is generally called by a brief name *Snags rim chen po.*
28. *Snags rim chen po,* op. cit., fol. 144a4-5.
29. *Dpal dus kyi 'khor lo'i cho ga yon tan kun 'byung,* Collected Works of Buston, Vol. CA (5), fol. 15a2 (p. 289).
30. *Vidhnantaka,* Tibetan-Sanskrit Dictionary, cf., *Bgegs mthar byed.*

digger's hoe has to be imagined as adorned with a *vajra.* It should be held in the right hand raised above and the left hand kept below, while the digger faces the south-east. Then, with a calm mind, the first four shovels of soil should be put inside the ritual cakes, and scattered, starting from the south-east. The fifth shovel of earth should be placed in the centre of the site. Thereafter, the labourers are permitted to dig out the site from all the sides and corners.[31]

Removing the Defects of the Soil

After having dug out the site, one has to remove the defects of the earth such as bones, ashes, stones, potsherds, chaff, charcoal, tree-stumps, thorny-brambles, etc., if any of these exist. As stated in the *Sarva-maṇḍalasāmānyavidhīnām-gūhya-tantra:*

> (One) should plough the land with a hoe and remove any defects in the soil. Land which possesses soil-defects will fail to fulfil the desired purpose. By soil-defects is meant potsherds, ashes, tree-stumps, and thorny-brambles. Remove them all, carefully.[32]
> *'jor gyis sa ni bslog bya shing / de nas zug rngu dbyung bar bya/ zug rngu bcas pa'i sa bzhi ni / las byas pa dag 'grub mi 'gyur //*

Furthermore, in the *Śrīvajrāḍaka-nāma-mahātantrarāja* text of the Kagyur Testament it is said:

> The various levels of minor *siddhis* and others [i.e. middle and superior *siddhis*] attainable are effected by the depth to which one digs—to the level of knee, groin, and navel, respectively. After removing the defects of the earth, such as chaff, stones, potsherds, charcoal, thorny-brambles etc., one should pat the soil firmly.[33]
> *dman sogs dngos grub bye brag gis / spus mo chu so lte ba'i bar / brkos la phub ma rdo dang ni / gyo mo sol ba zug rngu dang / tsher ma la sogs bsal la bcag //*

It is clearly important to strive to remove the defects of the earth to the maximum possible extent, as this enhances the possibilities of gaining *siddhis.*

31. *Collected Works of Buston*, op. cit., fol. 14b6.
32. Kagyur, op. cit., fol. 144a3.
33. Kagyur, op. cit., fol. 97b3-4.

Similarly, the disadvantages that will ensue from the existence of defects in the earth are explained in the *Vajrāvali-nāma-maṇḍalavidhi* as follows:

> If the place contains stones, a fierce wind will blow. If it contains bones, one will suffer from severe aches. If the land contains chaff and charcoal, one will be affected by infectious diseases. If it contains hairs, roots, and wood, etc., one will suffer poverty.[34]
> *sa de la rdo yod na rlung 'byung ngo / rus pa yod na zug gzer ro / gyo dum yod na klugs pa nyid do / phub ma dang sol ba yod na rims so / skra dang rtsa ba dang shing la sogs pa yod na / nye bar 'tsho ba phra mo'o zhes pas //*

Tsong Khapa, however, is of the opinion that the disadvantages will ensue from not removing the defects of the earth, rather than from their mere existence.[35]

If the land contains a lot of soil-defects and it is not possible to remove them completely, then the Tantric texts prescribe that the place be purified by means of *mantras,* until all the negativities associated with the defects are cleared away. As stated in the *Sarvamaṇḍala-sāmānyavidhīnām-gūhya-tantra:* "In case one is unable to remove all the defects of the earth, that land must be purified by secret *mantra* alone."[36] (*zug rngu'i nyes pa thams cad ni / gal te dbyung bar mi nus na / der ni gsang sngags kho na yis / sbyang ba legs par byas par 'gyur) //*

Thupten Legshay Gyatso adds: "If not through *mantra*, then the greatest purifier is (to establish everything as the direct realization of) interdependent origination (*pratītyasamutpāda)*, emptiness (*śūnyatā*), and so on."[37]

II. RITES DURING THE ACTUAL CONSTRUCTION

In the second stage, the following ritual activities must be performed during the actual construction of the stūpa:

---

34. Abhayakaragupta, op. cit., fol. 4b5.
35. *Sngags rim chen mo,* op. cit., fol. 144b2.
36. Kagyur, op. cit., fol. 144a.
37. Thupten Legshay Gyatso, *Gateway to the Temple*, p. 33.

Layout of the Actual Construction Ground

One commences the construction by smoothly plastering the entire surface of the ground, beginning from the north-east direction, with a mixture of cow dung, gathered before it falls to the earth, and cow urine. Then the eight major lines *(thig chen brgyad)*—two diagonals, two *Brahma*-lines *(tshang thig)*, i.e. the vertical and the horizontal axes, and the four outer borders—have to be established correctly. It is indeed noteworthy that the correctness at this point is crucial as a mistake here would affect the accuracy, and hence the religious value of the subsequent work. The method of establishing the eight major lines is exactly the same as that of the traditional artists, established in various Tibeto-Buddhist religious works.[38]

The eight directions (four cardinal and four intermediate) must be marked with eight pegs made of *Acacia catechu*[39] wood which measure eight spans each. One is also allowed to use Juniper *(deodar)* wood in place of the *Acacia catechu* wood if it is not available.[40] Before hammering on the pegs, one must recite over them the *mantra "Oṁ stom bandha svāhā"* one hundred and eight times.[41] While implanting each peg with a "vajra-hammer", one recites another *mantra* known as *"Namaḥ samantavajra akotayasame mahācantali phaṭ phaṭ sarvatrarakṣana trat mat mat phaṭ."*[42] The hammer is supposed to be made of half-burnt wood previously used at a cemetery for burning corpses. It would be excellent, if at this time, one or one's colleague performs the rites of cleansing, of beverage-offering, and of banishing troublesome land spirits.

Next, one should dig out three trenches of different depths followed by erection of their walls in order to strengthen the structure and prevent it from sinking. The innermost trench should be circular in shape, and should match the interior diameter of the dome. It should be deeper than the other two trenches. The second and the third

---

38. See Jackson's *Tibetan Thangka Painting: Methods and Materials*, op. cit., p. 115, for establishing the eight major lines.
39. *Seng ldeng*, Skt: *svadir*, Sarat Chandra Das, op. cit., cf. *Seng ldeng.*
40. *Rnying ma bka' ma rgyas pa*, op. cit., p. 560.
41. *Collected Works of Minling Lochen Dharmaśri*, Vol. XIII (PHA), fol. 12a1.
42. Ibid., fol. 12a1.

trenches should match the first step and plinth, respectively, both in size and shape (circular or square). The outermost trench should be the shallowest.

According to *Rnying ma bka' ma* text: "Next one must conceal vases filled with precious substances within the earth. If circumstances allow, one should obtain nine Nāga-vases *(klu bum dgu),* each filled with five kinds of jewels, medicines, perfumes, grains and food-essences *(snying po),* and place one vase each at the four cardinal directions, the four intermediate directions, and the centre. If one is incapable of obtaining nine vases, one can make use of the five Nāga-vases, one each at the four cardinal directions and the centre. In extremely difficult circumstances, only the centre vase is required. In all of the above cases, another vase, generally called the 'Lord of Earth-Vase' *(sa bdag bum pa)* must be placed in front of the centre vase. All the vases should be concealed in pits dug knee-deep and then encased tightly with stones, etc."[43] One then makes the thanks-giving offerings and apologizes for any errors or omissions that might have occurred during the ritual performances.

The twentyfive substances mentioned above are classified into five sets of five substances each. These are enumerated in Sahajavilāsa's commentary on *Vimaloṣṇīṣa,*[44] and are as follows:

1. The first set is of five kinds of jewels: coral, gold, silver, pearl and undamaged gems.[45]
2. The second set is of five kinds of medicinal substances:[46] *sadaghra, vyaghra* (castor oil), *girkarni* (probably *kantakari,* Wild Rubus, Solanum Jaquini), *pato*[47] and *hasdeva.*[48]

---

43. *Rnying ma bka' ma rgyas pa,* op. cit., p. 552.
44. Tangyur, Gyud drel, Derge, Vol. THU, fol. 291b3-4.
45. Mentioned a coral *(byu ru)* instead of the undamaged gem, *Bod rgya tshig mdzod chen mo,* cf., *Rin chen lnga.*
46. They consist of *sle tre (kughuci* or *guḍūcī), samūdraphen (rgya mtsho sbu ba), Indrahasta (dbang po lag pa),* Indra's arm, a viscid aromatic root of the Salep Orchid, and white *Aparājita (shu dag dkar po),* Ibid., cf. *sman lnga.*
47. Written *Patola,* Ibid., cf. *Patola.*
48. I am in no position to enumerate the Tibetan equivalent word to this.

3. The third set is of five kinds of grains: wheat, barley, unhusked rice, sesamum and *maśa (mon sran gre'u*[49]*).*

4. The fourth set is of five kinds of perfumes: *Sandal,* camphor, saffron or safflower,[50] nutmeg and *Agaru*[51] (Eagle wood or Aloe).

5. The fifth set is of five kinds of food-essences *(snying po lnga):* refined salt, unrefined sugar, butter and *śilaji (brag zhun).*[52]

Actual Construction of the Stūpa and its Accessories

The next step is the actual construction of the stūpa, beginning with the foundation and extending up to the main throne slab. This lower section of the stūpa is generally known as the 'Lion Throne' *(seng khri,* Skt: *siṁhāsana).* Its height should be four large units and its shape either square or octagonal, corresponding with the shape of the steps. The inside of the structure should be left hollow to accommodate the various kinds of articles like precious stones, medicinal things, grains, etc. There is a tradition of inserting *tsha tsha* in the Lion Throne's hollow, although it is uncertain whether such a practice was prevalent in ancient India, for I have not located any literary source which has made any reference to this custom.

Even my primary texts do not include a mere line in this regard, except the text of Minling Lochen Dharmaśrī. However, that too, is very meagre and perhaps may not meet our requirement. In his text entitled, *"Dri med rnam gnyis gzungs la rten te mchod rten bzhengs pa la nye bar kho ba'i cho ga bklags pas 'grub pa",* the only information given therein is as follows: "One should unmistakenly place the *dhāraṇī* in the lower section according to the existing instruction of the lineage."[53]

A similar practice is, however, mentioned in Sahajavilāsa's commentary on the *Vimaloṣṇīṣa* text: "Apparently, one may insert in

49. It grows in one of the sub-Himalayan regions called *Mon* which is presently in Arunachal Pradesh.
50. See Jackson's *Tibetan Thangka Painting: Methods and Materials,* op. cit., p. 115.
51. Mentioned a musk *(Bla rtsi,* Skt: *kasturi)* instead of *Āgaru, Bod rgya tshigs mdzod chen mo,* op. cit., cf. *dri lnga.*
52. Sesame oil *(til mar)* in place of *brag zhun,* Ibid., cf. *snying po lnga.*
53. *Collected Works of Min Ling Lochen Dharmaśrī,* op. cit., fol. 12a3-4.

the lower section of the stūpa a scroll containing the names of persons who intend to obstruct the deceased", for whom the stūpa is constructed.[54]

After placing various kinds of sacred objects and other articles within the hollowed structure, it then has to be covered by the main throne slab, which is shaped in the form of a large lotus.

Upon the Throne, the base of Ten-virtues and the four steps are to be erected, leaving their insides hollow, and then filled with as many *tsha tsha* and *dhāraṇī* as possible. It is said that the greater the number of *tsha tsha* put in a stūpa, the greater its power and blessings. Here many also house funeral ashes, old scriptures, paintings and so forth. The hollowed structure is then covered by the vase-base, which is also shaped like a lotus.

Method of Arranging the Vimaloṣṇīṣa Maṇḍala and Ritualistic Articles

One commences by smoothly plastering the surface of the vase-base and drawing upon it the *maṇḍala* of *Vimaloṣṇīṣa* with a coloured chalk. Alternatively, it is possible to engrave the *maṇḍala* on a stone-slab, properly colouring and coating it with hard varnish. This alternative method is offered solely for convenience's sake and to prevent defects such as fading. A blue canopy should be pitched above the *maṇḍala*. Finally, starting from the north-east, eight flowers are arrayed, each one of them marking one of the eight directions. Around the flowers, additional offerings are arranged: two types of water,[55] and five kinds of essential offerings consisting of flowers, incense, light, perfume and food. It is optimal if, surrounding the above offerings, six sets of essential offerings can be set up in each of the four cardinal directions, with an additional set of offerings in the east. However, one is only required to make one set of offerings in each of the four cardinal directions with an extra set of offerings in the east. It is extremely important to take the precaution of selecting optimum materials for the ritual offerings and containers, since these will be kept inside the stūpa for ever. Therefore, if available, one should use vessels which are not easily broken and corroded, i.e. bronze, copper, etc. If such a vessel is not available, then one can use earthenware.

---

54. Tangyur, op. cit.
55. They consist of *ārghyam (mchod yon)* and *pādyam (zhabs bsil)*.

In the vessel for the *arghyam* offering (the water offering for washing the mouth) one should first fill some refined-salt *(lan tshwa)*. Next fill the vessel with seven substances, viz.: (1) white flowers such as Magnolia *(campak)* or the flower of the *balu*[56] *(taliśa)* plant, whichever may be acquired; (2) white sesame; (3) white grains; (4) roasted rice; (5) *kuśa*; (6) scent; and (7) cheese, instead of milk (as there is a risk of curdling the milk). In the vessel for the *pādya* offering (the water offering for washing the feet) refined-salt should first be filled, and then the five kinds of original bark and some washing powder should be added. However, in Tibet, there has been a tradition of using the inner barks *(bar shun)* of the rhododendron *(ba lu)*, white willow *(lcang dkar)*, apricot *(kham bu)*, tamarisk *('am bu)*, and white sandal instead of the five original barks, due to their non-availability. The washing powder is made by grinding materials such as white peas *(sran dkar)*, *upabrśa (nye shing)* and rice-chaff *('bras pu bcad pa'i shun pa)*, etc. For the flower offering, artificial flowers should be made from brocade, if available. Otherwise, one should use white grain in place of the flowers. The incense-sticks are to be fixed on the incense-stand. The light offerings are to be arranged in an earthenware. In the case of the scented water *(dri chab)* offering, first after filling the refined salt one should then fill the vessel with powder of the five scents—saffron *(gur gum)*, camphor *(ga bur)*, clove *(li shi)*, nutmeg, and white sandal. The food offering is represented by *marzan,* a mixture of ground roasted barley, *tsam pa* and butter.

Outside the above offerings, eight ornamental banners (tiara, flag, banner and parasol etc., made from silk) are to be raised upon the ceramic-stands, eight in each of the eight directions, or at least one in each of the eight directions. A red curtain should encircle the banners. Next, the entire *maṇḍala* is surrounded by a wall (stone, cement or wood), at least an arm-length in height.

After enclosing the ritual offerings and *maṇḍala* within the above protection wall, the ritual musical instruments and offerings for the self-generating ritual are gathered in front of the *Vajrācārya.* Then the *Vajrācārya* performs the self-generating and front-generating ritual practices, in accordance with the treatises. The threefold ritual offering

56. *Balu* belongs to species of fragrant aborescent plants *(rhododendrons)* growing in the Himalayas and Tibet, the bark and leaves of which are used as incense in Tibet, its flowers are called *dali,* Sarad Chandra Das, op. cit., cf. *ba lu.*

cakes are brought in front of the *Vajrācārya,* and are offered, one by one, to the evil spirits. At this point, the *Vajrācārya* seeks help from *Kśetrapālas* and *Dikpālas* in order to pacify obstacles and hindrances.

Finally, the *Vajrācārya* recites the verses of auspiciousness and rings the ritual bell. He then circumambulates the *maṇḍala* three times and makes a request for the accomplishment of his own and others' wishes.

Method of Arranging the Raśmivimala Maṇḍala, Axle-pole and so forth

The day after completion of the *Vimaloṣṇīṣa* rites, one should add height to the dome structure. There are important deity preparatory practices, which accompany the construction of the *Raśmivimala Maṇḍala.* These rites should be done properly in accordance with the treatises.

Next, one must engrave the *maṇḍala* of *Raśmivimala* on a stone-slab and place it in the designated area within the dome of the stūpa. If the designated area is not large enough, the *maṇḍala* may be lodged in a nearby area inside the dome. Next , the axle-pole of standard size and carved with a miniature stūpa at the top and a half-*vajra* at the bottom has to be placed in its original orientation,[57] its bottom point almost touching the centre of the *maṇḍala.* There is a risk of breaking the *maṇḍala* slab, if one places a heavy axle-pole upon it. A method to prevent such breakage is to raise the axle-pole from its *vajra* portion towards all the directions with the help of supporting-beams. It is stated in the *Ārya Raśmivimala Viśuddha Prabhā Nāma Dhāraṇī* text that, "On the four sides of the axle-pole one should insert a scroll containing the mantra of the axle-pole written ninetynine times. The *mantra* is: *"Oṁ sarvatathāgata vipulayaṣṭi mañkanakarajeta vipusitayaṣṭi dhūru dhūru samante vilokite sarasara manasarvapava viśodhāni sambodhāni pravaryaṣṭi parimaniduṣṭah uruciramala viśuddhe huṁ huṁ svāḥā."*[58] One can also wrap a scroll of the same *mantra*, around the axle-pole.

The text further adds that a scroll of *hṛdaya-mantra* known as *"Oṁ sarva tathāgata malviśodhāni rudhāvale pratisatisamsara tathāgata dhātu*

57. In its original orientation is in reference to its standing position and the direction it faced when it was a living tree.

58. *Ārya raśmivimala viṣuddha prabhā nāma dhāraṇī,* op. cit., fol. 12a4-5.

dhāre dhūru dhūru sandhāra sandhāra sarvatathāgatādhiṣthanadhisthite svāḥā" should be written in a similar fashion and placed within the base of the axle-pole.[59]

Apropos the above, Minling Lochen Dharmaśri adds:

> Obtain an axle-pole of standard size. Then, one should engrave niches on the top, bottom, and on [the middle of ?] the four sides of the axle-pole to accommodate *dhāraṇī, mantras,* etc. In each niche on the four sides, one should place the mantra of axle-pole and the *dhāraṇī* of the *sgrib sel (Sarvanīvāraṇaviṣkambhina)* known as *"Namo bhagavate nava nava...."* each written 99 times. Likewise, in the top of the axle-pole insert *dhāraṇī* of the *Raśmivimala* (the longer one), *Uṣṇīṣavijayā* and relics, and in the bottom, *hṛdaya-mantra* of *Raśmivimala* and *Pratītyasamutpāda* are to be placed."[60]

It is excellent if genuine conch-shells *(dung chos)* are placed along the four sides of the *maṇḍala's snam bu* (outermost edge), for holding the precious substances. If conch-shells are not available then one has to make vessels out of stone or clay, and apply a coating of white-wash and hard varnish upon them. Inside, they should be filled with refined-salt and with five different types of scented powder. On the eastern *snam bu,* one should place three vessels containing incense of sandalwood, aloe-wood, juniper, and so on. In the south, one should place a conch-shell containing the above scents and an earthenware filled with flower and rice. On the western *snam bu,* one should place a painted vase filled with a certain porridge called *kri sa ra,* which is made from a mixture of black sesame, *māśaka* and rice. One is allowed to use white peas in case *māśaka* is not available. One should also place a vase filled with the three white foods, and an earthen plate containing 99 kinds of different fruits. On the northern *snam bu,* one should place an earthen plate holding a round ritual cake, white in colour, which is surrounded by different kinds of food, such as *mar thud,*[61] biscuits *(khur ba),* etc. One should also put here an earthen pot, decorated with

59. Ibid., fol. 13b2.

60. *Collected Works of Minling Lochen Dharmaśrī,* op. cit., fol. 13a3-7.

61. *Mar thud* is a very delicious kind of food made of butter mixed with cheese and treacle or molasses.

a scarf around its neck, and containing five scents and adorned with *kuśa* grass and peacock feathers. An earthen plate containing flowers and incense is also to be placed here.

At the north-western edge, beside the conch-shell of scent offerings, one must arrange on a semi-circular slate or wooden slab an image of Gaṇeśa with his elephant-face painted blue, and holding an axe and radish. Upon the head of the image one should place a butter lamp (made of silver if affordable, otherwise it would suffice to have bronze), nailing it firmly.

The outer surroundings of the *maṇḍala* should be anointed with a mixture of scented water and oil, and flower petals should be strewn around. Then one set of offerings is made at each of the four sides, with one or three additional sets offered in the west. If a full set of offerings is not available then the individual objects of offerings, i.e. *arghyam*, scented water, flowers, incense and food should be arranged as described above. Also, various types of biscuits and fruits, white peas-pap *(sran dkar gyi chan),* milk-porridge or cheese, and a butter lamp are to be arranged in a clockwise manner starting from the southwest. Outside the above offerings, one should build special altars, one in each of the four cardinal directions, for an *arghyam* offering. To represent the *arghyam,* one should place seven offerings such as *bzed zhal* (food offering), water offering etc. In the four intermediate directions, one should arrange one offering each of incense, butter lamp and food.

Finally, the *maṇḍala* is decorated with eight victory-banners (topped with peacock feathers) one in each of the four cardinal directions and the four intermediate directions. Each banner is of a different colour: the white one in the east, reddish yellow in the south-east, black in the south, dark brown in the south-west, red in the west, multi-coloured in the north-west, yellow in the north, and greenish-yellow in the north-east. It would be best if one could obtain the eight auspicious symbols *(bkra shis rtags brgyad).* If not, then each of them can be represented in the form of miniature pictures *(tsa ka li)* drawn on birch-bark or on a small circular slate, and hung around the neck of each victory-banner. All this should be encircled with red ribbon. Above the red ribbon, woven threads are stretched to the four outer altars and on these are hung silk hangings, flags, banners and bouquets of silk flowers.

At this stage, if circumstances allow, the *Vajrācārya* and his disciples should read or recite the *Raśmivimala-Dhāraṇī* text three times or more. However, they must read it at least once. Generally, it is best if one can arrange for a special person just to read the *dhāraṇī* and *sūtra.* Then one must start ringing the ritual bells, and playing of other ritual musical instruments accompanied with the recitation of the *Pūjāmeghā-mantra* (i.e. *Oṁ sarva tathāgata saparivarārghyam praticcha pūjāmeghā samudraspharanasamaye āh huṁ).* The threefold ritual cakes are offered followed by thanks-giving offerings, and a request is made for the perfect accomplishment of one's own and others' wishes. Next, auspicious verses such as the Refuge prayer and others, which are mentioned in the *sūtra* and *tantra,* are to be recited as many times as possible.

To conclude, if circumstances allow, the lengthy auspicious verses of the *Kriyātantra,* derived from the rite of the *Vimaloṣṇīṣa* text, and Aspirational prayers like the *Bhadrācārya* are to be recited extensively.

III. RITES AFTER THE COMPLETION OF THE CONSTRUCTION

The rites after the construction involve the Ritual of Consecration, which may only be performed after the completion of religious objects. The objects to be consecrated are Buddhist monuments, large or small, including stūpas, temples, images, photographs, statues, paintings of Buddhist deities, and the like.

The English translation of the *Ritual of Consecration* prepared by Sherpa Tulku and Michael Perrott says that, "The principal purpose of the Ritual of Consecration is to invite the wisdom beings from their pure Buddha-fields through the power of the practitioner's meditation, the potency of the rituals, and the devotion of the hosts. These wisdom beings are invited, drawn into the objects to be consecrated, and their presence is sealed by the procedures of the ritual."[62]

According to the Mahāyāna Buddhism, the basic reason for performing the Ritual of Consecration is to sanctify the places and objects of worship and Dharma-study, and to make them worthy for

---

62. Tibet Journal, op. cit., p. 36.

veneration. Therefore, as soon as the religious object is completed it should be consecrated as early as possible, as explained in the *Supratiṣṭha-tantra-saṁgraha* text: "Misfortune will ensue wherever there is a completed image, which remains for a long time without being blessed; unless it has been consecrated, it is not worthy for worship."[63] Likewise, the advantages derived from consecrating such things is also stated therein: "Invisible and visible results will be obtained due to the great merits of having done so [consecrated the objects]. On account of the characteristics of the sacred form the blessing will enter into it."[64] This Ritual of Consecration plays an important role in the achievement of whatever one desires, both in this and future lives, even including the attainment of the Buddhahood.

The length of the Ritual of Consecration is variable, depending mostly upon the kind of *maṇḍala* employed. If the coloured sand *maṇḍala* is used, the ritual performance is bound to be more elaborate as the *maṇḍala* itself requires extra days for construction. Alternatively, if a *maṇḍala* is drawn either on cloth or slate, the construction ritual may be somewhat abbreviated, yet the actual procedures for the Ritual of Consecration remain unaffected. Once the Ritual of Consecration has been completed, it is very important to properly maintain the object, and keep it always clean. If circumstances allow, the Ritual of Consecration should be re-performed at least once a year.

The procedures for the Ritual of Consecration are not mentioned here due to their lengthy and sacred nature. The detailed procedures may be studied in the Kagyur and Tangyur and in the texts of later Tibetan scholars.

63. Kagyur, op. cit., fol. 146b5.
64. Ibid., fol. 146b5-6.

3

Types of Stūpas, Structural Components and Proportional Differences

A mention of various types of Tibeto-Buddhist stūpa architecture is incomplete without making references to the eight stūpas associated with the eight major events in the life of Gautama the Buddha. Tradition, in fact, has sufficiently confirmed records that the eight stūpas were constructed in the eight sacred places where these events occurred. They are generally known as the eight stūpas of the Tathāgata *(de bzhin gshegs pa'i mchod rten rgyad)*. The ancient Indian literature is replete with information regarding their names, builders, localities and the events which they commemorated, although all kinds of divergences are found regarding their details.[1] But, surprisingly, the literature on the architectural formation of these stūpas has been comparatively neglected.

According to general opinion, the shapes and dimensions of the eight fundamental types of Tibeto-Buddhist stūpas as built today are somewhat transformed types of the Indian Buddhist stūpas, except for the modification imposed by the metre. Despite this transformation, the Tibeto-Buddhist stūpa has retained all the architectural aspects and religious significance as well as spiritual values and symbolical meanings which originated in the ancient Indian Buddhist culture.

---

1. See Chapter 1, for details.

The *Kriyāsamgraha* text has enumerated four types of stūpas, i.e. like a heap grains of rice *('bras spung lta bu*, Skt: *dhānyakaṭaka)*, like an alms-bowl *(lhung bzed lta bu*, Skt: *Khakkhara)*, like a vase *(bum pa lta bu*, Skt: *kumbha)*, and like a victory-banner *(rgyal mtshan lta bu*, Skt: *dhvaja)*. Among them, the victory-banner type of stūpa is further subdivided into two: the vase-shaped type of stūpa and the bell-shaped stūpa.[2] As I have discussed earlier, traditionally, the eight fundamental types of Tibeto-Buddhist stūpas were regarded as Mahāyāna stūpas having the victory-banner shape. Excluding the stūpa of Nirvāṇa, in the remaining seven stūpas, the structure of the dome (the principle part of the stūpa) is vase-shaped. In the case of the Nirvāṇa stūpa, the dome is bell-shaped without any steps. These two forms of dome structures are the basic features of the Tibeto-Buddhist stūpa architecture. But of particular interest is the flight of four or so steps found in the eight fundamental types of stūpas (excluding the stūpa of Nirvāṇa). In these steps, one can find distinct characteristic features of each type of stūpa. The steps are generally square, circular, octagonal or polygonal in shape. The remaining structural parts are similar in all the eight types of stūpas. Occasionally, though rarely, the structures of *harmikā*, vase-base and the base of ten-virtues and below (Lion Throne) are made in conformity with the specific structural shape of the steps.

I will discuss herein the detailed structural distinctions amongst the eight types of Tibeto-Buddhist stūpas followed by their main structural components and proportional differences as propounded in the various literary sources.

Types of Stūpas

The layout shown in figure 3, is the first type of stūpa called 'Enlightenment'. It has a flight of four perfect square steps which are free from embellishments, although there is a tradition of making all the upper edges of the steps bulge out by one-quarter part of their own height to have an attractive look.

The layout shown in figure 4, is the second type of stūpa called "Heaped Lotuses". It is also called the stūpa of "Auspicious Appear-

2. 'Tangyur, Gyud drel, Derge, Vol. KU (Toh. 2531), fol. 352a7-b1.

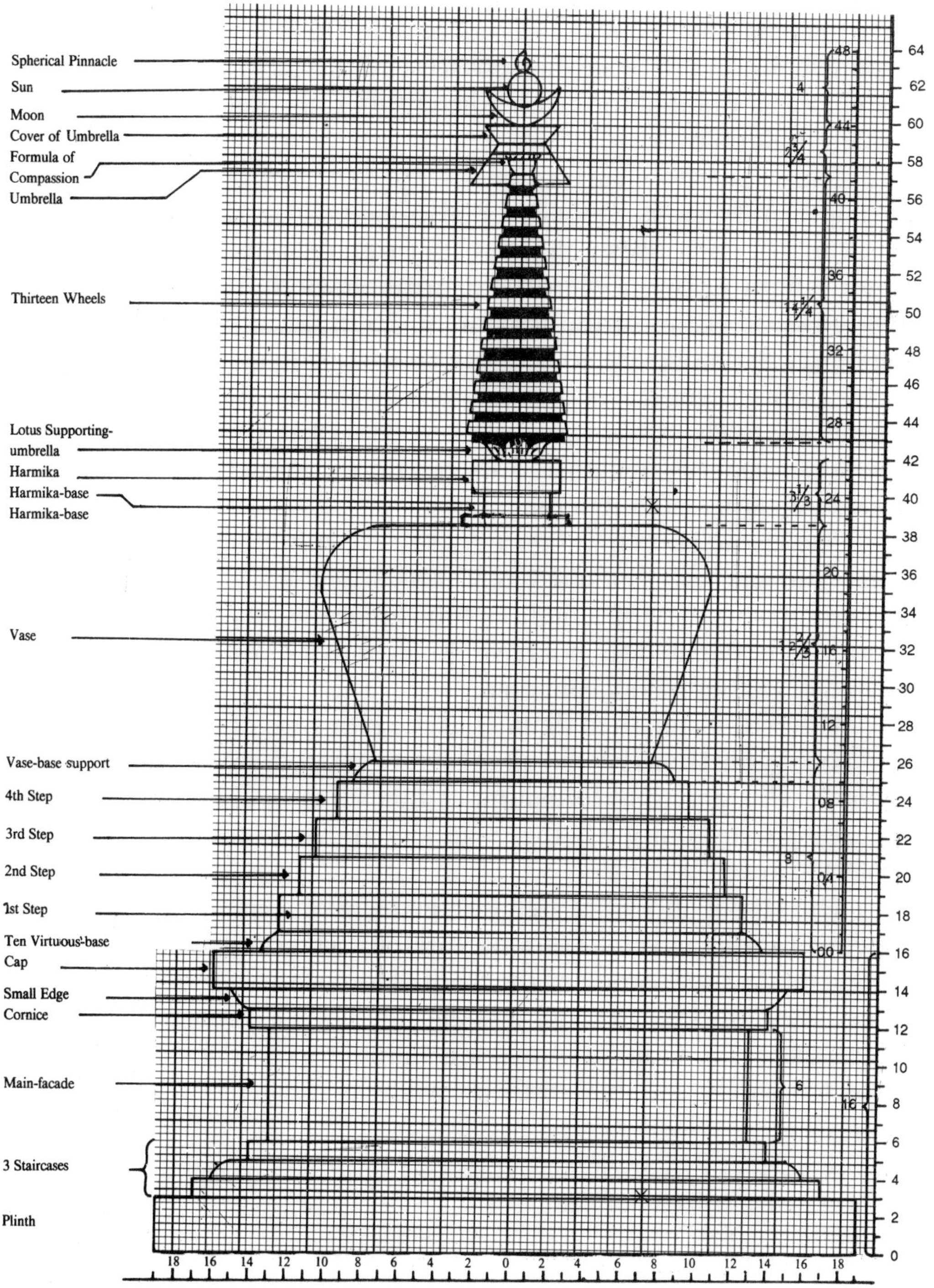

Figure 3. Stūpa of Enlightenment type

ance",[3] and "Appearance of Sugata".[4] It comprises a flight of four circular steps adorned with heaped lotuses. There is also a tradition of making a maximum of seven steps to symbolize the seven paces that the Gautama Buddha took immediately after his birth in the Lumbini garden of Kapilavastu.

The layout shown in fi+ gure 5, is the third type of stūpa called the "Multiple Auspicious Doors", or also called the stūpa of "Divine Wisdom"[5]. It comprises a flight of four square steps and each sides' centre bulges out by one-third the size of their width. These stūpas have 108 doors or niches at the maximum, 56 in the medium and 16 in minimum. Symbolically, four doors on each side symbolize the four Noble-truths, eight doors on each side symbolize the eight doors of liberations, twelve doors on each side symbolize the twelve links of interdependent origination and sixteen doors on each side symbolize the sixteen types of emptiness.

The layout shown in figure 6, is the fourth type of stūpa called "Great Miracle", or "Conquest of Tirthīkas", which is identical to the preceding ones (having a flight of four square steps projected in their centre), although it does not have doors or niches on the steps and is devoid of further embellishments.

The layout shown in figure 7, is the fifth type of stūpa called the "Descent from Heaven", or alternatively named stūpa "Offered by Devas"[6]. The structural formation of this stūpa is also similar to the preceding ones, but it has three ladders in the centre of each side's projected area.

The layout shown in figure 8, is the sixth type of stūpa called "Reconciliation", which is comprised of four octagonal steps formed by cutting off the four corners of the flight of four steps to form eight even sides. They are free from all embellishments. Occasionally, though rarely, there is a tradition of making all the upper edges of the steps projected out by one-third of their own height.

---

3. Chenga Lodos Gyaltsen, *Mchod rten gyi tshad ston pa legs shad gser gyi phreng ba,* Vol. CA, fol. 16b3.
4. *Ibid.,* fol. 16b3.
5. *Ibid.,* fol. 16b4.
6. *Ibid.,* fol. 17a2.

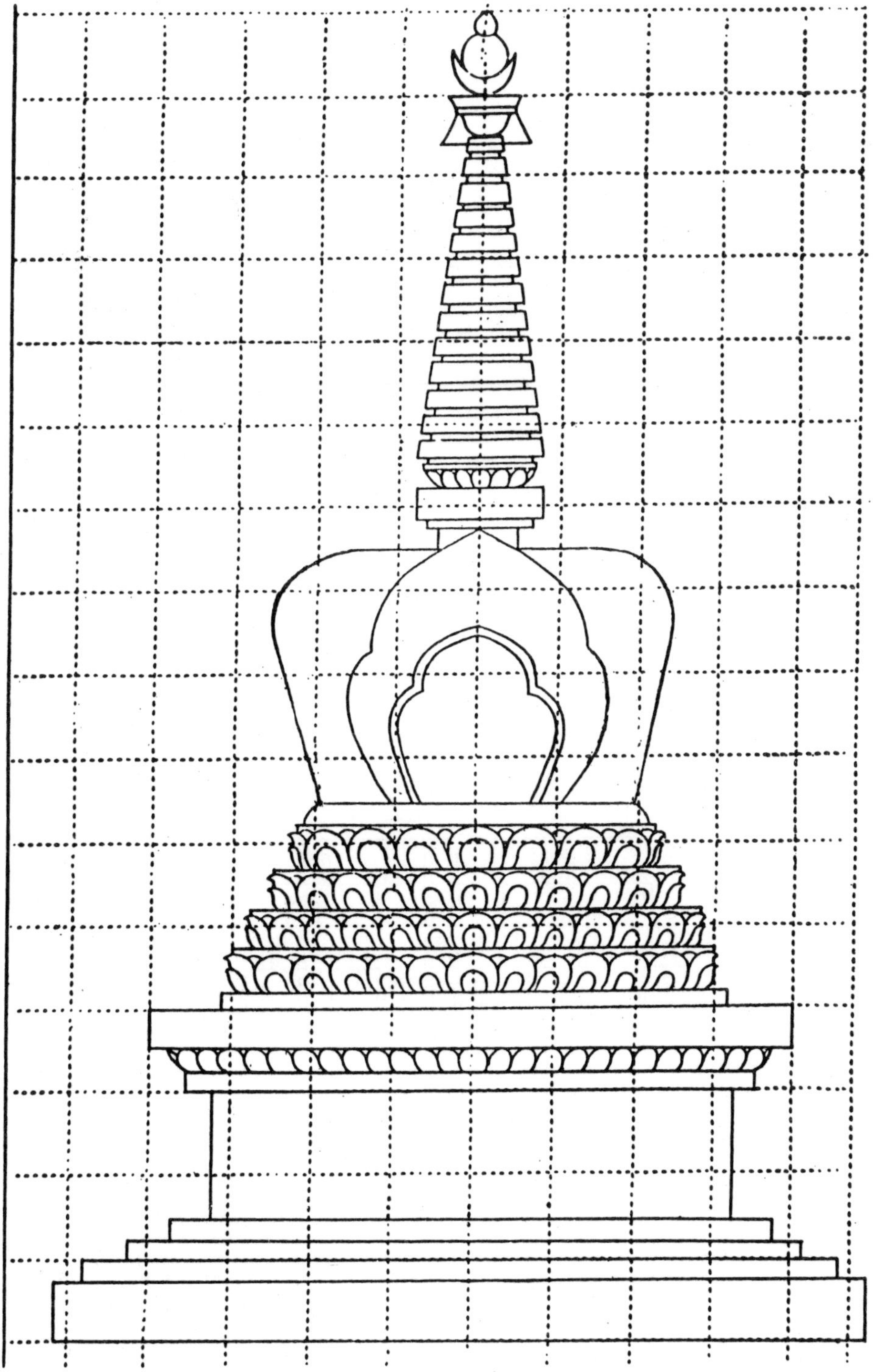

Figure 4. Stūpa of Heaped Lotuses type

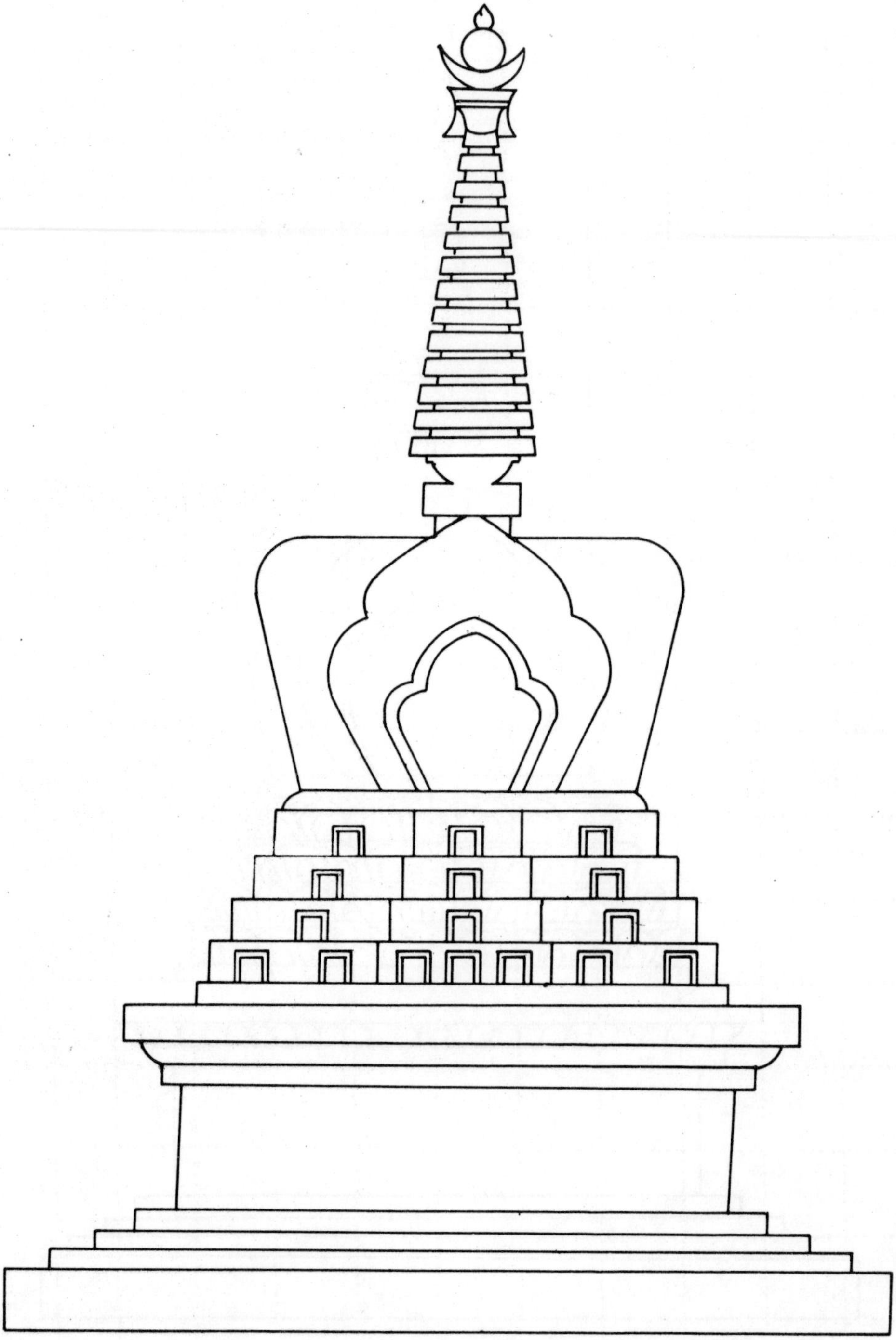

Figure 5. Stūpa of Multiple Auspicious Doors type

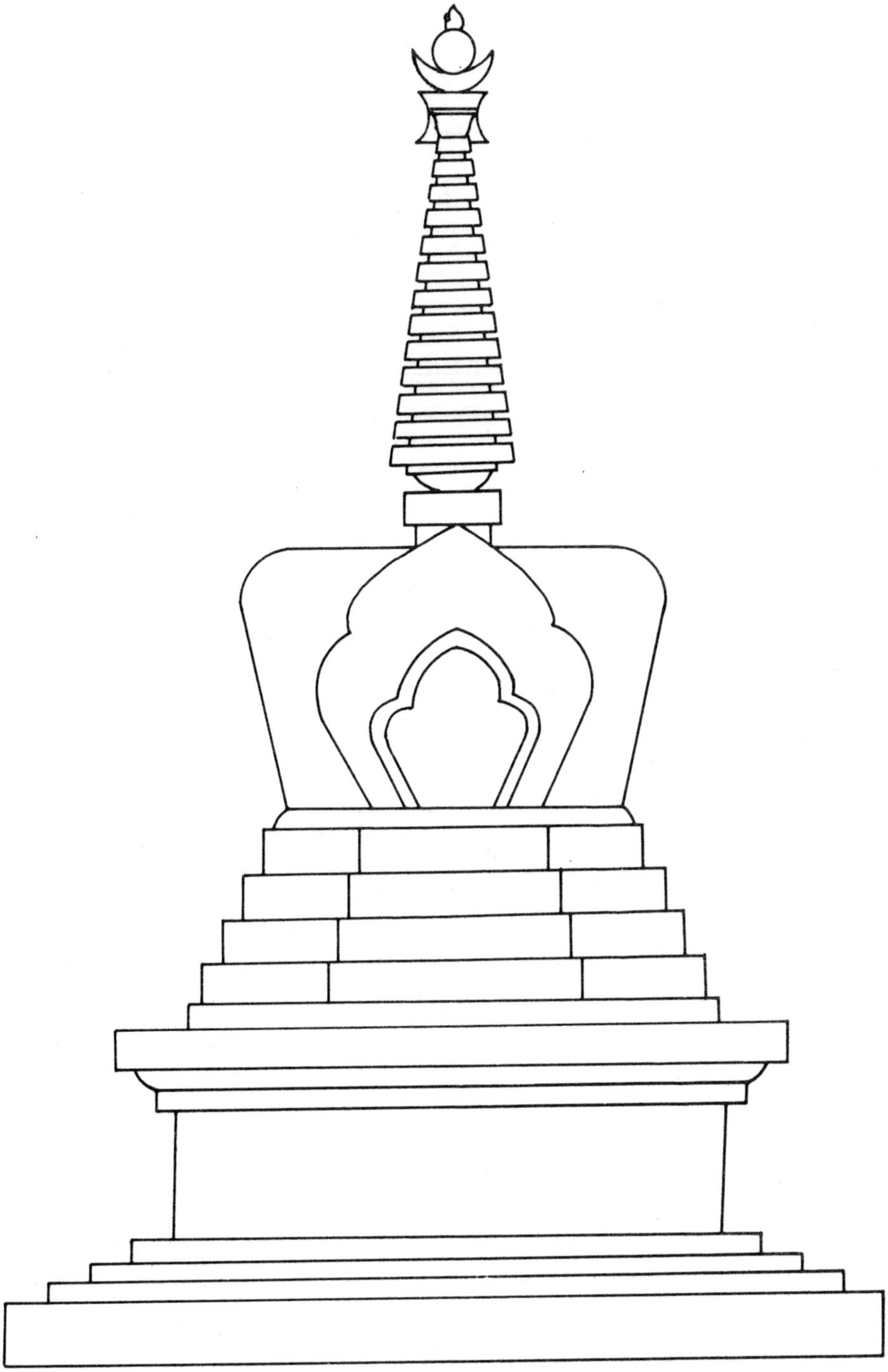

Figure 6. Stūpa of Great Miracle type

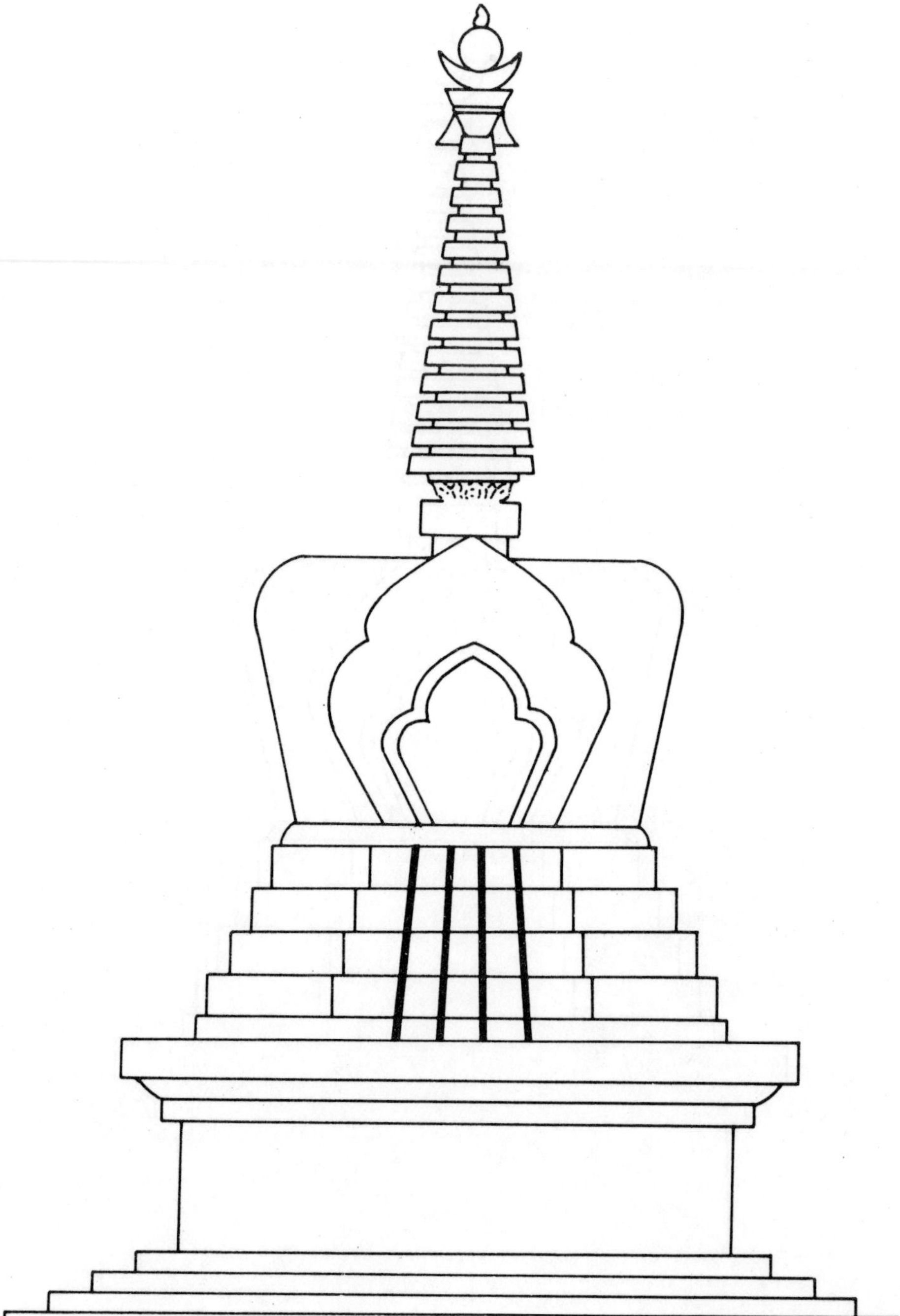

Figure 7. Stūpa of Descent from Heaven type

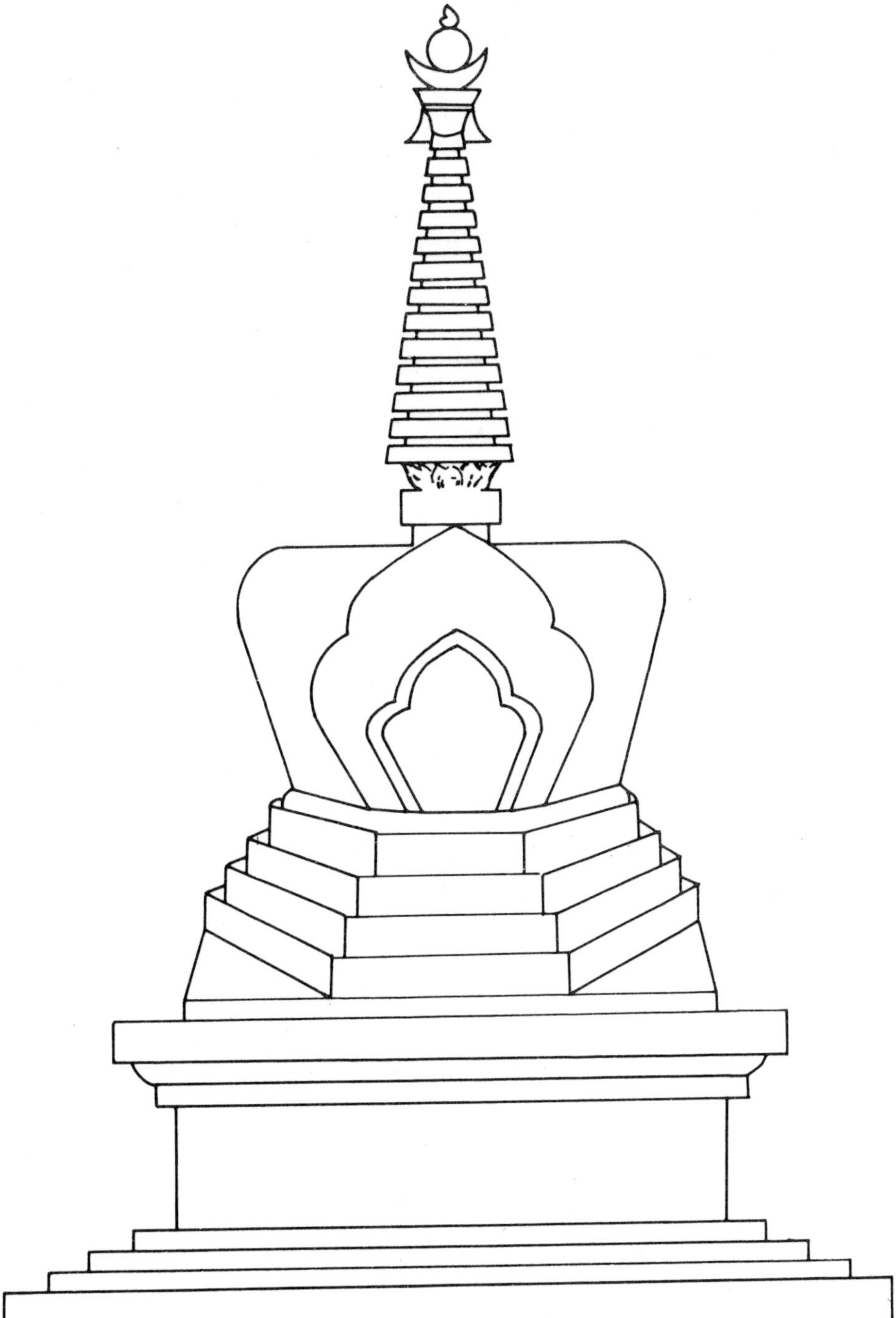

Figure 8. Stūpa of Reconciliation type

Figure 9. Stūpa of Victory type

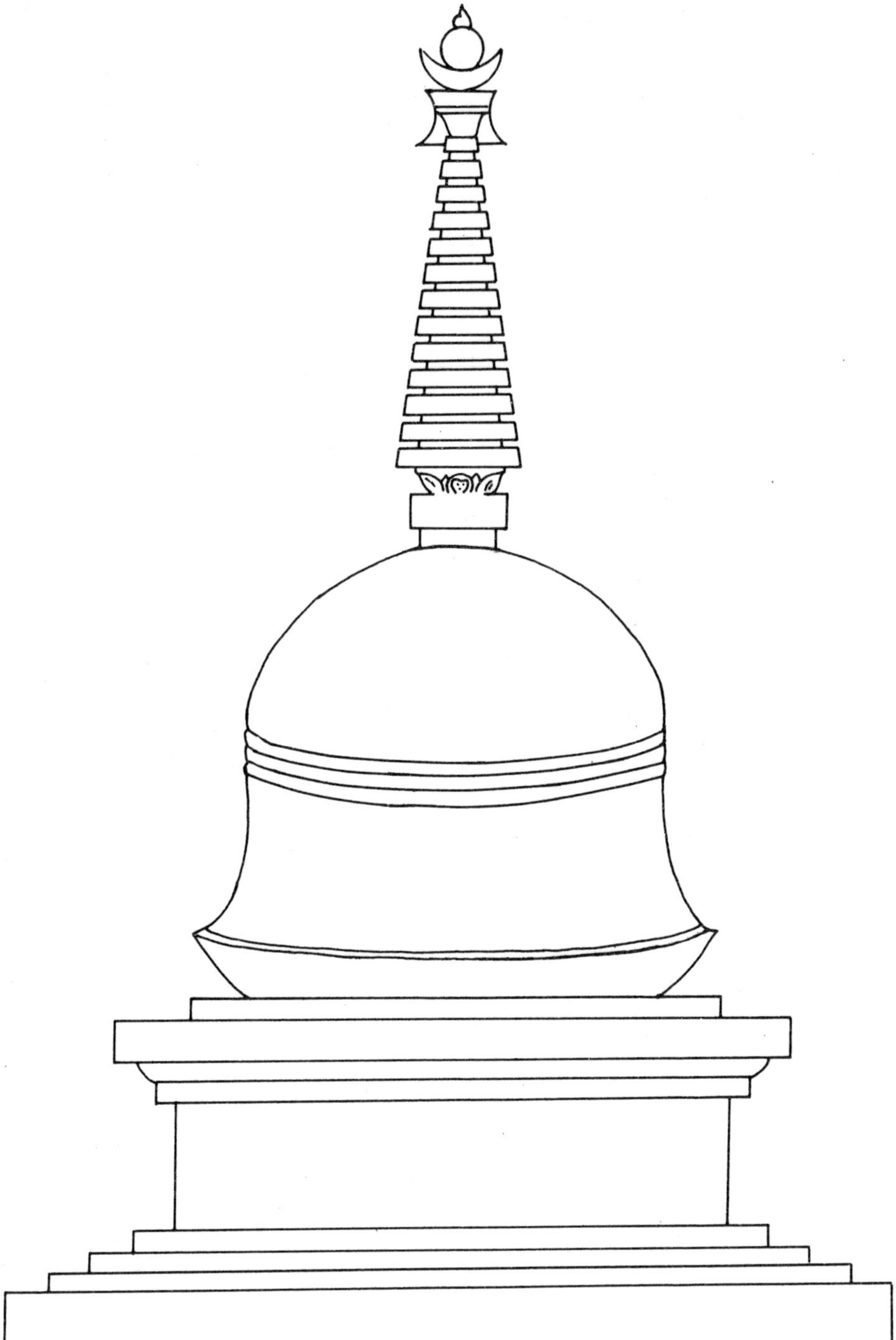

Figure 10. Stūpa of Nirvāṇa type

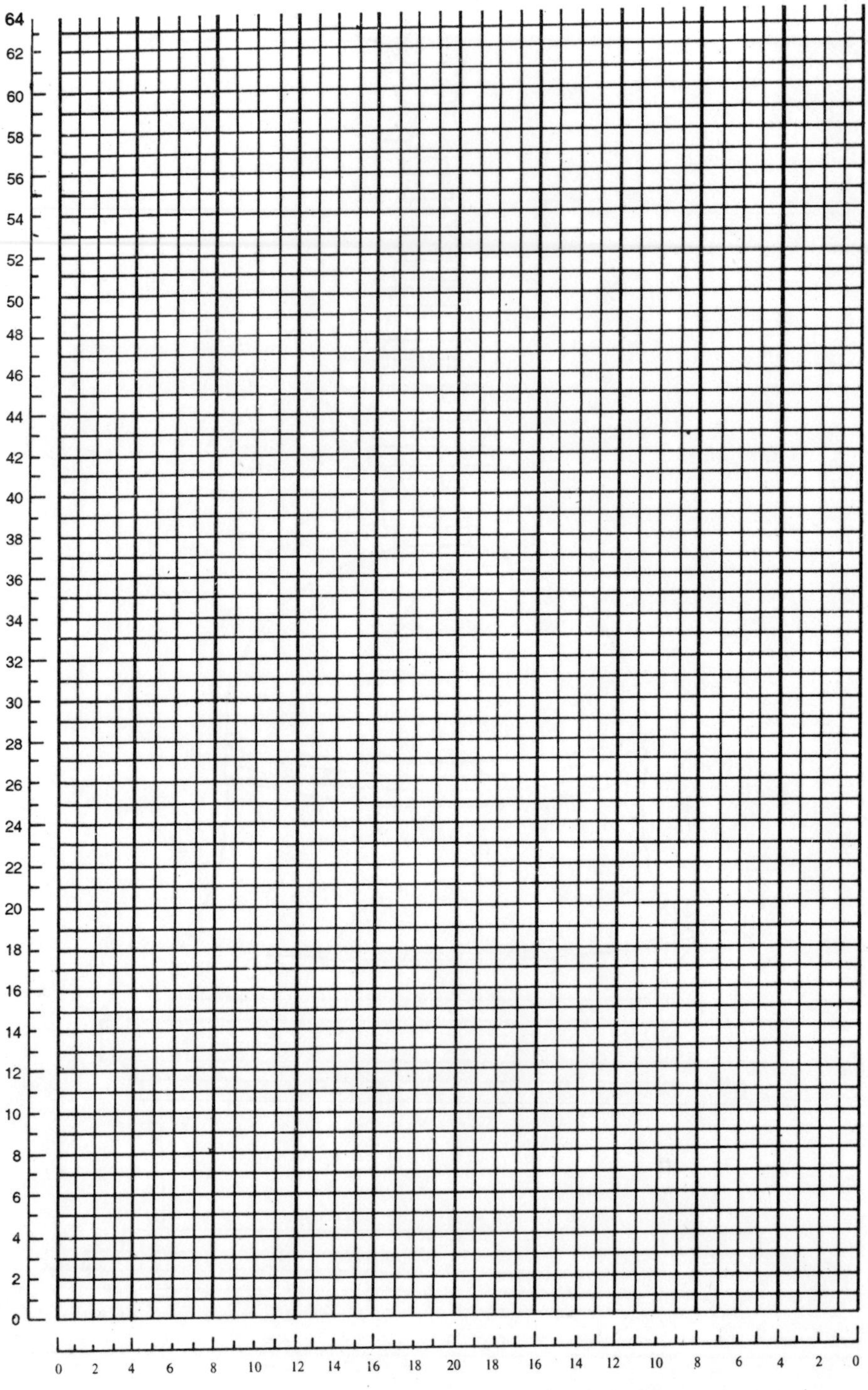

Figure 11. Main Orientation Line of Stūpa

The layout shown in figure 9, is the seventh type of stūpa called "Victory". It has three circular steps rather than four. Even the base of ten-virtues and the vase-base are circular.

The layout shown in figure 10, is the eighth type of stūpa called "Nirvāṇa". It is rather a unique type of stūpa because of its "bell-shaped dome" in which mouth rests directly on the "base of ten-virtues" without any steps.

Traditionally, the eight types of Tibeto-Buddhist stūpas just mentioned can be both a *"nang rten"*, or a *"phyi rten"*, (internal or external receptacle). Among them, the stūpa of Enlightenment is most frequently built in our community.

Apart from these eight types of stūpas, there are other types of Buddhist stūpas associated with the different categories of Buddhist order, i.e. the stūpas of Pratyekabuddha, Śrāvaka (true-hearer), *Anāgāmin* (never-returner), *Sakṛḍagāmin* (once-returner), *Śrotāpanna* (stream-enterer) and virtuous layman, although they are hardly built in the Tibetan community. The basic archetype of stūpa for the said Buddhist order is more or less similar. The only variation seen amongst them is limited to the number of the entitled umbrellas or wheels.

Structural Components of the Stūpa Proper

The Tibeto-Buddhist stūpa, in all its styles, comprises three main structural bodies: (1) the Lion Throne *(seng khri)*, (2) the intermediate section (or the later extremity), and (3) the upper section (or the upper extremity).

The Lion Throne

The Lion Throne is the lower section of the stūpa, which consists of six symbolic structures from the ground plinth *(sa stegs)* up to the frame *(ba gam)*. The structural shape of the Lion Throne can be broadly classified into two: i.e. the one dependant upon and the other not dependent upon the specific structural shape of the steps. The former can be seen in different shapes, depending on the specific structural shape of the steps; however, it is not in common practice, although it looks more attractive than the latter because of its well matching features. For example, if the structural shape of the steps is octagonal, the Lion Throne should also be made octagonal in shape. The same rule is applied to other shapes, as well, however, a circular Lion Throne is rarely made. Those not dependent upon the steps are widely prevalent in practice. In these cases, the structural shape of the Lion Throne is perfectly square and does not depend upon the structural shape of the steps.

There is a practice of either carving or drawing various figures, such as animals and eight auspicious symbols, on the four cardinal surfaces of the Lion Throne. The animals are usually represented by two figures each of a lion, *garuḍa,* horse and peacock. I could not, however, gain access to any indication of these practices in the texts so far studied. In fact, according to the tradition, the structure of the Lion Throne is to be dedicated to lion's figures, as practised in the ancient period.

The practice of erecting the Lion Throne was not an ancient tradition of Tibet as none of the earliest construction manuals or allied works mention it. It was obviously added later by the Tibetan architects and has now become one of the prominent structural parts of the stūpa. There are two necessary implications behind its presentation viz., showing respect for the holy shrine or the person for whom it was constructed and showing respect for its aesthetic considerations. Its proportion and structural parts are also similar to the other Lion Thrones constructed in honour of the ruler, the incarnate lama and the high priest in Tibet.

The Intermediate Section

The Intermediate Section or in architectural terminology the "later extremity" comprises six symbolical structures from the "base of ten-virtues *(rmang dge ba bcu)",* up to the *harmikā.* Structurally, the base of ten-virtues represents the foundation of the main structure of the stūpa proper of the ancient period. It is either circular or square in shape and the circular structure has to be inscribed with the lotus petal designs. It is also called the "seat of ten-virtues *(gdan dge ba bcu)".* Upon this, there is a flight of four or so steps which shorten progressively towards the top while maintaining equal height. In the case of the stūpas of Victory (and very rarely, of Nirvāṇa), there are three steps instead of four but, the Nirvāṇa stūpa in the later period has no steps at all. The steps are generally square, circular, octagonal or projectional in shape.

To identify the structural differences between the eight fundamental types of Tibeto-Buddhist stūpas, one must rely solely upon the structural formation of the steps. One must comprehend at first that basically every style of the stūpa has the same architectural shape with regard to the structure of the vase-base and above, and that of the base of ten-virtues and below. The exception lies in the case of the steps (which are in between the base of ten-virtues and the vase-base), where one can notice a distinct characteristic feature in each of the eight fundamental types of stūpas (excluding the stūpa of Nirvāṇa, as it does not have any steps at all).

The 'vase-support *(bum rten)*' is circular in shape and has to be inscribed with lotus petal designs. Upon it stands the 'vase-shaped dome', which broadens gradually from the 'vase-base *(bum rtsa)*' up towards the 'vase-belly *(bum lto)*', until it reaches its full width which is equal to that of the third step. From here, it curves[7] inwards until it becomes equal in width to the vase-root. In the case of the 'bell-shaped dome', its structure is like the mouth of a bell placed on the base of ten-virtues, and it is without any steps. So naturally, the dome is thinnest at the upper part and broadest at the lower part; in addition, it reaches higher than the vase-shaped dome. The dome is topped by the *harmikā*-base and the *harmikā,* which are rectangular in shape or sometimes, projectional in shape.

In this manner, the total height of the later extremity must equal the width of the first step. According to the *Vimaloṣṇīṣa* commentary of Sahajavilāsa: "The height of the 'later extremity' *(gnam 'phang phyi ma),* is [equal to] the measurement of [one] side of the first step."[8] To interpret this, Buston, Phreng Khapa, etc., had established the proportion of the later extremity as equal to the measurement between the top of the *harmikā* and the base of the first step.[9] But, Desid set up the proportion as similar to the size between the lower part of the first step

7. It seems that there is a tradition of cutting-off the height of the vase shoulder from both the extent points of the vase-belly and the uppermost part of the vase. But, none of the construction manual inform us to follow such method. The vase-belly in a distended form (*bum pa'i lto ba idir ba lta bu*) is generally deemed as a salient feature of the vase in our tradition.
8. Tangyur, Derge, op. cit., fol. 313b5.
9. *Collected Works of Buston*, op. cit., fol. 3a2 (p. 555).

and the upper part of the 'Lotus Supporting-umbrella'[10]. There is no doubt that both systems maintained the idea of equalizing the measurement of the later extremity with the width of the first step, but neither system gave any justification for or explanation regarding their variant ways of calculating the measurement of the later extremity.

The Upper Section

The upper section or 'upper extremity' consists of all the structures from the 'Lotus Supporting-umbrella *(gdugs 'degs pad)*' up to the 'Spherical Pinnacle (*tog*)'. The Lotus Supporting-umbrella has to be inscribed with lotus petal designs all along its circumference. Upon this, there is a tier of thirteen wheels or umbrellas in the shape of thirteen disks or rings that taper off in height and circumference towards the topmost wheel. All the wheels are of equal height, and surround the "axle-pole *(srog shing*, Skt: *yaṣṭi*)'.

The axle-pole is an important part of the structure of a stūpa. One needs a great deal of care and caution in selecting an appropriate specimen of wood for the axle-pole and proper arrangement should be made in locating its original cardinal direction and correct position while placing it inside the stūpa. This is quite imperative for the purpose of accumulating merits and blessings, and for preventing calamities and inauspiciousness.

If available, the axle-pole should be made out of sacred wood like Sandal, Juniper, Cedar, etc. If not possible, then the wood of other hard and straight trees should be used, but not from poisonous or coarse trees. After the process of its selection, it is necessary to mark the east side of the selected tree before it is cut off. After this the axle-pole should be made into a square shape, thinner at the top and broader at the bottom, and carved with a miniature stūpa of the Victory type at the top and that of half-*vajra* at the bottom. As the axle-pole tapers upwards the top it should have the thickness of one-third the size of the bottom. Finally, the axle-pole has to be placed in its proper original form facing the correct cardinal directions and resting in the correct upper and lower positions: its base touching the fourth step and its top at the base

10. *Vaidurya dkar po las 'phro pa'i snyen sgron dang dri len g.ya' sel bzhugs so,* op. cit., fol. 292a1.

of the moon. Thus, the east side of the axle-pole should correspond with the east side of the stūpa, and its upper and lower positions should correspond to the top and bottom positions of the stūpa, respectively.

It is believed that in cases, where the axle-pole is either longer or shorter than its required size, or when it is mistakenly fixed in the reverse position, it is considered to be inauspicious.

Atop the thirteenth wheel rests the structure of "Formula of Compassion *(thugs rje mdo gzungs*, Skt: *karuṇāsūtra dhāraṇī)."* It is in the form of the offering cup *(mchod ting)* which holds oblation water and is placed before the images of deities in Tibeto-Buddhist chapels. The one-third of its upper part has to be encircled by many coil-shaped in bas-relief. The "Umbrella *(gdugs)"*, should equal the seventh wheel; the "Cover of Umbrella *(gdugs khebs)"*, the width of the sixth wheel, and the *"za ra tshags*", the height of the *harmikā*. The crown structures of the latter two are usually made of ornate perforated metal, although sometimes it is produced in a non-perforated form. The Formula of Compassion and the Umbrella are hidden within the ornate metal crown. The moon which stands upon the Formula of Compassion is in the shape of a crescent, and the radius of sun is a bit bigger than the moon. The Spherical Pinnacle is found in two shapes: one is similar to the crest of a young bud of blue lotus *(utpala)* and the other is in a small vase-shaped structure topped by a single or double spherical structure similar to the *āmalaka-kalaśa*—termination of the modern Nepalese stūpa.

Proportional Differences

Before discussing the proportional differences among the stūpas described in various sources, an important task is to determine the establishment of their main orientation lines preceded by the eight major lines *(thig chen brgyad)*, in order to make the stūpas proportionate.

Whatever type of stūpa one may plan, irrespective of its size, one has to make five equal parts on both the right and left sides of the central vertical axis *(tshang thig)*, totalling ten equal parts. Similarly, eight equal parts are made in both the upper and lower sides of the central horizontal axis, totalling sixteen equal parts from the bottom to top. Each one of these parts constitutes a "large unit" *(cha chen)* and is further divided into four equal parts vertically and horizontally, a quarter part of ạ large unit constituting a "small unit" *(cha chung* or *cha phran).* This total height of sixteen large units (equivalent to sixtyfour small units) and breadth of ten large units (equivalent to forty small units) on both the right and left sides of the vertical axis is common to all styles of the stūpas (Figure 11). The bases are all perfectly square and the circular parts are all perfectly round in shape, having circumference equal to three times the diameter.

All the Tibetan scholars have unanimously established the measurement of sixteen large units (corresponding to sixtyfour small units) as the maximum height of the whole structure of the stūpa measuring from the structure above the plinth up to the spherical pinnacle. However, some minor dissimilarities in the measurement of some parts of the main structures of the stūpas can be found amongst the proportions established in various sources. For instance, in the case of the height of a vase: Buston established the measurement of twelve small units and one-third of a small unit.[11] However, Desid set up its proportion as three large units and one-third part of a small unit (equal to thirteen small units and one-third part of a small unit) which matches with the measurement of two-thirds the length of the fourth step.[12] Likewise, Buston propounded the measurement of eighteen small units for the height of the thirteen wheels including the "Lotus Supporting-umbrella" (below the first wheel) and the "Formula of Compassion" (above the thirteenth wheel).[13] But, Desid established the measurement of fourteen small units for the height of the thirteen wheels and one small unit each for the "Lotus Supporting-umbrella" and the "Formula of Compassion", totalling sixteen small units.[14]

In both the cases, the measurements do not concur with each other. It is even more surprising that the height of the vase (i.e. the dome) established by Buston contradicts the measurement in the *Vimaloṣṇīṣa,* on which Buston's proportional manual was based. According to the commentary on *Vimaloṣṇīṣa* by Sahajavilāsa: "The

11. *Collected Works of Buston,* op. cit., fol. 3a2 (p. 555).
12. *Vaidurya dkar po las 'phro pa'i snyen sgron dang dri len g.ya' sel bzhugs so,* op. cit., fol. 291b3 (p. 715).
13. *Collected Works of Buston,* op. cit., fol. 3a5-6 (p. 555).
14. *Vaidurya dkar po las 'phro pa'i snyen sgron dang dri len g.ya' sel bzhugs so,* op. cit., fol. 291b3-4 (p. 715).

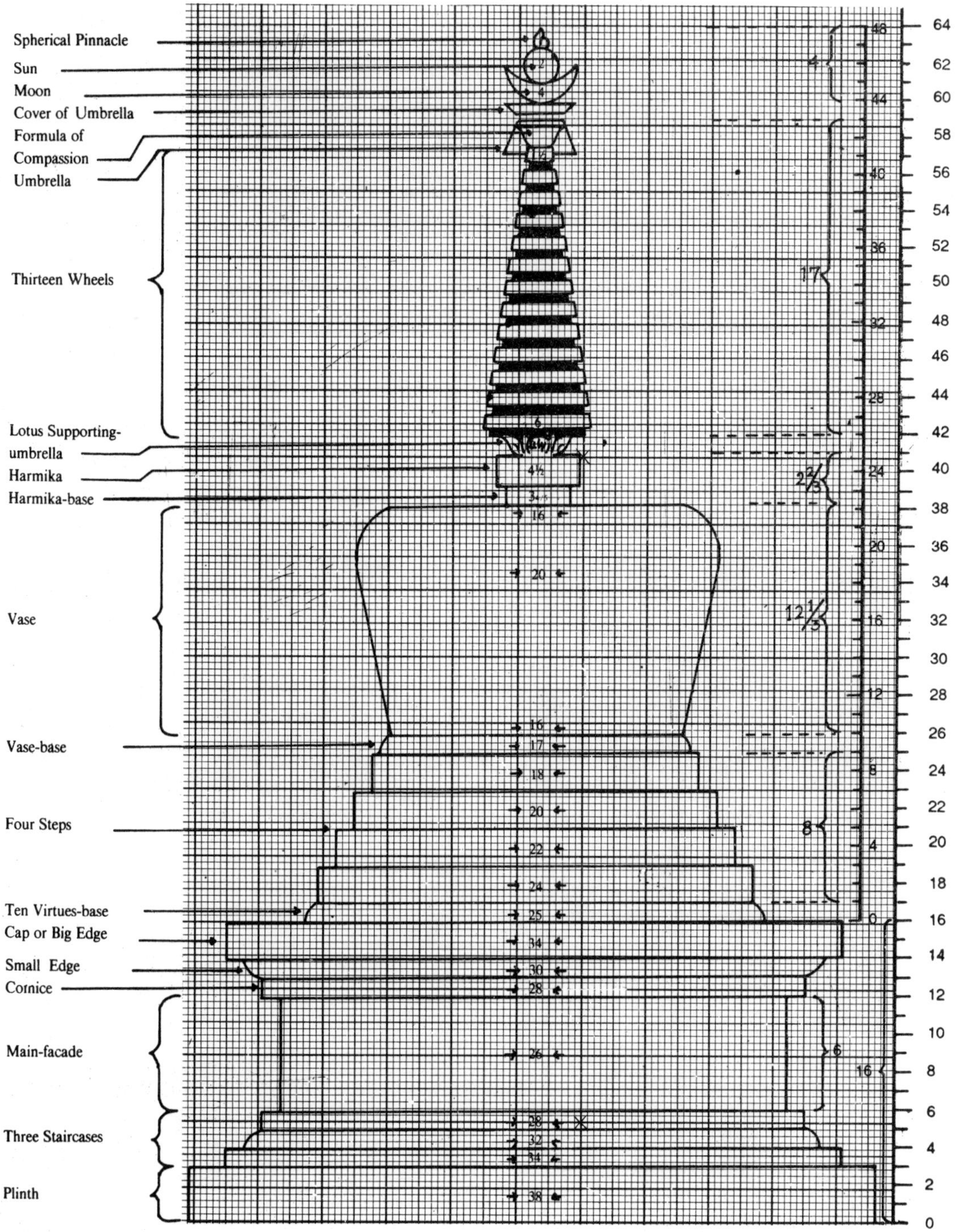

Figure 12. Buston's Proportion for the Stūpa of Enlightenment

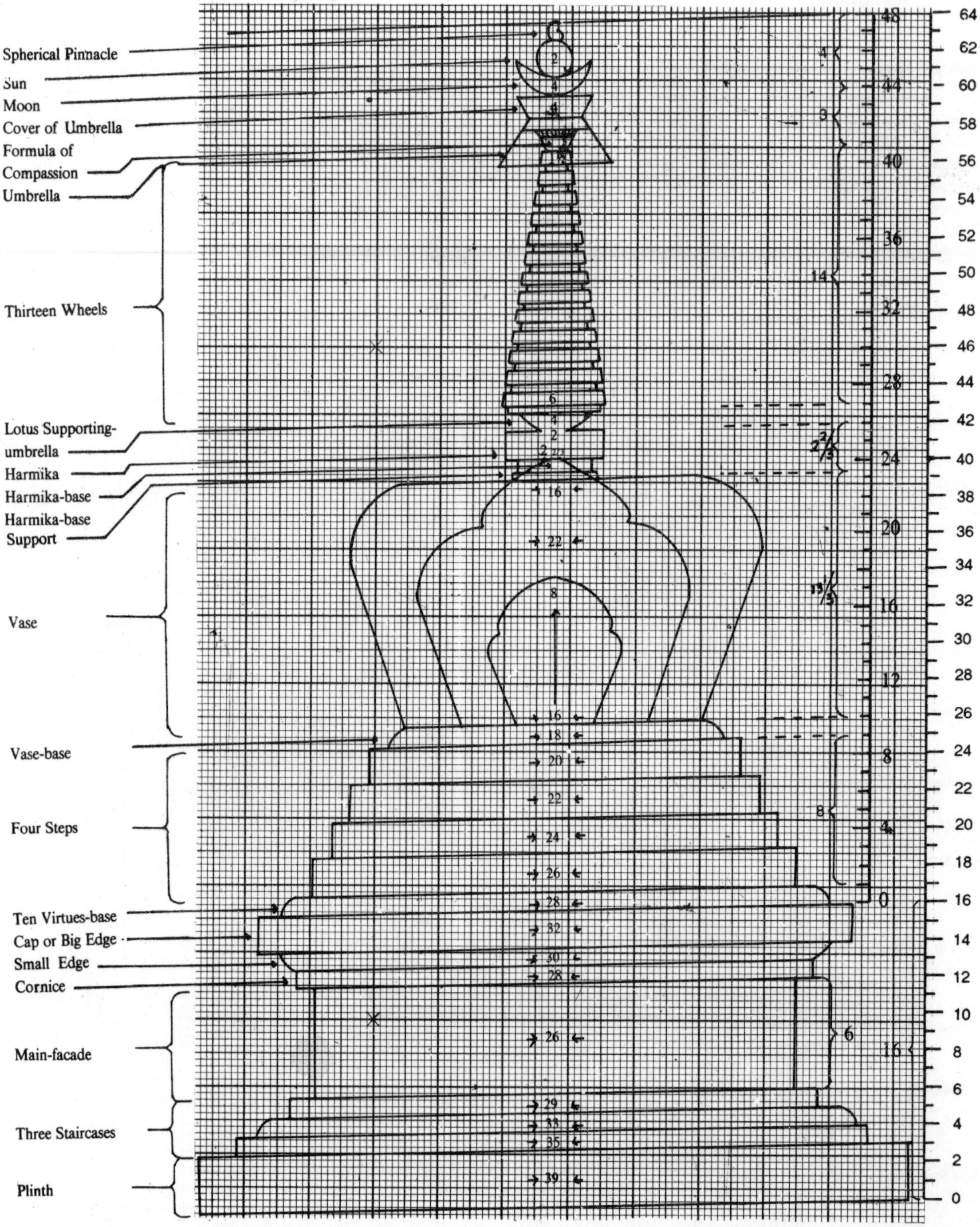

Figure 13. Desid's Proportion for the Stūpa of Enlightenment

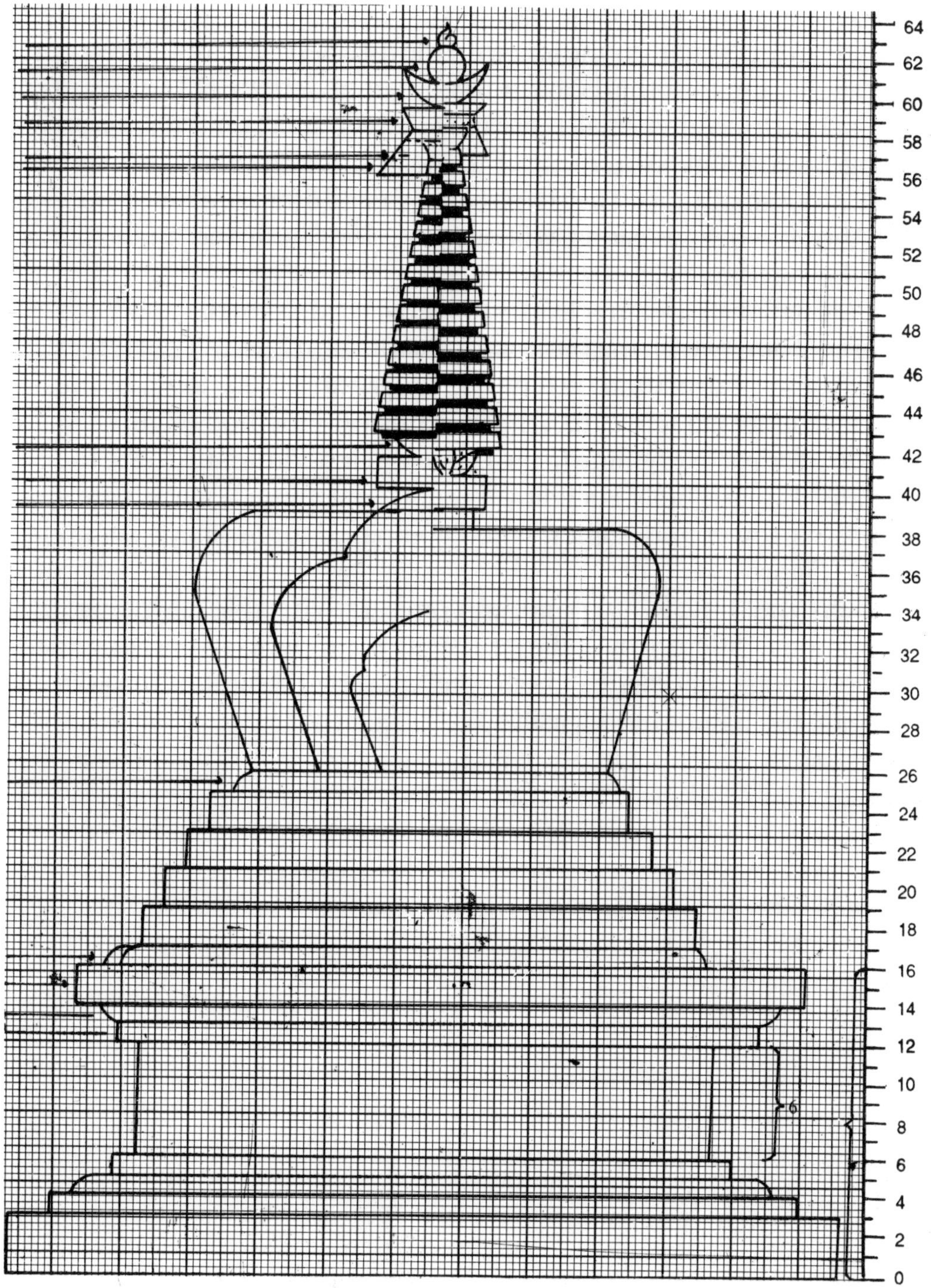

Figure 14. Comparative Measurement of Buston's and Desid's Stūpa

vase is two-thirds of the first step and the height of the thirteen wheels should be three-quarters the length of the first step."[15] To interpret these quotations, the two-thirds and three-quarters length of the first step correspond to sixteen small units and eighteen small units respectively, taking Buston's measurement of the length/width of the first step as twenty four small units. The shape of the vase, if arranged in accordance with the above dimensions, will become elongated, and much higher than the custom.

Most of the Tibetan scholars (except Desid, Namkha and Yodzer) are in conformity with the proportions of Buston (Figure 12). However, in the sense of structural beauty, the proportions laid down by Desid are much more attractive than those of Buston's method (Figure 13). In Buston's format everything from the base of ten-virtues up to the fourth step and the vase-belly is slightly thinner. The thirteen wheels are also slightly narrower and higher, when compared to the shape set up by Desid (Figure 14).

On the following page, a comparative table showing the proportional differences of the structural components as propounded by the various scholars has been prepared by the author in order to compare the datum more easily.

---

15. Tangyur, Derge, op. cit., fol. 313b7.

TABLE SHOWING DIFFERENT PROPORTIONS PROPOUNDED BY VARIOUS TIBETAN SCHOLARS

Structural Components	Buston		Phrengkha		Lobsang		Jamyang		Namkha		Desid		Yodzer	
	S. Unit H	S. Unit W	S. Unit H	S. Unit W	S. Unit H	S. Unit W	S. Unit H	S. Unit W	S. Unit H	S. Unit W	S. Unit H	S. Unit W	S. Unit H	S. Unit W
Spherical Pinnacle	1	1	1	1	1	1	1		1	1	1	1	$1\frac{1}{2}$	1
Sun	2	2	2	2	2	2	2		2	2	2	2	$2\frac{1}{2}$	$2\frac{1}{2}$
Moon	1	4	1	1	1	E. Um	1		1	4	1	4	$1\frac{1}{2}$	4
Cover of Umbrella	$\frac{1}{2}$	E. 6W	$\frac{1}{2}$	E. 6W	$\frac{1}{2}$	E. 6W	$\frac{1}{2}$	E. 6W			$1\frac{1}{2}$	4 3	1	
Za ra tshags		E. Ha	E. Ha		E. Um				$2\frac{1}{2}$	E. Um 6		E. Um 6		$1\frac{1}{2}$
Umbrella	$\frac{1}{2}$	E.7W	$\frac{1}{2}$	E. 7W	$\frac{1}{2}$	E. 7W	$\frac{1}{2}$	E. 7W	$\frac{1}{2}$	$3\frac{6}{8}$	1	6	1	
Formula of Compassion	1	$1\frac{1}{5}$	$1\frac{1}{5}$	1	1	$1\frac{1}{2}$	1	$1\frac{1}{2}$ 1	1	2 E. 13W	1		1	2 $1\frac{1}{3}$
13th Wheel 13 Wheels 1st Wheel	 $15\frac{4}{5}$ 	$\frac{3}{4}$ 6	 $15\frac{4}{5}$ 	$1\frac{1}{2}$ 6	 16 	$1\frac{1}{2}$ 5	 16 	1 6	 14 	$\frac{1}{4}$ 5	 14 	1 5	 13 	2 6
Lotus Supporting-umbrella	1		1	4 2	1	4 2	1	4 2	1	4 3	1	4 3	1	$2\frac{1}{2}$ 1
Harmikā Harmikā-base Harmikā-base Supporter	$1\frac{2}{3}$ 1	$4\frac{1}{2}$ $3\frac{3}{8}$	$1\frac{2}{3}$ 1	$4\frac{1}{2}$ $3^{8/10}$	$1\frac{2}{3}$ 1	$4\frac{1}{2}$	$1\frac{2}{3}$ 1	$4\frac{1}{2}$ $3^{8/10}$	$1\frac{2}{3}$ $\frac{2}{3}$ $\frac{1}{3}$	$5\frac{1}{3}$ 4 $4\frac{2}{9}$	$1\frac{2}{3}$ $\frac{2}{3}$ $\frac{1}{3}$	$5\frac{1}{3}$ 4 $4\frac{2}{9}$	2 $\frac{1}{2}$ $1\frac{1}{2}$	6 5 4
Vase-shoulder Vase-belly Vase Vase-root	 $12\frac{1}{3}$ 	16 20 16	 $12\frac{1}{3}$ 	16 20 16	 $12\frac{1}{3}$ 	16 18 16	 $12\frac{1}{3}$ 	16 20 16	 $13\frac{1}{3}$ 	16 22 16	 $13\frac{1}{3}$ 	16 22 16	 13 	20 16
Vase-base	1	17	1	17	1	17	1	17	1	18	1	18	1	17
4th Step	2	18	2	18	2	18	2	18	2	20	2	20	2	18
3rd Step	2	20	2	20	2	20	2	20	2	22	2	22	2	20
2nd Step	2	22	2	22	2	22	2	22	2	24	2	24	2	22
1st Step	2	24	2	24	2	24	2	24	2	26	2	26	2	24
Ten-virtues base	1	25	1	25	1	25	1	25	1	28	1	28	1	26

Abbreviations

S. Unit = Small Unit E. 6W = Equal to 6th Wheel E. Ha = Equal to Harmikā

H = Height E. 7W = Equal to 7th Wheel E. Um = Equal to Umbrella

W = Width E. 13W = Equal to 13th Wheel

4

Stūpa Architecture of the Upper Indus Valley

Presented here is a survey of the stūpa architecture of the Upper Indus Valley of Ladakh or more precisely, of those stūpas which are found between the monasteries of Spituk and Hemis. These stūpas are in many diverse forms and sizes, are mostly built of inferior material, and can be found in every habitat and monastic site. So far, no attempt at a systematic study of these stūpas, with respect to their architectural aspects and chrono-historical determinations, has been made.

The survey carried out by the author is limited to a small number of stūpas within the regional limits of Ladakh, due to time restraints and financial constraints.

The Leh district, nestled in the middle of the Upper Indus Valley, has been more closely investigated. A large number of stūpas in this area definitely evince a Tibetan origin; the few exceptions being some older stūpas, which are of unknown origin.[1]

1. During the last decade of the 13th century and the early quarter of the 14th century, the famous scholars Buston, Tag tsang Lotsawa, Tulku Phrengkhaba, etc., collaborated to compose a construction manual for stūpas, in order to encourage uniformity in their construction. In the present volume, the term "later stūpa" refers to a stūpa which was definitely constructed after the implementation of this 14th century codified text. The term "early stūpa" refers to a stūpa which was probably constructed before the 14th century, or in any case was not clearly influenced by the above mentioned codification. It is not certain whether the early stūpas were built in accordance with the then prevailing Tibetan custom (pre-codification) or before the introduction of the Tibeto-Buddhist architectural tradition into Ladakh.

The later Ladakhi stūpas are of the standard types, identical to the eight fundamental transformed types of Tibeto-Buddhist stūpas. Thus, they are undoubtedly of the Tibetan origin. Structurally, they are less ponderous, more slender and elegant than their earlier counterparts, especially in their view of the "dome" and its upward parts. In the earlier stūpas, the dome, raised on a square or circular or polygonal base, is hemispherical in shape, (like an inverted alms-bowl) resting upon the vase-base; whereas in the later stūpas, the dome is an inverted, truncated cone, often known as a "vase-shaped dome", and is more elongated on account of its reduced diameter.

Basically, all the eight types of stūpas have the same architectural shape with regard to the structure of the "vase-base" and above, and that of the "base of ten-virtues" and below. But the "Stūpa of Nirvāṇa" is an exception because it has a "bell-shaped dome" instead of the usual "vase-shaped dome" and it has no steps at all.

Plate I. Eight transformed fundamental types of stūpas located on a mountain slope just below the Tiktse Monastery.

The main structural variations found within the eight fundamental transformed types of stūpas are limited to the steps, which can either be square, circular, octagonal, or polygonal in shape. Normally, these stūpas have four steps, although occasionally the number is found to vary. (The Stūpa of Nirvāṇa is, of course, an exception.) The best examples of the above types are located just below the Tiktse Monastery, where one finds a row of the eight fundamental transformed types of stūpas, built of superior material (Pl. I).

Of the eight types of stūpas, the "Stūpa of Enlightenment" is most commonly found. It has a flight of four steps which are perfectly square in shape and are free from embellishments. Stūpas of this type are preponderant throughout Ladakh. Among them, the most representative stūpa of this pattern, located on top of the Shey palace, contains all the usual structural components and seems to be of a relatively recent date (that is, *circa* 17th century A.D., Pl. II). Local inhabitants say that the stūpa was built by king Senge Namgyal in memory of his father Jamyang Namgyal, the second king of the Namgyal dynasty of Ladakh.

Plate II. Rear view of the Shey Palace with a Stūpa of Enlightenment at the centre. On the right is a row of eight impaired states of stūpas.

Often one can see stūpas of this pattern erected over a free standing gateway, the most inspiring architecture I have come across in the region of the Upper Indus Valley. The gateways are not at all functional; they have no doors, thus can neither be opened nor shut. They consist of simple thick walls erected on either side of the access lanes, on which rests a square lintel surmounted by a *chorten* (stūpa) proper. As a rule, the *maṇḍala* and Buddhist pantheons are represented on the underneath surface of the lintel (which is made of lumber).

The gateway-stūpas are all found around the access lanes leading into the old palaces and their monasteries. Three of them can be found in Leh proper and one each at Stok, Tiktse, Hemis and Spituk. Of them, the one seen at the very beginning of the old access lane leading into the Leh palace seems to be the earliest (Pl. III). The *harmikā* and the parts above are missing, perhaps having deteriorated over the course of time. On the centre surface of each of the four sides of its Lion Throne there is an image of a lion in bas-relief.

Plate III. The oldest gateway-stūpa in Leh proper.

In contrast, the other two gateway-stūpas located near the Leh palace still exhibit all the usual structural components and appear to be of later date (Pl. IV). However, the one situated nearest to the Leh palace has in embossed *Lantsa* script, the renowned six-syllable *mantra,* i.e. *"Oṁ maṇi padme huṁ",* around the umbrella-tower. This umbrella-tower is made of moulded terracotta pieces (Pl. V), and is the most inspiring and unique umbrella-tower that the author has ever seen. A *maṇḍala* surrounded by various deities is painted on the underneath surface of the lintel (Pl. VI).

On the Lion Thrones of both the stūpas, one can see carved on each side in each of the four cardinal directions, two figures of four different animals; i.e. clockwise from the East: *garuḍa,* lion, horse and peacock, respectively.

Plate IV. The gateway-*stūpa* closest to the Leh Palace.

Plate V. A moulded terracotta umbrella-tower embossed with *Lantsa* script around it.

The Stok Gateway-stūpa, which is similar to the above two stūpas in all other respects, has an inscription in *Lantsa* characters on its Lion throne instead of the animal figures (Pl. VII).

Jan Pieper is of the opinion that the gateway-stūpas are not erected for the purpose of worship, but for what may be called their "signal value"[2]. His assumption is quite possible. However, the symbolical significance behind this customary practice still remains

2. Jan Pieper, *Stūpa Architecture of the Upper Indus Valley*, Anna Libera Dallapiccola (ed. et al.), *The Stūpa: Its Religious, Historical and Architectural Significance*, Franz Steiner Verlag, Weisbaden, 1980, p. 129.

indeterminate and is a matter of special query before us, requiring systematic study.

Plate VI. A *maṇḍala* surrounded by various deities painted on the underneath surface of the lintel

The stūpa of the "Descent from Heaven" is another redeeming type, which is also rather frequent and is almost always found in ancient habitats. It is perhaps the only type of stūpa consisting of structures, which must have played either a leading role in the dissemination of the stūpa architecture of Ladakh or must have predominated before the standard types of stūpas were introduced in the region. For example, in the sandy plain of Shey, known locally as Shey Thang, one can find enormous impaired stūpas of different sizes built of inferior material. The types of stūpas most frequently represented in the site are those symbolizing the "Descent from Heaven" and "the Enlightenment".

However, the former showing varied structures can be broadly classified into four main groups, i.e. the stūpas consisting of a double flight of four polygonal steps, of a double flight of four circular multi-projected steps, of a single flight of four polygonal steps, and of a single flight of four square steps. The detailed descriptions of the structural differences amongst them will be categorically specified below.

Plate VII. The gateway-stūpa situated at the access lane leading into the Stok palace.

The first group of stūpas consists of a square base having a length approximately equal in measurement to the bottom (first) step, on which stand the double flight of four polygonal steps that diminish in width and are furnished with a ladder at their centre. On both of the top steps, there is a polygonal structure approximately equal to the height of a step devoid of embellishment.

The polygonal structure above the topmost step is capped with a squared structure which is slightly bigger as well as higher than the structure on which it rests. Above this, there are two other circular

Plate VIII. Stūpa of double flight of four polygonal steps located at Shey Thang.

structures[3] of different sizes erected one upon the other surmounted by a vase-shaped dome and furnished with a niche which is chiefly meant to enable the devotees to pay their devotion by inserting *tsha tsha* within the stūpa which is hollow on the inside. Upon the dome stands the *harmika* without the elevation of umbrellas etc. (Pl. VIII).

The second group of stūpas consists of a huge square base, on which stand other smaller square structures having niches at the centre surmounted by two circular structures one upon the other, of which the lower structure is shorter as well as thicker than the upper one. Upon these rest the double flight of four circular multi-projected steps along with a polygonal structure sandwiched between the two flights. Both flights of four steps successively diminish in width and are furnished with a ladder at their centre. On the circular base of the dome above

3. Occasionally, the two circular structures are omitted, and the dome is raised directly on the square structure. It is also possible for the square structure to be omitted, in which case the dome rests directly upon the polygonal structure.

Plate IX. Stūpa of double flight of four circular form of multi-projected steps symbolizing the Descent from Heaven type at Shey Thang.

Plate X. Stūpa having a single flight of four polygonal steps symbolizing the Descent from Heaven type.

Plate XI. Stūpa consisting of a single flight of four square steps symbolizing the Descent from Heaven type.

the topmost step, stands the culminating part of this stūpa—the vase-shaped dome, which is more slender than the dome of the previous stūpa (Pl. IX).

There is a close similarity between the third and fourth groups of stūpas; however, in the former the flight of steps is polygonal (Pl. X), and in the latter, square (Pl. XI). Both types of stūpas evince traces of the central ladder, as it is the distinct characteristic feature of the "Descent from Heaven" type.

In addition to these four groups, a Nepalese type of "Descent from Heaven" stūpa is situated between the left side of the main road and the rear of the Shey palace on a natural amphitheatre visible from all sides. It consists of a large polygonal base, upon which rise three diminishing polygonal steps marked with a ladder at the centre of each side. The hemispherical "dome" rests on two circular seats (diminishing in size), and is topped by a *harmikā* perfectly cubic in shape. From the centre of the *harmikā* rises the axle-pole surrounded by a pyramid-shaped tower made of kiln-fired bricks representing thirteen umbrellas or rings. The umbrella-tower is in turn capped by a circular metal crown

Plate XII. Nepalese type of stūpa of Descent from Heaven located at the rear of the palace-fort of Shey on a natural amphitheatre.

known as a *za ra tshags* which is topped by an inverted crescent moon, a sun disc, and a small "Spherical Pinnacle" which are also made of metal (Pl. XII).

In addition, in the eastern side of Leh, there is a big dilapidated yellow stūpa known locally as the *Mani sermo (Mani gsermo).*[4] Architecturally, it is in the form of a "Descent from Heaven" stūpa (Pl. XIII). However, the architectural components as well as the formation of this stūpa are distinct, differing much from all the above mentioned stūpas of the "Descent from Heaven" type. A detailed description of this stūpa will be presented later in this chapter.

The stūpa of the "Reconciliation" type has octagonal steps formed by cutting off the four corners of the flight of four steps to form eight even sides. It is not frequently found, although it is not extremely rare either, as there is a limited number of well preserved stūpas of this type from different periods. Four were located in three different places, i.e. one each in Hemis and Leh, and two in Tiktse. The structures from the

4. *Mani gsermo* means yellow jewel; "jewel" stands for stūpa.

harmikā part upwards are similar amongst these stūpas except in the case of the Hemis stūpa.

However, a minor variation can be seen in one of the Tiktse stūpas which is situated on the mountain slope in front of the monastery.

Plate XIII. Mani Sermo, the stūpa of Descent from Heaven type located near the Leh polo-ground.

The peculiarity of this stūpa lies in its two structural features. In the first place, the "base of ten-virtues" and the "vase-base" are octagonal in shape, matching with its flight of four steps. Secondly, the umbrellas of this stūpa rise in a parallel like fashion on account of its reduced diameter from the lower section (Pl. XIV).

The stūpa of Reconciliation type at Leh, located on the left side of the Leh palace on a rocky mountain is evincibly more attractive than the rest of the stūpas of this pattern found in Ladakh. Among these, only the Leh Stūpa exhibits two figures each of four different animals in between the ornamental designs at the four cardinal directions of the Lion Throne, i.e. clockwise from east: Garuḍa, lion, horse and peacock; respectively (Pl. XV).

Plate XIV. Stūpa of Reconciliation type found at Tiktse.

While in the Hemis stūpa, the umbrellas made of moulded terra-cotta pieces are in a poor state of preservation, and the ornate metal crowns are missing, the stūpa at Hemis differs in period, structural formation, and material composition from the three other standard stūpas. From the stand-point of its architectural and material composition, the Hemis stūpa is of earlier vintage than its above mentioned counterparts. The Hemis stūpa has four diminishing octagonal steps, which are bulging out on the upper edge of each step by one quarter of the step's height. On the circular vase-base above the fourth step stands the hemispherical egg-shaped dome. Four wooden niches are

Plate XV. The stūpa of Reconciliation type located on the left side of the Leh palace on a rocky mountain.

carved out on the outer surface of the four cardinal directions of the dome which formerly must have contained Buddhist images, but none of these images remain now (Pl. XVI). In the three standard stūpas mentioned above, the dome is an inverted, truncated cone known as a "vase-shaped dome" and has only a single engraved niche.

The stūpa "of Victory" consists of a flight of three circular steps; "the base of ten-virtues" and "the vase-base" are also circular. This type of stūpa is not found frequently, although a limited number of these stūpas of recent origin are found in the villages of Tiktse and Leh.

Plate XVI. Stūpa of Reconciliation type in the Hemis Valley.

For instance, in the village of Tiktse, there are two stūpas of the standard type. One stands at the end of a *Manthang*[5] (Mani-wall). The upper edges of its steps bulge out and the umbrellas or rings made of kiln-fired bricks are in a poor state of preservation. Some of its upper rings and crowning parts are missing (Pl. XVII).

The second "Victory" stūpa, located near the main crossing of the Tiktse Monastery, along with two other stūpas, symbolizing "the Reconciliation" and "of Enlightenment" is in complete form (Pl. XVIII).

5. A *Manthang* is a sort of a wall comprising many small stone-slabs individually engraved with *mantras*, such as *Oṁ maṇi padme huṁ* (See Plate XVII).

Plate XVII. Stūpa of Victory type at Tiktse village along with Mani wall.

These three stūpas together are traditionally known as the "stūpas of the three guardians *(Trikulanatha-stūpa, rigs gsum mgon po'i mchod rten).*" Around the Leh bus station, one can find three more "Victory" stūpas; two are without the elevation of umbrellas, and the remaining one is of the standard type, but with signs of more recent accumulation of elegance (Pl. XIX).

In addition, in the northern side of the Hemis valley there is another "Victory stūpa" (Pl. XX), although its dome differs from that of the forementioned stūpas. In this stūpa, there is a hemispherical egg-shaped dome attached with four projected wooden niches, one in each of the four cardinal directions, which formerly must have contained the

Plate XVIII. The stūpa "of Victory" along with two other stūpas symbolizing "the Reconciliation" and "of Enlightenment", located near the main crossing of the Tiktse Monastery.

Plate XIX. Stūpa symbolizing the Victory type of more recent origin located near the Leh bus station.

Plate XX. The Stūpa of Victory located in the northern side of Hemis valley.

Buddhist images, but none of these images remain now. The stūpa itself is in a poor state of preservation. The upper part of the umbrella-tower, made of moulded terracotta pieces, and the ornate metal crowns are missing. Thus, on the basis of these evidence, one can safely conclude that this stūpa predated the forementioned stūpas of this type.

The stūpa of "Multiple Auspicious Doors" is in fact the most monumental amongst the eight types. It consists of four square steps which project at the centre by one-third part of their own sizes. This stūpa generally consists of a maximum of 108 doors, 56 is the average number of doors, and 16 is the minimum number of doors. Occasionally, though rarely, the number of these steps and doors may be varied.

For instance, the most representative stūpa of "Multiple Auspicious Doors" situated in the village of Changspa is the only stūpa of this pattern. It consists of a huge polygonal base surmounted by five diminishing polygonal steps which contain as many as 80 doors (Pl. XXI). A detailed description of this stūpa will be presented later in this chapter.

Plate XXI. The Stūpa of Multiple Auspicious Doors at Changspa.

The stūpa "of Miracles" or "Conquest of Tīrthikas (non-believers)", is characterized by a flight of four square steps, which project at the centre by one-third part of their own widths; it is free from embellishments. We have a very limited number of stūpas of this type. The most representative one of this pattern is situated on the main street of the Leh market (opposite the main office of the Indo-Tibetan Border Police), and is of the standard type. It also has signs of recent accumulation of elegance (Pl. XXII).

Plate XXII. Stūpa of Miracle type at Leh market opposite Indo Tibetan Border Police Office

The stūpa of "Heaped Lotuses" has four circular steps rather than square ones, and is carved with lotus-petal designs. Of all the eight types of stūpas, this one is most rare in Ladakh. Only one stūpa of this pattern has been located and it is of recent origin. It is situated just below the Tiktse Monastery along with the other seven stūpas of the standard types, and it is built of superior materials (see plate I).

The stūpa "of Nirvāṇa" is a unique type of stūpa because of its "bell-shaped dome" which rests directly on the "base of ten-virtues". It has no steps at all. There are only three stūpas of this type. All of them are located within the Hemis area, two in the Hemis valley, and one near the Hemis Monastery. The one located at the very beginning of the

Plate XXIII. The Nirvāṇa stūpa having a low dome with pyramid-shaped umbrella-tower at Hemis valley.

Hemis valley differs a lot from the other two stūpas. It consists of a low dome surmounted by a rather flat *harmikā* from which rises the axle-pole adorned with a pyramid-shaped umbrella-tower (Pl. XXIII).

The second "Nirvāṇa" stūpa in the Hemis valley has a dome raised on an elongated Lion Throne, which bulges out at the centre as well as at the base. The centre surface of the dome is inscribed with designs of pendant ornaments called *dra ba dra phyed.* On the front side of the dome facing towards the Hemis Monastery, there is a niche furnished with a narrow ladder for reaching to the top of the dome. The *harmikā* standing upon the dome has elongated shape and is wider in dimension (compared to earlier ones), and is provided with a niche on each of the four sides. Inside each of the niches is an image of Lord Buddha engraved on black slate in the postures of *"bhūmisprśa"* in the west and north, and the *"dharmopadeśa"* in the east and south directions. The niches are finally enclosed with a diamond-shaped wooden trellis.

The ceremonial umbrellas made of moulded terra-cotta pieces fitted around the axle-pole are in a ring-shaped umbrella-tower instead of the pyramid-shape. The ornate metal crown known as the *za ra tshags* is hanging down and terminates on a small vase-shaped structure and spherical pinnacle, which are also made of metal (Pl. XXIV).

Plate XXIV. The Nirvāṇa stūpa having elongated dome and *harmikā*, and ladder inside the dome at Hemis valley.

With regard to the structure of the Lion Throne, it is rather similar to the earlier ones, although it has various designs inscribed on all the surfaces of the Lion Throne, i.e. going clockwise from east, the figures of the lotus, sword, *ratna* and *vajra* are carved on the centre surface of all the four projecting structures. And on the eight recess surfaces of the four sides one figure out of "eight auspicious symbols *(bkra shis rtags brgyad)*" has been exhibited.

The third stūpa of "Nirvāṇa" located near the Hemis Monastery, is almost identical to the aforementioned ones. However, it does not have a niche on its dome (Pl. XXV).

Plate XXV. The Nirvāṇa stūpa having elongated dome with a ring-shaped umbrella-tower, located near the Hemis Monastery.

Mani Sermo : The Stūpa of Descent From Heaven

Half a kilometre to the east of Leh, there is a big dilapidated yellow stūpa. It is situated on a slightly lop-sided mound just near the Polo Ground and is known locally as the *Mani sermo* (Pl. XXVI). It is particularly respected as one of the earliest and most ancient monuments in the Ladakh region. The present inhabitants of Leh say that it was erected during the period of the great *Lotsaba* (Translator) Rinchen Zangpo (964-1054 A.D.). This belief may be given credence, for the material composition of the stūpa attests that it cannot be much later than the 15th century, and it might well have been built earlier.

Plate XXVI. Mani Sermo, the stūpa of Descent from Heaven type at Leh.

One clue as to its date rests in the fact that the brick masonry, in the form of adobe for the stūpas and other monuments in Ladakh was most probably introduced in much later period. We do not find the use of the brick masonry during the earlier period.

In the case of this stūpa, not a single adobe has been used. The whole structure is made of roughly-cut stone masonry laid in regular courses and covered with a thick layer of clay plaster. In order to produce uniformity, stone slabs were sometimes laid in between some of the adjoining horizontal layers of the masonry. There are many stūpas of more recent origin that are attached to or around it.

Technical Description of Structural Formation

This "Descent from Heaven" stūpa is distinct from other stūpas of its type, perhaps a singular representative in Ladakh. This stūpa has a perfect square base, about 6'-10" in height and 22'-2" in width. Above this, there is a circular structure with "images of lions in bas-relief"[6] on the four sides, resembling a Lion Throne. It is about 2' in height and 15'-1" in width, corresponding to 45'-3" in circumference. Upon this rests another circular structure, which is somewhat shorter as well as smaller in dimension than the former one, and which is surmounted by two stacked polygonal structures with clear traces of projectional steps accompanied with ladders at their centre. The ladders recede progressively from the base up to the middle part. However, the lower ladder appears wider and has more steps than the upper one. The front side of the upper polygonal structure does not have steps and ladders, rather it has a niche with a complete image of a seated Buddha in the "Earth-touching" *(bhūmisprśa)* posture.

This upper polygonal structure was interpreted by Francke as a dome, which formerly must have had niches on the four sides.[7] His postulate is possible, as there exists a common practice of placing an image of a Buddhist deity on the front niche of the dome. There is also a tradition of making niches on the four sides of the dome, although it is not as prevalent. Thus, on the basis of such practices, it is possible to interpret this part of the stūpa as a dome.

However, in this particular instance, the architectural formation of the upper polygonal structure resembles a flight of steps rather than a dome, because there are clear traces of projectional ladders (narrowing towards the top) at the centre of the other three sides. Each side also has a flight of steps on their bases. All these features argue against the hypothesis that it is a dome structure. In addition, a dome is clearly

6. Those images of lions in bas-relief have quite escaped the notice of Francke who does not mention them in his work, *Antiquities of Indian Tibet,* Part I. See his description of the *Mani sermo,* p. 75.
7. *Ibid.*, p.75.

present just above the upper polygonal structure. It is in a hemispherical egg-shape, and is without the adornment of *harmikā*, umbrellas, and crowning parts.

The author was informed that a banner *(rgyal mtshan)* made of multi-coloured cloth was recently raised on the top of this stūpa by the members of the SOS Tibetan Children's Village, Choglamsar, a few weeks before the commencement of his survey there.

The Changspa Stūpa of "Multiple Auspicious Doors" *(Tashi Gomang)*

About two kilometres south-west of Leh, there is a gigantic pyramidal stūpa of the type called "Multiple Auspicious Doors" (Pl. XXVII). It stands on a low hill in a wide valley with a dense forest and buildings in the background. As a result it is hard to see the stūpa even from a short distance. The history of this stūpa is quite obscure, both regarding the exact date of its construction and its builder.

Plate XXVII. The stūpa of Multiple Auspicious Doors at Changspa.

The author's interest in the genesis of this stūpa was further piquant by Francke's assertion that the stūpa belonged to the early period.[8] He visited the stūpa several times but could not find any inscription or cogent record which could testify it as belonging to the early antiquity. This stūpa closely resembles the *kubum chorten*[9] which stands near the Gyantse Monastery in Tibet, thus, confirming Tibetan influence. On this basis, one cannot date the stūpa's construction as being prior to the introduction of the Tibeto-Buddhist culture in Ladakh.

Surrounding this massive stūpa, there are 108 small stūpas without the elevation of umbrellas and crowning parts. They indirectly serve as a boundary, enclosing a path for the clockwise ceremonial circum-ambulation *(pradakṣiṇāpatha)*, being a chief form of reverence paid to the relics contained within the central stūpa. None of these small stūpas are supposed to have contained any relics or other sacred things like *tsha tsha* etc., as nothing was found from a few of these ruined stūpas. Very close to the central stūpa from a front side open chamber, one can see three different stūpas of more recent date[10] accompanied by portraits of five Buddhist deities depicted on all the interior walls.[11]

Technical Description

The gigantic stūpa of "Multiple Auspicious Doors" is built on a large polygonal base, on which stand five diminishing polygonal steps or stages furnished with as many as 80 doors or niches, each step carrying 16 doors[12] on the four sides of the step. Upon this rests the circular base of the dome surmounted by the principal part of the stūpa called the dome which is an inverted, truncated cone known as the "vase-shaped dome". On the front side of the dome facing towards the Leh market, there is a niche provided with a wooden door which is engraved with a symbol of *daṣakaro vaśi (rnam bcu dbang ldan)*. In this case, the niche does not have an image, instead it has a narrow ladder for reaching the top of the dome, which is surmounted by a cubic *harmikā*.

8. Francke, op. cit., p. 80.
9. *Kubum chorten;* literally meaning, "the stūpa of one hundred thousand images".
10. Starting from left symbolizing the stūpas "of Victorious", "of Enlightenment", and "of Reconciliation". Traditionally, they are called the "stūpas of the three protectors".
11. The portraits on the central interior wall represent *trikulanatha,* i.e. starting from right: *Mañjuśri, Avalokiteśvara* and *Vajrapāṇi*, and the remaining portraits depicted on the left and right interior walls represent *Amitābha* and *Nīlasiṁhavaktrā* (the Lion faced goddess in blue colour) respectively.
12. Carrying 16 doors, each representing the 16 Emptinesses *(Śunyatā)*.

Up to the *harmikā*, the structures piled one upon the other are made of solid blocks of roughly-cut masonry covered with a thick layer of clay plaster, and coated white. It is still being regularly whitewashed simply by pouring lime-water slowly upon the stūpa with the help of a small vessel (Pl. XXVIII). The usual method of coating by brush is not customarily practised in Ladakh, particularly not with stūpas plastered with clay, in order to prevent splitting of the clay plaster.

Plate XXVIII. The scene of pouring lime-water upon the clay plastered stūpa at Changspa.

The *harmikā* is capped with the "Lotus Supporting Umbrellas" in the shape of lotuses. Above the lotus blossoms, there is a ring attached with embossed crescents. The thirteen umbrellas are erected on top of this ring, tapering off towards the top. All of them, including the "Lotus Supporting-Umbrellas", are made of moulded terracotta pieces fitted around the axle-pole. The latter rises from the centre of the dome and is adorned with an ornate doily crown known as a *za ra tshags* (Pl. XXIX) supported by a double wooden cross-bar. Finally, the stūpa terminates in a small vase-shaped structure topped by a "Spherical Pinnacle" made of gilded copper. The combination of such a termination

Plate XXIX. Ring-shaped umbrella-tower adorned with crowning parts of Changspa stūpa.

structure is often found in the Nepalese stūpa and is known as *āmalaka-kalaśa* termination.

Pointed rods of iron are fixed both on top of the spherical pinnacle and the upper borders of the ornate crown to prevent birds from resting on them. In addition, two long chains (one on each side) are hung from the wooden cross-bar, reaching down to the upper part of the dome. Upon the chains, prayer-flags are fastened and two small bells are dangled.

The section from the "Lotus Supporting-Umbrellas" upto the pinnacle was presumably added after the first decade of the present century. As evident from the earlier photographs of this stūpa found in Francke's text,[13] the axle-pole rose alone from the centre of the *harmikā*, being devoid of all the terracotta embellishment, the ornate metal crown, and other accessories.

Tsha Tsha With Stūpa Images

The following *tsha tsha* were found in the stūpas at Shey Thang, Spituk and Tiktse.

1. ***Shey Thang*** (Pl. XXX). This most remarkable *tsha tsha* is in

Plate XXX. A unique stūpa of Descent from Heaven type with a long circular stand.

13. Francke, op. cit., plate XXXI, p. 81.

the shape of the "Descent from Heaven" stūpa, although it differs much from the standard type. As can be seen in the photo, this *tsha tsha* consists of a tall circular stand upon which rest the two twelve-sided bases with three polygonal steps each, and a projected ladder at the centre of each of the four main sides. Rising above this are three octagonal structures surmounted by an egg-shaped dome. The *tsha tsha* culminates with two square structures, which resemble the *harmikā*-base and the main *harmikā,* respectively.

There are five holes, one each on the four corners of the uppermost polygonal structure and one on the top of the *harmikā*, presumably for erecting flags and axle-pole respectively. Broken sticks are still lodged in some of these holes.

From the base up to the top of the dome, this *tsha tsha* is painted with gold-lacquer. When the author first discovered this *tsha tsha*, its tall circular base was decorated with blue and red paint; however, upon handling the colour wore off, despite extreme care. It must be remarked that this *tsha tsha* is undoubtedly one of the finest one, both in respect of its material compositions and structural appearances that the author has ever come across.

Plate XXXI. A big stūpa of Enlightenment type at the centre surrounded with different stūpas found at Shey Thang.

2. ***Shey Thang*** (Pl. XXXI). There is a big stūpa at the centre, resembling the type called "Enlightenment", without umbrellas and crowning parts, and encircled by lotus flowers at its base. On each of the steps are four smaller stūpas of different types, corresponding to the "Heaped Lotuses", "Great Miracles", "Descent from heaven", and "Victory" types. There is no inscription.

3. ***Tikste*** (Pl. XXXII). This *tsha tsha* is identical to the preceding one, although it is slightly larger and has an inscription in Tibetan *Lantsa* characters just above the circle of lotuses.

Plate. XXXII. A large stūpa of Enlightenment surrounded at the centre with different stūpas, accompanied by Tibtan *Lantsa* characters found at Tiktse.

4. ***Shey Thang*** (Pl. XXXIII). Around a large stūpa of the "Descent from Heaven" type (without umbrella), there is in each of the cardinal directions a "Descent from Heaven" stūpa and in each of the four intermediate directions, a stūpa of "Victory". On the open space around the base of the steps and just above a circle of lotus petals, there is an inscription in Tibetan *Uchen* characters of the typical *"Ye dharmā* ...." formula[14].

Plate XXXIII. A large stūpa of Descent from Heaven type surrounded with eight other smaller stūpas and containing *Ye dharmā* ...formula in Tibetan *Uchen* characters.

14 The *Ye dharmā* ..... formula, the *mantra* of the twelve link of dependent origination *(dvādasangapratītyasamutapāda)* is often found in *tsha tsha* which are in the form of stūpas. This *mantra* is often found to be used in the ancient *tsha tsha* of Northern India and especially favoured by the Hīnayāna school of Buddhism.

5. ***Shey Thang*** (Pl. XXXIV). Upon a ring of lotus petals stands a big stūpa, perhaps of the "Great Miracle" type, and yet without umbrellas. Surrounding it, there are eight unidentifiable smaller stūpas accompanied by stūpas of the "Enlightenment", and "Victory" types at the four cardinal directions and at the four intermediate directions, respectively. On the stūpas of the four cardinal directions are twelve smaller stūpas of similar shape, imprinted three each upon each of the four stūpas' steps. The structural formation of these stūpas is quite difficult to distinguish. Each one of them is in the form of three diminishing

Plate XXXIV. A large stūpa of Great Miracle type surrounded by eight unidentifiable smaller stūpas and four each stūpas of Enlightement and Victory found at Shey Thang.

Plate XXXV. A large Stūpa of Great Miracle type surrounded by eight unidentifiable smaller stūpas and four each Stūpas of Enlightenment and Victory types found at Shey Thang.

successions of steps, upon which rested the dome devoid of *harmikā* and without the elevation of umbrellas. There is no inscription. The whole structure is painted in red.

6. ***Spituk*** (Pl. XXXV). This *tsha tsha* is identical with the preceding

Plate XXXVI. A tablet containing an inscription of *Ye dharmā* ....formula in Tibetan *Uchen* characters.

one but slightly bigger and unpainted. Inside it is contained a very neat and clear tablet made of unfired clay with an inscription in Tibetan *Uchen* characters of the *"Ye dharmā ..."* formula (Pl. XXXVI).

7. ***Spituk*** (Pl. XXXVII). Rising from the centre is a big stūpa (without umbrellas) in the style "of Reconciliation". Surrounding it, there are eight unclearly formed smaller stūpas of the standard type. Each of these stūpas rest on one of the eight sides of the main figure, not quite reaching the top of the steps and the proportions of their steps are somewhat higher than the dome. There is an inscription in Tibetan *Lantsa* characters of the *"Ye dharmā ...."* formula, which is inscribed just above a ring of lotus flowers.

Plate XXXVII. A big stūpa of the Reconciliation type, at the centre with an inscription of the *Ye dharmā*... formula in Tibetan *Lantsa* characters found at Spituk.

8. ***Shey Thang*** (Pl. XXXVIII). A single big stūpa at the centre of the *tsha tsha,* which is probably modelled after the type called "Multiple Auspicious Doors". It exhibits the usual standard flappings, umbrellas, sun and moon. On either side, it has a *"Ye dharmā..."* inscription in *Rañjanā* characters, and the script is datable to the 9th and 10th century.

Plate XXXVIII. A typical Multiple Auspicious Doors type of stūpa with an inscription of *Ye dharmā* ....formula in *Rañjanā* script, found at Shey Thang.

9. ***Tiktse*** (Pl. XXXIX). This *tsha tsha* has 20 "Enlightenment Stūpas" in four rows, each adorned with the standard designs including five umbrellas. Starting with the lowest and moving to the top, there are

Plate XXXIX. Twenty Enlightenment stūpas with an inscription of early Indian characters, found at Tiktse.

5 stūpas, then 6, then 5, and then 4 in each row. There is an inscription in early Indian characters just below the stūpas, but the state of preservation of the *tsha tsha* does not allow us to be certain about the script.

10. ***Tiktse*** (Pl. XL). This *tsha tsha* exhibits nineteen stūpas in a way similar to that of the preceding *tsha tsha*, but their sizes vary. The five stūpas in the lowest row are bigger having four steps each; the middle one is the largest and adorned with all the standards. The remaining fourteen stūpas are smaller and have only three steps each. Below the stūpas, there is an inscription in early Indian characters, which is illegible.

Plate XL. Nineteen stūpas of unidentifiable type with illegible inscription of early Indian characters, found at Tiktse.

11. ***Shey Thang*** (Pl. XLI). This *tsha tsha* sports a single stūpa, probably of the "Great Miracles" type. There is a niche in the centre of the dome. On both sides of the stūpa there are two similar inscriptions of two syllables possibly of early Indian characters.

12. ***Shey Thang*** (Pl. XLII). This *tsha tsha* exhibits a stūpa of the "Descent from Heaven" type, adorned with all the usual standards. The preceding two syllables of the Indian script repeated on both the sides of the *stūpa* are accompanied with some additional writings below the stūpa.

13. ***Shey Thang*** (Pl. XLIII). Three stūpas of similar type and size are represented here with all the standard features. They seem to be either the "Reconciliation" or the "Great Miracle" type. Between the upper and lower parts of their bases are contained inscriptions in early Indian characters similar to the *Aśokan Brahmi.* In addition, on each side of the middle stūpa, there are two designs which probably symbolize tridents, and on top of them stand the symbols of the Buddhist Trinity.[15]

15. In the gateway of Sāñcī stūpa 1, we noticed this symbol, which is interpreted by scholars as a symbol of Buddhist Trinity i.e. Buddha, Dharma, and Saṅgha.

Plate XLI. Single stūpa of Great Miracle type found at Shey Thang with two syllables of illegible characters.

Plate XLII. Single stūpa of Descent from Heaven type found at Tiktse, with some illegible characters.

Plate XLIII. Three stūpas similar to Reconciliation or Great Miracle type, found at Shey Thang with an inscription similar to *Aśokan Brahmi.*

14. ***Tiktse*** (Pl. XLIV). On this *tsha tsha* is depicted a single stūpa of the type called "Descent from Heaven", with umbrellas and adorned with the sun and the moon. On both sides of the stūpa, there is an inscription in the Tibetan ornamental script called *'brug rtsa.* The state of preservation of this *tsha tsha* does not allow us to be certain about the content of the inscription.

Plate XLIV. Stūpa of Descent from Heaven type found at Tiktse, with an inscription of Tibetan ornamental *'brug rtsa* script.

15. ***Tiktse*** (Pl. XLV). On a lotus flower stands a tall stūpa of the type called "Descent from Heaven" having all the standards. On the front side of the *harmikā*, there is a miniature image of seated Lord Buddha. The dome of this stūpa is comparatively smaller in size than that of the usual ones, which is sandwiched in between the steps below and the *harmikā* on top of it.

Plate XLV. Stūpa of Descent from Heaven type, with a miniature statue of Lord Buddha found at Tiktse.

APPENDIX A

Transliteration of the *Caitya Vibhaṅga Vinayoddhṛta Sūtra*[1]

De nas mchod rten gyi don bshad bde/ bsags par bya ba yin pas bsags pa'o / yang na bsags su rung ba'i phyir yang bsags pa zhes bya'o/ yang na don gi skabs su 'dir dran par bya ba yin pas na[2] *dran par zhes bya ste/ de bzhin gshegs pa chos kyi sku'i bdag nyid dran pa nye bar bzhag pa dang/ yang dag par spong ba dang/ lam gyi yan lag dang/ ye shes dang/ stobs dang/ ma 'bres pa'i dran pa nye bar bzhag pa dang/ snying rje chen po zhes bya ba'i yon tan de dag yun ring po nas thabs kyi bye brag gi bsags pa dang/ sngon yang dag par ma bsgoms kyang don gyi skabs dag tu 'dul ba rnams kyis dran par bya ba'i phyir na brtsigs*[3] *pa zhes bya ba'am dran pa zhes bya ste/ de dag gi gzugs brnyan la mchod rten zhes bya'o/ chos kyi sku'i gzugs brnyan zhes bya'o//* (174a3-7)

De'i bang rim bzhi dang/ bum rten dang/ bum pa dang/ pu shu dang/ srog shing dang/ 'khor lo brtsegs[4] *ma bcu gsum dang/ char kheb rnams ni mchod rten gyis dbyibs yin no//* (174a7-b1)

de la bang rim dang po ni dran pa nye bar gzhag pa bzhi ste/ 'di ltar lus dran pa nye bar gzhag pa dang/ tshor ba dang/ sems dang/ chos dran pa nye bar gzhag pa'o //

---

1. *Mchod rten gyi cha dbye ba 'dul ba las byung ba'i mdo,* Tangyur, Gyud, Narthang, Vol. TU, fol. 174b4-175a5.
2. Written as *yin pa nas,* Ibid.
3. *btsags,* Ibid.
4. *rtseg,* Ibid.

bang rim gnyis pa ni yang dag par spong ba bzhi ste[5] / *'di ltar sdig pa mi dge ba'i chos skyes pa rnams spong ba'i phyir brtson pa dang/ sdig pa mi dge ba'i chos ma skyes pa rnams mi*[6] *bskyed pa'i phyir brtson pa dang/ dge ba'i chos ma skyes pa rnams bskyed pa'i phyir brtson pa dang/ dge ba'i chos skyes pa rnams gnas par bya ba'i phyir brtson pa'o //*

bang rim gsum pa rdzu 'phrul gyi rkang pa bzhi ste/ 'di ltar 'dun pa'i ting nge 'dzin spong ba'i 'du byed dang ldan pa'i rdzu 'phrul gyi rkang pa dang/ sems kyi ting nge 'dzin dang/ brtson 'grus kyi ting nge 'dzin dang/ dpyod pa'i ting nge dzin spong ba'i 'du byed dang ldan pa'i rdzu 'phrul gyi rkang pa'o //

bang rim bzhi pa dbang po lnga ste/ 'di ltar dad pa'i dbang po dang/ brtson 'grus gyi dbang po dang/ dran pa'i dbang po dang/ ting nge 'dzin gyi dbang po dang/ shes rab kyi dbang po dang// (174bl-4)

bum rten ni stobs lnga ste/ 'di ltar dad pa'i[7] *stobs dang/ brtson 'grus kyi stobs dang/ dran pa'i stobs dang/ ting nge 'dzin gyi stobs dang/ shes rab kyi stobs so //*

bum pa ni byang chub kyi yan lag bdun te/ 'di ltar dran pa yang dag byang chub kyi yan lag dang/ chos rnams par 'byed pa dang/ dga' ba dang/ shin tu sbyang pa dang/ ting nge 'dzin dang/ brtson 'grus dang[8]/ *btang snyoms yang dag byang chub kyi yan lag do//* (174b4-5)

pu shu[9] *ni lam yan lag brgyad*[10] *pa ste/ 'di ltar yang dag pa'i lta ba dang/ yang dag pa'i rtog pa dang/ yang dag pa'i ngag dang/ yang dag pa'i mtha' dang/ yang dag pa'i 'tsho ba dang/ yang dag pa'i rtsol ba dang/ yang dag pa'i dran pa dang/ yang dag pa'i ting nge 'dzin to//* (174b6-7)

srog shing ni shes pa bcu ste/ 'di ltar kun rdzob shes pa dang/ pha rol gyi sems shes pa dang/ chos shes pa dang/ rjes su rtogs par shes pa dang/ sdug bsngal shes pa dang[11] / *'gog pa shes pa dang*[12] / *kun 'byung*

5. *dang,* Ibid.
6. *mi* is missing, Ibid.
7. *ba'i,* Ibid.
8. This sixth division missing in the xy1.
9. *pu shu* is synonym to either *bre* or *mgul chu* according to other sources.
10. They should be called as "*'phags lam yan lag brgyad*".
11. "*sdug bsngal shes pa dang*", is missing in the text.
12. "*'gog pa shes pa dang*", is missing, Ibid.

shes pa dang/ lam shes pa dang/ zad pa shes pa dang/ mi skye ba shes pa'o// (174b7-175a1)

'khor lo dang po ni gnas dang gnas ma yin pa mkhyen pa'i stobs so// 'khor lo gnyis pa ni las bdag gir mkhyen pa'i stobs so// 'khor lo gsum pa ni bsam gtan dang rnam par thar pa dang ting nge 'dzin dang snyoms par 'jug pa mkhyen pa'i stobs so// 'khor lo bzhi pa ni dbang po mchog dang mchog ma yin pa mkhyen pa'i stobs so// 'khor lo lnga pa ni mos pa sna tshogs mkhyen pa'i stobs so// 'khor lo drug pa ni khams sna tshogs mkhyen pa'i stobs so// 'khor lo bdun pa ni thams cad du 'gro ba'i lam mkhyen pa'i stobs so// 'khor lo brgyad pa ni sngon gyi gnas rjes su dran pa'i stobs so// 'khor lo dgu pa ni 'chi 'pho ba dang skye ba mkhyen pa'i stobs so// 'khor lo bcu pa ni zag pa mkhyen pa'i stobs so// 'khor lo bcu gcig pa ni ma 'dres pa'i dran pa nye bar bzhag pa dang po ste/ gang gis de bzhin gshegs pa'i 'khor rnams la chos ston pa na slob ma thams cad mthun par gus par nyen pa la dga' ba'i[13] *sems mi 'byung ba'o// 'khor lo bcu gnyis pa ni ma 'dres pa'i dran pa nye bar gzhag pa gnyis pa ste/ slob ma thams bcad mthun par gus par mi nyen pa la khong khro ba mi 'byung ba'o// 'khor lo bcu gsum pa ni ma 'dres pa'i dran pa nye bar bzhag pa gsum pa ste/ gang gis de bzhin gshegs pa'i*[14] *'khor rnams la chos ston pa la slon ma la la gus par mnyen la/ la la gus par mi nyen pa rnams la dga' ba dang/ khong khro ba gnyis mi 'byung ba'o//* (175a1-b1)

char kheb ni snying rje chen po ste/ gang gis de bzhin gshegs pa'i 'dul ba'i rgyun smin pa dang/ ma smin pa dang/ da ltar smin pa rnams kyi don dpyod cing/ 'jig rten la[15] *phan pa'i phyir/ de bzhin gshegs pa'i* [16] *chos kyi sku ma lus pa dus kyi khyad par dag tu yang dag 'dzin pa 'di ni mchod rten gyi rang bzhin no//*
(175b1-2)

de la rdo ring rnams ni mi 'jigs pa bzhi bstan te/ 'di ltar zag pa zad pa dang/ yang dag par rdzogs pa'i sangs rgyas dang/ bar du gcod pa'i chos rnams phyin ci ma log par bstan pa dang/ nges par 'byung ba'i lam phyin ci ma log pa bstan pa'o //

---

13. *dga'i,* Ibid.
14. *de bzhin gshegs pa,* Ibid.
15. *jig rten pa,* Ibid.
16. *de bzhin gshegs pa,* Ibid.

them skas kyis ni bsrung ba med pa bzhi bstan te/ 'di ltar sku'i phrin las yongs su dag pa dang/ gsung gi phrin las yongs su dag pa dang/ thugs kyi phrin las yongs su dag pa dang/ 'tsho ba yongs su dag pa'o//

chu srin rgyal mtshan rnams kyis ni/ bdud kyi rgyal mtshan bsnyal bar bstan te/ 'di latr lha'i bdud bsnyal ba dang/ nyon mongs pa'i bdud bsnyal ba dang/ phung po'i bdud bsnyal be dang/ 'chi bdag gi bdud bsnyal ba'o //

me tog gi phrang bas ni bla na med pa'i tshul khrims kyi phung po bstan to //

'jig rten skyong ba rnams kyis ni 'phags pa'i bden pa bzhi bshad pas/ 'jig rten bzhi la phan 'dogs par bstan to/ 'di ltar so so'i skye bo la phan 'dogs pa dang/ rgyun du zhugs pa la phan 'dogs pa dang/ lan cig phyir 'ong ba la phan 'dogs pa dang/ phyir mi 'ong ba la phan 'dogs pa'o //

dril bu rnams ni tshang pa'i dbyangs bstan te/ gang gis de bzhin gshegs pas tshigs[17] *chung ngus stong gsum gyi stong chen po'i 'jig rten gyi khams su chos bstan pa'i sgra skad kyis kun tu 'gengs pa'o //*

gdugs kyis ni 'gro ba thams cad kyi spyi bor gyur par bstan te/ de bzhin gshegs pa sems can rkang pa med pa dang/ rkang pa gnyis pa dang/ rkang mang dang/ gzugs can dang/ gzugs med pa rnams kyi mchog ces bya bar gyur pa'o //

zla bas bla na med pa'i ye shes kyi snang ba bstan te/ gang gis de bzhin gshegs pa mun pa'i 'jig rten du bla na med pa'i shes rab kyi mig bskyed par mdzad pa'o //

dar gyi cod pan gyis ni bla na med pa'i yang dag par rdzogs pa'i byang chub kyi cod pan thogs pa bstan te/ gang gis de bzhin gsheg pa thams cad du thogs pa med pa'i ye shes kun tu 'jug pa'o //

ba dan rnams kyi ni bla na med pa'i chos kyi grags pa'i ba dan bstan te / gang gis de bzhin gshegs pa chos kyi 'khor lo bskor ba'i grags pas 'jig rten gyi dkyil 'khor non par gyur pa'o //

mchod rten gyi cha dbye ba 'dul ba las byung ba'i mdo rdzogs so// (175b2-176a5)

---

17. *tshegs,* Ibid.

ENGLISH VERSION OF THE *CAITYA VIBHAṄGA VINAYODDHṚTA SŪTRA*[18]

Here, the significance of the *mchod rten* (stūpa) will be explained. [The *mchod rten*] is called "the accumulation" because [it represents the essences] to be accumulated. Or it is called "the accumulation" because [these essences] can be accumulated. Or, in respect of its meaning, it is called "the mindfulness" because it is to be remembered. The essence of the Tathāgata's *Dharmakāya* is application of mindfulness (*smṛtyupasthāna*), perfect abandonments (*samyakprahāṇā*), faculties (*indriya*), forces (*bala*), factor of enlightenment (*bodhyāṅga*), factors of the noble paths (*mārgāṅga*), wisdom (*jñāna*), forces (*bala*), absolute unshared (*asamsṛsta smṛtyūpasthāna*), and great compassion (*mahā karunā*). These are qualities which were accumulated through various means and instances over a long period of time. Even though, it was not contemplated perfectly earlier. In the context of its meaning, it is called either built-up or mindfulness because of realising them through those who are tamed. The reflected images of these are called the stūpa; as well as the reflected images of the *Dharmakāya*. (174a3-7)

The flight of four steps, vase-base, the vase (dome of the stūpa), the *harmikā*, axle-pole, thirteen wheels, and the rain-cloak comprise the physical structure of the stūpa. (174a7-b1)

The first step [symbolises] the four close mindfulnesses (*catvāri smṛtyūpasthāna ādhāra vedī*) viz.,

(1) The close mindfulness of body (*kāyasmṛtyūpasthāna*),
(2) The close mindfulness of feeling (*vedanā smṛtyūpasthāna*),
(3) The close mindfulness of mind (*citta smṛtyūpasthāna*), and
(4) The close mindfulness of wisdom (*dharma smṛtyūpasthāna*).

The second step [symbolises] the four perfect abandonments (*catvāri samyak-prahāṇani dvitīyā vedī*) viz.,
(1) Effort to abandon the non-virtues that have arisen,
(2) Effort to prevent the non-virtues that have not yet arisen,
(3) Effort to produce the virtues that have not yet arisen, and
(4) Effort to retain the virtues that have already arisen.

---

18. *Mchod rten gyi cha dbye ba 'dul ba las byung ba'i mdo,* Tangyur, Gyud, Narthang, Vol. TU fol. 174b4-175a5.

The third step [symbolises] the four stages of miraculous powers (*catvāri ṛddhipādās tṛtīyā vedī*) viz.,

(1) A miraculous power possessed of compositional factor renouncing an aspiration of meditative concentration or meditative concentration of desire,
(2) A miraculous power possessed of compositional factor renouncing a meditative concentration of mind,
(3) A miraculous power possessed of compositional factor renouncing a meditative concentration of effort, and
(4) A miraculous power possessed of compositional factor renouncing a meditative concentration of analysis.

The fourth step [symbolises] the five (moral) faculties (*śraddhādīni pañcendriyāni cathurthā jaṃghā vedī*) viz.,

(1) Moral faculty of faith (*śraddhā indriyā*),
(2) Moral faculty of effort (*vīrya indriyā*),
(3) Moral faculty of mindfulness (*smṛti indriyā*),
(4) Moral faculty of meditative concentration (*samādhi indriyā*), and
(5) Moral faculty of wisdom (*prajñā indriyā*). (174b1-4)

The vase-base [symbolises] the five (moral) powers (*śraddhādīni pañca balāni kaṇṭhakam*) viz.,

(1) The (moral) power of faith (*śraddhā bala*),
(2) The (moral) power of effort (*vīrya bala*),
(3) The (moral) power of mindfulness (*smṛti bala*),
(4) The (moral) power of meditative concentration (*samādhi bala*), and
(5) The (moral) power of wisdom (*prajñā bala*).

The vase (dome of the stūpa) [symbolises] the seven factors of enlightenment (*sapta bodhyāṅgāni kuṃbhaḥ*) viz.,

(1) The factor of enlightenment to the perfect mindfulness (*smṛti samyak bodhāṅga*),
(2) The factor of enlightenment to the perfect dharma (*dharma pravicaya samyak bodhāṅga*),

(3) The factor of enlightenment to the perfect joy (*prīti samyak bodhāṅga*),
(4) The factor of enlightenment to the perfect effort (*vīrya samyak bodhāṅga*),
(5) The factor of enlightenment to the perfect suppleness (*praśrabdhi samyak bodhāṅga*),
(6) The factor of enlightenment to the perfect meditative concentration (*samādhi samyak bodhāṅga*), and
(7) The factor of enlightenment to the perfect equanimity (*upekṣā samyak bodhāṅga*). (174b4-5)

The *harmikā* [symbolises] the Eightfold Noble paths (*aṣṭāṅga mārgo harmikā*) viz.,

(1) Right view (*samyak dṛṣṭi*),
(2) Right thought (*samyak saṅkalpa*),
(3) Right speech (*samyak vāk*),
(4) Right action (*samyak karmānta*),
(5) Right livelihood (*samyak ajiva*),
(6) Right endeavour (*samyak vyāyāma*),
(7) Right mindfulness (*samyak smṛti*),
(8) Right meditative concentration (*samyak samādhi*). (174b6-7)

The axle-pole [symbolises] the ten knowledges (*daśa jñānāni yaṣṭih*) viz.,

(1) Knowledge of conventional phenomena (*samvṛti jñāna*),
(2) Knowledge of others' mind (*paracitta jñāna*),
(3) Knowledge of dharma (*dharma jñāna*),
(4) Knowledge of realization of subsequent (*anvaya jñāna*),
(5) Knowledge of sufferings (*duhkha jñāna*),
(6) Knowledge of cessation (*nirodha jñāna*),
(7) Knowledge of sources of origination (*samudaya jñāna*),
(8) Knowledge of paths (*mārga jñāna*),
(9) Knowledge of exhaustion (*kṣaya jñāna*), and
(10) Knowledge of non-productivity (*anutpatta jñāna*).
(174b7-175a1)

(1) The first (bottom) wheel [symbolises] the power of

understanding what is approrpriate and inappropriate (*sthānāsthānajñāna bala*),

(2) The second wheel [symbolises] the power of understanding that one is responsible for one's own deeds or action (*karma-svakajñānabala*),

(3) The third wheel [symbolises] the power of understanding, concentration, liberation, meditative stabilization and meditative absorption (*dhyāna vimokṣa samādhi jñāna bala*),

(4) The fourth wheel [symbolises] the power of understanding the superior and inferior faculties (*indriyā parāpara jñāna bala*),

(5) The fifth wheel [symbolises] the power of understanding the various mental inclinations (*nānā dhimukti jñāna bala*),

(6) The sixth wheel [symbolises] the power of understanding various mental faculties/constitutions (*nānā dhātu jñāna bala*),

(7) The seventh wheel [symbolises] the power of understanding the paths leading to all goals (*sarvatra gāminī pratipatha jñāna bala*),

(8) The eighth wheel [symbolises] the power of understanding the recollection of former existence (*pūrva nivāsānusmṛti jñāna bala*),

(9) The ninth wheel [symbolises] the power of understanding deaths and births (*cyutyutpatti jñāna bāla*),

(10) The tenth wheel [symbolises] the power of understanding the exhaustion/cessation of contaminations (*āsrava kṣaya jñāna bala*),

(11) The eleventh wheel [symbolises] the first peculiar close mindfulness [of the Tathāgata], that by which, when the Tathāgata teaches the dharma to his retinue, he does not get pleased when all his disciples listen with great respect,

(12) The twelfth wheel [symbolises] the second peculiar close mindfulness, that by which, when the Tathāgata teaches the dharma to his retinue, he does not get angry when all his disciples do not listen with due respect, and

(13) The thirteenth wheel [symbolises] the third peculiar close mindfulness, that by which, when the Tathāgata teaches the

> dharma to his retinue, he neither becomes joyful nor angry when part of his disciples listen with respect and part do not listen with respect. (175a1-b1)

The rain-cloak [symbolises] the great compassion by which the Tathāgata examines the mental disposition of his trainees who are mature, immature or maturing. For the benefit of universal people, a perfect apprehension of all the truth bodies (*dharmakāya*) at all the different occasions is the nature of the stūpa. (175b1-2)

[In addition, there are requisite ritual offering articles which are related to the Tathāgata's *dharmakāya* such as pillars, staircases, crocodile victory-banner (*makaradhvaja*), flower garlands, guardians of the world, bell, parasol, moon, tiara flag, flag, etc.]

The four pillars represent the four grounds of self-confidence (*catvāra vaiśaradyāni stambhaḥ*), i.e. (1) Extinction of contamination (*kṣīṇāsrava*), (2) *Samyaksaṃbuddha*, (3) Unmistakenly explained the intervening facts (*antarāyika dharma samākhyāne*), and (4) unmistakenly explained the path of renunciation (*nairyānika mārga samākhyāne*).

The staircases [represent] the four unguarded actions (*catvāri araksyaṇi sopāni*), viz., (1) Absolute purification of the virtuous activity of the body, (2) Absolute purification of the virtuous activity of Speech, (3) Absolute purification of the virtuous activity of Mind, and (4) Absolute purification of the virtuous activity of livelihood.

The *makaradhvaja*, etc. [represents] the victory of overcoming evils, i.e. (1) Overcoming the evil of Devaputra (Cupid), (2) Overcoming of affliction (*kleśamāra*), (3) Overcoming of the aggregates (*skandhamāra*), and (4) Overcoming of the Lord of death (*mṛtyūpatimāra*).

The flower-garlands [represent] the aggregate of [highest] morality (*anuttara śīla skandhāḥ puṣpamamālāh*).

The guardians of the universe [represent] the beneficiaries to the four worldly inhabitants by explaining the four noble truths, i.e.

(1) Beneficial to ordinary people,
(2) Beneficial to stream-enterer (*śrotāpanna*),
(3) Beneficial to once-returner (*sakṛdagāmin*), and
(4) Beneficial to never-returner (*anāgāmin*).

The bells [represent] the *Brahma*-sound by which even a word spoken by the Tathāgata is filled with the sound of promulgation of the religion in every direction of the great thousand worlds of the three thousand (*ārya ratnam idaṃ gāthā dvayasattva viṣayātma gataṃ ghaṇṭa dvayaṃ*).

The umbrella [represents] the Tathāgata a leader of all sentient beings, because the Tathāgata became the supreme among the living beings without legs, among those having two legs, many legs, and among those who are corporeal and incorporeal.

The moon [represents] the brightness of the unsurpassed wisdom by which the Tathāgata generates the eyes of the unsurpassed knowledges in the darkness of this world.

The tiara-flag [represents] the crowning tiara of unsurpassed perfectly accomplished enlightenment by which Tathāgata infuses non-obstructed wisdom in all.

The flags [represent] the flag of unsurpassed glory of the Dharma by which the sphere of the world is subdued through the fame of the turning the Wheel of Law (Dharma) by the Tathāgata. Completed the text *Caitya Vibhaṅga Vinayodbhāva Sūtra*. (175b2-176a5)

APPENDIX B

Transliteration of the Commentary on *Vimaloṣṇīṣa* of Sahajavilāsa[1]

Gcan gzan la sogs pa ni rgyu de phan gdags pa'o / kun nas sgor 'jug pa la sogs pa ni bzlas pa'i grangs gsungs te / lan stong ni shi ba la phan gdags pa'i bzlas brjod kyi grangs so / khri ni 'chi ba slu[2] *ba'i tshes brgyad nas nye'i bar du dge slong la sogs pa gang zag bcus byed pa'i grangs so / 'bum ni bsnyen pa'i bzlas brjod kyi grangs so / 'bum bris te mchod rten gyi nang du bcug ces pa ni snying po 'ba zhig gur gum dang gi wang*[3] *dang tsan dan la sogs pas sngon bzhin bris nas tsha tsha'i nang du bcug pa'o / 'bum tshang nas mchod rten chen po gcig gi nang du bcug ste shing bu bsgreng zhing rgyen btags nas mchod do zhes pa ni 'bum gter chen po'i ring bsrel lo //* (313a2-4)

De la mchod rten gyi rim pa ni /
ri'am thang ngam ljongs gang dag /
dur khrod la sogs spangs pa yi[4] */*
yid yong gnas su rgyal ba yi /
sku gdung mchod rten brtsig pa bya /
yang na sa'am rdo dag la /
mkhas pas tshul bzhin brko bar bya /
sa'am rdo'am shing dag gam /
yang na tshogs pas brtsig par bya// (313a4-5)

---

1. Sahajavilāsa, op. cit., fol. 313a2-314a5.
2. *blu* in Narthang xylograph, Vol. TU, fol. 179a2.
3. *gi wam,* Ibid., fol. 179a3.
4. *yang pa med,* Ibid., fol. 179a5.

de la sangs rgyas kyi mchod rten ni khri 'phang bcu gsum yan chad sum bcu rtsa gnyis man chad do / rang sangs rgyas kyi dgu yan chad bcu gcig man chad de char kheb[5] *dang tog kyang med do / dgra bcom pa'i khri 'phang bzhi yan chad do 'khor lo lnga pa'o / rgyun du zhugs pa nas phyir mi 'ong ba'i bar gyi khri 'phang gsum kho na'o 'khor lo gdun pa'o / so so'i skye bo'i khri 'phang gnyis 'khor lo bzhi'o //* (313a5-7)

de las sangs rgyas kyi sku gdung cha brgyad du bgos pa'i mchod rten chen po brgyad ni grong khyer ser skyar rgyal po zas gtsang gis yon bdag byas nas dpal lha las babs pa'i mchod rten brtsigs so / yul ma ga dha' (Magadha) dbus 'gyur tshal du rgyal po ma skyes dgras[6] *yon bdag byas nas byang chub chen po'i mchod rten brtsigs so / grong khyer rtsa mchog tu gyad rnams kyi yon bdag byas nas cho 'phrul chen po'i mchod rten brtsigs so / yul vwa rwa na si*[7] *ru ser skye'i rgyal po tshang byin*[8] *gyis yon bdag byas nas dpal chos kyi 'khor lo'i mchod rten brtsigs so / yul yangs pa can du rgyal po li tsa bi gzhon nus*[9] *yon bdag byas nas dpal ka ni ka'i mchod rten brtsigs so / yul mnyen yod*[10] *du rgyal po gsal rgyal*[11] *gyis yon bdag byas nas dpal bkra shis sgo mangs brtsigs so / yul chang ger*[12] *rgyal po 'dun 'dzin ta las*[13] *yon bdag byas nas dpal 'od can gyi mchod rten brtsigs so / yul ti ka tsa shir*[14] *rgyal po ain dra va mis*[15] *yon bdag byas nas mchod rten pad ma can brtsigs so / slan chad kyang de dag gi rjes su 'brangs te brtsigs par bya'o //*
(313a7-b4)

De la byang chub chen po'i mchod rten gyi tshul du brtsigs na/ sku gdung gi rmang[16] *yod na rmang rten ji ltar mtho ba bzang*

---

5. *char khab,* Ibid.
6. Ajātśatru.
7. Varanasi.
8. Brahmadatta.
9. Licchavi prince.
10. Śrāvasti.
11. Prasenajit.
12. *Tshad ge* has been interpreted in an English translation of Tucci's Indo-Tibetica I, p. 121.
13. Śuncidala, Ibid.
14. Tikacaśi, Ibid.
15. Indravami(n).
16. According to Chenga Lodos Gyaltsen's interpretation, it has been quoted as "*sku gsdung gi rten*", rather than "*sku dgung gi rmang*". His interpretation has more sense than the counterpart.

ngo/ / rten med na bang rim dang po'i sum cha'i tshad do / de'i steng du dge bcu ni phyir bskyed pa dang rngams bang rim dang po'i rngams phyed do / gnam 'phang phyi la bang rim dang po'i ngos tshad do / de yan chad srog shing ste bang rim dang po'i bzhi gsum gyi tshad do / bang rim bzhi 'phang mnyam mo / bang rim rngams kyi phyir tshad khri 'phang ngo / bum rten khri 'phang gi phyed[17] *tshad do / bum pa ni bang rim dang po'i sum gnyis kyi tshad do / stod kyi skyed ni bang rim gsum pa dang mnyam mo/ bre rten gyi rgya ni bang rim bzhi pa'i lnga cga gcig go / bre ni bang rim bzhi pa'i bzhi cha gcig go / de gnyis ka'i 'phang ni bang rim gyi sum gnyis dang bang rim gyi phyed do/ bang rim bzhi pa'i*[18] *shar dang lhor gsal khung bang rim nyid kyi brgyad cha'o / srog shing gi rtsa ba bang rim bzhi pa la reg go / 'khor lo bcu gsum gyi 'phang du bang rim dang po'i bzhi gsum gyi tshad do / 'khor lo dang po ni bre'i zur bzhi la slebs so / de bzhi chas 'khor ba'i tshad ni 'khor lo bcu gsum pa'o / bcu gcig po yang rim gyis gzhol ba'o / rtseg par thams cad ni ci mdzes su bya'o / thugs rjes mdo gzungs 'phang khor lo chung ba dang mnyam mo / de'i smad du rngams kyi bzhi gsum ni 'jam po nyid stod du bzhi cha gcig ni phreng ba'i sul bcu drug pa'o / de'i steng du 'khor lo bcu gsum nyid kyi shing phyed tshad yang rtse phra ba bang rim nyid kyi 'phang phyed do / yang srog shing 'phang du bre phyed*[19] *tsam steng du zla ba'i rste mo gdugs dang mnyam srog shing la bskor te rtse mo bgrad*[20] *do / gdugs ni 'khor lo bdun pa dang mnyam mo / gdugs khebs*[21] *'khor lo drug pa dang mnyam mo / za ra tshags ni bre'i 'phang dang mnyam mo / yang srog shing 'phang du bre'i sum cha'i tshad kyi steng du nyi ma zla ba las khyad yud*[22] *tsam mo / nyi ma'i steng du tog ni*[23] *ut pal gsar pa'i*[24] *tog bu 'dra ste ci mdzes su bya'o / nyi ma dang*

---

17. *phyed* is missing in the text.
18. *pa'i* is missing in the text.
19. *ched* is written in the text.
20. *dgrad* is written in the text.
21. *khabs* is written in the text.
22. *yungs* is written in the text.
23. *gi* is written in the text.
24. *po'i* is written in the text.

zla ba dang tog thams cad kyi zur la bya mi chags[25] *par bya ba'i phyir lcags kyi thur ma rnon po gzer bar bya'o //* (313b4-314a4)

Tog ni ser po nyi ma ni dmar po / zla ba ni dkar po / gdugs khebs ni dkar po'o / gdugs ni sngon po / gdugs kyi phyogs bzhir rigs bzhi'i[26] *phyag rgya bri'o / thugs rje'i sul*[27] *ni dmar po'o / thugs rje nyid dang shes bcu ni ser po'o / 'khor lo thams cad dang*[28] *srog shing dmar po'o / rmang dang rmang rten ljang gu'o / mchod rten brtsig pa'i rim pa'o //* (314a4-5)

---

25. *'chags* is written in the text.
26. In the English translation of Tucci's Indo-Tibetica I, in footnote 1, p. 125, elucidated therein a list of four races *mahāmudrā*, i.e. Ratnasambhava, Amitābh, Amoghasiddhi and Akṣobya corresponding their directions to south, west, north and east respectively.
27. *phul* is written in the Xyl.
28. *'khor lo thams cad dang* is missing in the text.

ENGLISH VERSION OF THE COMMENTARY ON *VIMALOṢṆĪṢA* BY SAHAJAVILĀSA[29]

"Carnivorous animals, etc.", show that the cause is beneficial. *"Samantamukhapraveśa* etc." mentions the number of recitations. One thousand time is the number of recitations for benefiting the deceased. Ten thousand is the number of recitations for rescuing from death, which is to be done by ten persons such as *Bhikṣūs*, etc., from the eighth day to the full-moon day. One hundred thousand is the number of recitations for the propitiation of one's deity.

"By writing one hundred thousand *mantras* and putting them inside the stūpa", means that the *hṛdaya-mantra* alone is written as before with saffron (*gur gum*), yellow pigment (*gi wang,* Skt: *garocna*) and sandalwood, etc., and is to be inserted in the *tsha tsha.* "After the completion of one hundred thousand *tsha tsha*, they are to be placed inside a large stūpa "a wooden pole should be raised, decorated and worshipped" refer to the relics of the one hundred thousand treasures.[30]

(313a2-4)

---

29. Sahajavilāsa, fol. 313a2-314a5.
30. In the *Vimaloṣṇīṣa* text of Kagyur, Gyud, Derge, Vol. PHA, fol. 258b4 elucidates a detail context of their contents as follows: "A group of birds will be completely liberated, if [one] recites the *hṛdaya-mantra* of the *Vimaloṣṇīṣa* to them. Even the dog, tortoise, snake and different kinds of insects will be completely liberated, if one recites it to them.

    By reciting 21 times on sand and strewing [the sand] over the cemetery, whosoever's bone is struck will be completely liberated from the hell, where they took birth and will be reborn in the higher realm (*svargaguṇa*). That person who is born in the higher realm will be showered with flower petals upon his body. Carnivorous animals and various kinds of birds whoever [may] walk in that cemetery will be reborn in the state of fortunate beings (*sugati*). Wild animals and birds whoever [may] wander in the hill will be reborn in the state of fortunate beings, if [the sand is] strewn [over the hill].

    The person who has committed the five heinous actions (*pañcānatarīya*) shall be liberated immediately after experiencing the scorching heat of the boundless hell (*avīci*), if [one] recites the *hṛdaya-mantra* of *Vimaloṣṇīṣa.* If [one] recites [the *hṛdaya-mantra*] one hundred thousand times, that person will immediately be reversed from the place of *Yama,* even if he has been taken tied with a rope on his neck. He will be completely liberated from great fear, etc. That person will happily proceed to the realm of *Sukhavatī* or *Sugavati* by

That the stages of constructing the stūpas are:

The stūpa of the relics of the Victor
should be erected in an attractive place(s);
(such as) somewhere on a hill or a plain or a valley,
(avoiding) other than a cemetery, etc.
or on earth or stones.
A stūpa should be engraved properly by an expert,
or by the earth, stone or wood,
or by an assemblage of these a stūpa should be erected.

(313a4-5)

The stūpa of the Awakened One has to be (made) above thirteen *Khri phang*[31] and below thirtytwo. For the Pratyekabuddha it should be

---

leaving his body as the snake changes his skin or as the path of concentration changes. He will not see the sufferings of *Yama*. If one puts in the stūpa one hundred thousand copies of the *hṛdaya-mantra* that stūpa will blossom completely after containing one hundred thousand *hṛdaya-mantra*. Even oneself will blossom and surely become an irreversible aspirant (*apratyudavārtaya*). One will dwell in the ten grounds (*daśa bhūmi*). One will obtain prophecy by producing the virtuous deeds for Tathāgata, equal in number to the sand of the Ganges river. It will be called as a stūpa of one hundred thousand essence-relics of Tathāgata, if when [one] raises the wooden pole and one inserts one hundred thousand *tsha tsha* containing the same number of [*hṛdaya-mantra*] inside the large stūpa.

31. The literal meaning of *khri 'phang* is "the height of a throne". Although in architectural terminology it has been interpreted by Bodhisattva in his text entitled," *'phags pa kun nas sgor ' judg pa'i 'od zer gtsug tor dri ma med par snang ba'i gzungs bklag cing mchod rten brgya rtsa brgyad dam mchod rten lnga gadp pa'i cho ga mdo sde las bsdus pa",* Tangyur, Gyud, Vol. PU, Toh. fol. 162b6, as a step by the following reference: *"khri 'phang dang po dran pa nyer bzhag bzhi",* and so forth.

But, in this case, the word *"khri 'phang"* in the first instance perhaps may be interpreted as a wheel and in the latter undoubtedly refers to the step. Normally, scholars have unanimously agreed that the stūpa for the Awakened One has to be made atleast thirteen wheels in the minimum and thirtytwo in the maximum, or in other interpretation it can have more than hundred or so. So, on the basis of above theory, the word *"khri 'phang"* is improper to use for the wheel.

above nine and below eleven, having no cover of umbrella and spherical pinnacle. For an *Arhat* it should have four *Khri phang* and five wheels. For a *Śrotāpanna* to an *anāgāmin* it should have only three *Khri phang* and seven wheels. For an ordinary person *(pṛthagjana)* it should have two *Khri phang* and four wheels.

(313a5-7)

That the eight great stūpas emerged from the division of the Buddha's relics into eight parts which are:

(1) The stupa of "Descent from Heaven" was built under the sponsorship of king Śuddhodana at the city of Kapilavastu.
(2) The stūpa of "Enlightenment" was built under the sponsorship of king Ajātaśatru at the central garden of the Magadhan city.
(3) The stūpa of "Miracles" was built under the sponsorship of Mallas at Kuśinagara.
(4) The stūpa of "Turning the Wheel of Law" was built at Kāśi under the sponsorship of Brahmadatta, king of Kāśi.[32]
(5) The stūpa of "Kanika" was built under the sponsorship of the Licchavi prince of Vaiśāli.
(6) The stūpa of "Multiple Auspicious Doors" was built under the sponsorship of king Prasenajit of Śrāvasti.
(7) The stūpa of "Luminosity", was constructed under the sponsorship of king 'dun 'dzin ta la[33] at the city of Tshad ge.
(8) The stūpa of "Lotus-shape", was constructed under the sponsorship of king Indravami at the city of Ti ka tsa shi[34].

(313a 7-b4)

Thus, the stūpa should be constructed by following them. If a stūpa of Enlightenment is to be built it should be done as follows:

If there is a receptacle of relics,[35]

32. In the text it is stated as the king of Kapilavastu instead of the Kāśi king.
33. Śuncidala has been interpreted by Dr. Lokesh Chandra in his introduction note of the English translation of Tucci's Indo-Tibetica I text, p. vi.
34. Tikacaśi, Ibid.
35. "Receptacle of relics", is quoted in the Chenga Lodos Gylatsen's work, which is more appropriate than the "Foundation of relics" as it does not make sense. Probably, it was wrongly translated.

It is better for the foundation support to be as high as possible.
If there is no receptacle, the size should be one-third the length of the first step.
Upon that, the base of ten-virtues tapers out,
its width being half of the first step's length.
The height of the later sphere is, [equal to] the length of one side of the first step.
Above it is the axle-pole, three-quarters the length of the first step.
The four steps are equal in height, while half of the outer width or thickness of the steps is the height of a single step.
The vase-support is half the height of a step.
The vase is two-thirds of the first step.
The upper waist (vase belly) is equal to [the length of the] third step.
The length of the *harmikā*-base is one-fifth of the fourth step.
The *harmikā* is one-quarter [the width] of the fourth step, and the height of both is two-thirds and half of the steps' [height].
Windows on the east and south of the fourth step are an-eighth part of the step itself.
The base of the axle-pole should touch the fourth step.
The height of the thirteen wheels is three-quarters the length of the first step.
The first wheel should reach at the four edges of the *harmikā*, one-quarter of its circumference size is the thirteenth wheel.
The [remaining] eleven should gradually taper off.
All the built-up one upon another should be made as attractive as possible.
The height of the Formula of Compassion (*karuṇāsūtra dhāraṇī*) should be [made] equal to the smallest wheel.
At its lower part, three-quarters of the thickness is in smooth, and one-quarter of its upper part is in a form of sixteen plaits of coil.
The wooden [pole] is half the size of the thirteenth wheel, and its pointed tip is half the height of a step.
The axle-pole having the height of about half of the *harmikā*, is topped by the moon the tips of which are equal in width to the umbrella, and surrounding the axle-pole.

The umbrella is equal to the sixth wheel.
The *za ra tshags* is equal to the height of the *harmikā*. Upon the axle-pole (which is one-third the height of the *harmikā*) stands the sun, which is a bit bigger than the moon.
The spherical pinnacle topped upon the sun is similar to the crest of a budding *utpala*.
On the edges of the sun, moon, and the spherical pinnacle, sharp iron nails should be fixed to prevent birds from resting thereupon. (313b4-314a4)

The colour of the spherical pinnacle is yellow, the sun is red, the moon and the cover of umbrella are white. The umbrella has to be blue and on its four directions there should be drawn the symbols of the four races.[36] The plait of compassion is red, the compassion itself and the ten-fold knowledges are yellow. All the thirteen wheels and the axle-pole are red. The stūpa itself is white, the base of ten-virtues is yellow, and the foundation and the foundation-support are green in colour. These are the stages for the construction of a stūpa. (314a4-5)

36. They are recorded as *Ratnasambhava* at south, *Amitābha* at west, *Amoghasiddhi* at north and *Akṣobhya* at east in the English translation of the Indo-Tibetica text, Vol. I, p. 125.

APPENDIX C

Transliteration of Buston's Proportional Manual of the Stūpa of Enlightenment[1]

Mchod rten sgrub pa' cho ga byin rlabs dpal 'bar zhes bya ba / sans rgyas dang byang chub sems dpa' thams cad la phyad 'tshal lo //

sngon 'phags pa sha ri'i bu'i[2] *rings bsrel rnams khyim bdag mgon med zas sbyin gyis khyer te / rang gi khyim gyi nang gi phyogs mthon po zhig tu bzhag ste, de la mchod pa dang, skye bo'i tshogs chen po gzhan rnams kyis kyang der 'ong te mchod/ dus re zhig kyim bdag ri bor zhig tu bya ba cung zad cig la sgo bcad de song ba na, skye bo'i tshogs rnams kyis mchod pa bya sa ma byung bar bdag cag gi bsod nams kyi bar chad byas so zhes 'phya ba de kyim bdag gis thos nas khyim bdag gis bcom ldan 'das la bdag gis sha ri'i bu'i mchod rten phyogs snang gyel can zhig bgyis la mchod pa dgyid du rtsal to / bka' stsal pa, gnang gi byos shig / Ji ltar bya ba mi shes nas zhus pas / Bka' stsal pa, rim gyis bang rim bzhi byas la / de nas bum rten bya'o / de nas bum pa dang, bre dang, srog shing dang, gdugs gcig dang, gnyis dang, gsum dang, bzhi bya ba nas bcu gsum gyi bar du bya zhing char khebs dag bzhag par bya'o / bcom ldan 'das kyis mchod rten de lta bu bya'o zhes gsungs pa dang / des ci, 'phags pa sha*

1. *Byang chub chen poi' mchod rten gyi tshad bzhugs so,* Collected Works of Buston, Vol. 14 (PHA), pp. 551-58.
2. Śāriputra.

ri'i bu 'ba' zhig la mchod rten rnam pa de lta bu bya'm. 'on te 'phags pa (552b7) *thams cad la bya ba mi shes nas skabs der*[3] *bcom ldan 'das la dge slong dag gis gsol ba dang / bka' stsal ba, khyim bdag re zhig de zhin gshegs pa'i mchod rten ni rnam pa thams cad yongs su rdzogs par bya'o / rang sangs rgyas kyi ni char khebs mi bzhag par bya'o,*[4] *dgra bcom pa ni gdugs bzhi'o, phyir mi 'ong ba'i ni gsum mo, phyir 'ong ba'i ni gnyis so / rgyun du zhug pa'i ni gcig go,*[5] *so so'i skye bo dge ba rnams kyi ni mchod rten byi bor bya'o*[6] */ zhes lung du gsungs pas //*

de la byang chub chen po'i mchod rten gyi phyag tshad gtsug tor dri med[7] *kyi 'gral pa nas 'byung ba bzhin brjod par bya'o / de la tshangs thig zur thig rnams legs par btab ba la / tshangs thig nas zur thig tu byas nas tub pas cha chen bcu gnyis su 'gyur la / phyi nas cha chen re re bsnan la bcu bzhi ru bya'o / de re re la cha chung bzhi bzhir bgo bar bya'o //*

rmang rten yod na, ji ltar mtho ba bzang ste 'on kyang thig khongs su mi rtsi la / rmang rten med na, rmang gi dpangs tshad cha chen gnyis yin la rgya tshad dngos su ma gsung kyang dgan dge ba bcu las[8] *rgya che ba tsam la / 'og tu them skas dang steng du ba gam la sogs pa ji ltar mdzes pa'o //*

Ji skad du; *sku gdung gi rten*[9] *yod na /*
rmang rten ji ltar mtho ba bzang ngo /

---

3. *de* written in the text.
4. According to Buston's note *"bse ru lta bu yin gi, tshogs spyod nyan thos dgra bcom dang 'dra'o"*, which implies that the number of umbrellas should be made equal to the Śrāvaka Arhat.
5. According to Buston's note, In the *"['dul ba] mdo rtsa (Vinayasūtra)* written by [Guṅaprabha] and Viśākhadeva's (Sa ga'i lha) *'dul ba tshig le'ur byas pa (Vinaya kārikā)* text mentioned *" 'bras bu'i tshad pas gcig gis mang bar bshad pas lung ma dag gam snyam"*, see page 144, footnote 29.
6. Buston mentioned in his footnote that *byi bo* means without having axle-pole. This implies absense of umbrellas or wheels.
7. *Vimaloṣṇīṣa.*
8. *bas* in xyl.
9. *rmang* is attributed instead of *rten* in the commentary on *Vimaloṣṇīṣa* of Sahajavilāsa and *Mchod rten gyi cha rnam par dbye ba* of unspecified author.

rmang rten med na [10] /
bang rim dang po'i sum cha'i tshad do zhes so //

de'i steng du gdan dge ba bcu ni dpan̄gs su cha phran gcig rgyar gyas gyon du cha phran phyed dang bcu gsum ste, nyi shu rtsa lnga'o //

Ji skad du; *de'i steng du dge ba bcu ni* /
phyir bskyed pa dang /
rngams bang rim dang po'i rngams phyed do zhes so //

de'i steng du bang rim dang po dpangs su cha chung gnyis rgyar gyas gyon du cha chen gsum gsum ste, drug go / *de'i steng du bang rim gsum dpangs su cha chung gnyis gnyis te, dpangs mnyams* / *zheng gyas gyon du cha chung re re phri ba yin te* / *bang rim bzhi ka'i rngams kyi rgyar cha chen gcig yin la* / *de'i phyed bang rim gyi dpangs su yod de* //

Ji skad du; *bang rim bzhi dpangs mnyam mo* /
bang rim rngams kyi phyi[11] *tshad khri 'phang ngo zhes so* //

de'i steng du bum rten dpang su cha chung gcig rgyar gyas gyon du cha phran phyed dang dgu ste, bcu bdun no / *de'i steng du bum pa'i rtsa ba gyas gyon du cha chen gnyis gnyis te, bzhi la* / *bgas kyi 'phel bas stod kyi rked gyas gyon du cha chen phyed dang gsum ste, lnga la*/ *de yan chod bgas kyis zhum pa'i zlum zhing mdzes pa ste* / *rtsa ba dang rgya mnyam pa* / *dpangs su cha chen gsum dang cha phran gcig gi sum cha'o* / *de'i steng du bre rten gyi gyar gyas gyon du cha chung re re'i lnga char byas pa'i dgu dgu dpangs cha chung gcig* / *de'i steng du bre gyas gyon du cha phran gnyis gnyis dang cha phran bzhi zha re ste, cha chen gcig dang cha phran phyed do* / *dpangs cha phran gcig dang cha phran gsum gnyis te* //

Ji skad du; *bum rten khri 'phang gi phyed do* [12]/

---

10. *rten med na* is attributed in the VIM and MCHOD.
11. *phyir* is attributed in the VIM and MCHOD.
12. *phyed tshad do* in the VIM and *tshad do* is elucidated in the MCHOD.

bum pa ni, bang rim dang po'i sum gnyis kyi tshad do /
stod kyi rked ni, bang rim gsum pa dang mnyam mo /
bre rten gyi rgya ni, bang rim bzhi pa'i lnga cha gcig go /
bre ni, bang rim bzhi pa'i (554b7) *bzhi cha gcig go /*
de gnyis ka'i 'phang ni, bang rim sum gnyis dang bang rim gi phyed do[13] */ zhes gsungs te //*

'de'i go rim bzhin sbyar na, bre rten dpangs mtho ba zhig snang mod kyi / mchod rten gzhan dang gzhan kun la bre rten dpangs dma' bar yod pas 'gyur gyi skyon du mngon no / de ltar na, bang rim dang po'i rgya dang bang rim dang po nas bre'i rtse mo tshun chad mnyam pa ste //

Ji skad du; *gnam 'phang phyi ma bang rim dang po'i ngos tshad do zhes so //*

bum pa'i dpangs tshad dngos su ma gsungs kyang, phyi'i tshad ni sngar gi shugs las go'o / bang rim bzhi pa'i shar dang lhor skar khung bang rim gyi brgyad cha yod pa bya zhing / srog shing ni, rtsa ba bang rim bzhi pa la reg ste / de yan chad cha chen bzhi dang chan phran gnyis ni 'khor lo bcu gsum gyi dpangs te //

Ji skad du; *bang rim bzhi pa'i shar dang lhor gsal khung*
bang rim nyid kyi rgyad cha'o /
srog shing rtsa ba bang rim bzhi pa la reg pa'o[14] */*
'khor lo bcu gsum gyi, phang du /
bang rim dang po'i bzhi gsum gyi tshad do zhes so //

'khor lo dang po'i rgya tshad gyas gyon du cha phran gsum gsum ste, thad kar drug, zlum por skor ba'i mtha' bskor du bco brgyad do / 'khor lo bcu gsum pa ni, gyas gyon du cha phran bzhi gsum nas bskor bas thad kar phyed dang gnyis, mtha' bskor du phyed dang lnga'o /

---

13. It should perhaps be interpreted as *bang rim gsum gnyis kyi phyed do.*
14. *reg go* in xyl. VIM and MCHOD.

de'i bar gyi 'khor lo bcu gcig po rnams rim gyis je phra je phrar gyur pa ste / 'khor lo bcu gsum po dpangs mnyam pas 'khor lo re re'i dpangs cha chung bco rgyad la bcu gsum gyis bgos pai' cha re re ste / 'on kyang 'khor lo dang po'i 'og du 'degs kyi pad ma cha chung gcig dang thugs rje mdo gzungs dpangs 'khor lo chung ba dang mnyam par bya ste// (555b7)

Ji skad du; *'khor lo dang po ni,*
bre'i zur bzhi la slab bo[15] */*
de bzhi chas 'khor ba'i tshad ni,
'khor lo bcu gsum pa'o /
bcu gcig po yang rim gyi gzhol ba'o /
brtsegs[16] *par thams cad ci mdzes su bya'o /*
thugs rje mdo gzungs 'khor lo chung ba dang mnyam mo zhes so //

thugs rje mdo gzungs kyi smad du bzhi gsum 'jam po nyid la cung zad gyen du gyel ba la, stod bzhi cha gcig phrang ba'i sul bcu drug pa utpala'i 'dab ma'i rnam pa can te //

Ji skad du; *de'i smad du rngams kyi bzhi gsum ni,*
'jam po nyid /
stod du bzhi cha gcig ni,
phreng ba'i sul bcu drug pa'o zhes so //

de las,[17] *cha phran bco rgyad kyi gcig 'khor lo 'deg pa'i pad ma la btang nas, lhag ma bcu bdun cha mnyam par dgos pa'i 'khor lo re re'i 'phang la cha phran re re dang cha re'i gcig bzhi cha gsum mo / de'i bar ci mdzes 'og tu gsungs kyang sum gnyis sum gnyis la 'khor lo sum cha bar gyi cha bar stong du bzhag pa la rdo rje la sogs pa'i rked bris ci mdzes so / thugs rje mdo gzungs kyi steng du ka shu shing gi sboms su 'khor lo'i dpangs kyi phyed, dkrus su cha phran gnyis te, gyas gyon du bang rim gyis phra ba gyen du gyel ba bzhi rgya gram btang ba ste //*

Ji skad du; *de'i steng du 'khor lo bcu gsum pa nyid kyi srog*

15. *slebs so* in xyl. VIM and MCHOD.
16. *rtseg* in xyl. VIM and MCHOD.
17. *des na* in xyl.

[shing.] gi phyed tshad[18] *yang rtse phra ba bang rim nyid kyi 'phang phyed do zhes so //*

gdugs kyi dbugs bug bar srog shing gi cha phran sum gnyis kyi rtse mor zla ba'i rtse mo gdugs dang mnyam pa, gyas gyon du rtse mo bgrad pa / de'i steng du nyi ma zla ba las che tsam / de'i steng du tog ste utpal gsar pa'i tog bu 'dra ba / gdugs ni, 'khor lo bdun pa dang mnyam pa / za ra tshags bre'i 'phang dang mnyam pa / gdugs khebs 'khor lo drug pa dang mnyam pa ste // (556b7)

Ji skad du; *yang srog shing 'phang du bre phyed*[19] *tsam, steng du zla ba'i tse mo gdugs dang mnyam, srog shing la bskor te rtse mo bgrad*[20] *do / gdugs ni*[21], *'khor lo bdun pa dang mnyam mo / gdugs khebs*[22] *'khor lo drug pa dang mnyam mo / za ra tshags ni, bre'i 'phang dang mnyam mo / dpangs*[23] *srog shing 'phang du bre'i sum cha'i steng du nyi ma zla ba las kyad yud*[24] *che tsam mo / nyi ma'i steng du tog ni, utpal gsar pa'i tog bu dang 'dra ste, ci mdzes so / nyi ma dang zla ba dang tog thams cad kyi zur la bya mi 'chags par bya ba'i phyir lcags kyi thur ma rnon po gzer bar bya'o // tog ni ser po, nyi ma ni dmar po, zla ba ni dkar po, gdugs khebs ni dkar po'o, gdugs ni sngon po'o / gdugs kyi phyogs bzhir rigs bzhi'i phyag rgya bri'o / thugs rje'i sui*[25] *ni, dmar po'o / srog shing dmar po'o / dge bcu yang ser po'o / rmang dang rmang rten ljang khu'o zhes so //*

Mchod rten sgrub pa'i cho ga byin rlabs dpal 'bar zhes bya ba

---

18. *shing phyed tshad* in xyl. VIM and MCOD.
19. *ched* in xyl. MCHOD.
20. *dgrad* in xyl. VIM and MCHOD.
21. Buston has attributed in his note section the following passage: *"gdugs dang gdugs khebs kyi dpangs su cha phran phyed phyed, zla ba la cha phran gcig, nyi ma gnyis, tog la gcig ste, cha phran bzhi po de steng gi cha chen bcu bzhi pa la 'don no."* This passage indicates the proportion of the final structures of the stūpa.
22. *khabs* in xyl. VIM and MCHOD.
23. *yang* in xyl. VIM and MCHOD.
24. *gyung* in xyl. MCHOD.
25. *phul* in xyl.

Bu ston gyis bkod pa'i yi ge pa ni dge slong sgra tshad pa rin rnam yin no //

ENGLISH VERSION OF BUSTON'S PROPORTIONAL MANUAL OF THE STŪPA OF ENLIGHTENMENT[26]

A method for accomplishing the construction of the stūpa designated as "Flaming Splendour of Blessing".

Prostration to all Buddhas and Bodhisattvas.

Previously, the relics of Ārya Śāriputra were taken away by the *gṛhapati* (householder) Anāthapiṇḍaka and were placed on a high place [altar] of his house and worshipped. Many other people also came there for worship. On a certain occasion, the householder locked the door and went to hill-site to do some minor work. When he returned, an assemblage of people, who had been deprived of the chance to worship accused him of obstructing their merits. Consequently, the householder approached the Buddha to seek his permission for constructing a stūpa of Śāriputra at an easily visible spot [or accessible to people] for making offerings to it. The Buddha said: "Permission granted, and may it be done." Not knowing how should he do it, the householder asked again. The Buddha elaborated, "Successively, four steps should be made, then the vase-base should be made. After that, the vase (dome) of the stūpa, the *harmikā* or *droṇa*,[27] the axle-pole, one, two, three, and four to thirteen umbrellas should be erected, and the cover of the umbrella(s) should be placed [on it]." In this way, the stūpa should be built as expressed by the Buddha. It was, however, still not clear for whom the stūpa should be built—only for Ārya Śāriputra, or for all Āryas. So, at that time, the *Bhikṣūs* raised the matter with the Buddha. The Buddha commanded, "House-

26. *Byang chub chen po'i mchod rten gyi tshad bzhugs so,* Collected Works of Buston, op. cit., pp. 551-56.
27. In Tibetan *called bre, which is quadrangular in shape used to measure grains in Tibet.*

holder, the stūpa for the Tathāgata has to be built in a very complete form. For the Pratyekabuddha, the cover of the umbrella should not be placed.[28] For the Arhat there should be four umbrellas; for the never-returner (*Anāgāmin*) only three; for the once-returner (*Sakṛḍagāmin*) two; and only one for the stream-enterer (*Śrotāpanna*).[29] The stūpas for the Virtuous laymen are to be constructed as *byi bo*."[30] Thus it is mentioned in the text.[31]

The proportions of the "Stūpa of Enlightenment" shall be explained according to the commentary upon the *Vimaloṣṇīṣa* text.[32] According to this text, the central axes and the border lines are to be drawn accurately; twelve large units are formed by making divisions between the central axes and the border lines. Then, by adding one large unit to each of the extremities [top and bottom], we get [a total of] fourteen large units. Each of these large units should also be divided into sixteen (4 x 4) small units.

---

28. Buston mentions in his footnote that the *Pratyekabuddha* here refers to the "rhinoceros-like-Pratyekabuddha" and that the *"Pratyekabuddha* living in the gathering (*Vargacarin*)" is similar to the *Śrāvaka Arhat.*
29. Buston mentions in his footnote that the *Vinayasūtra* of Guṇaprabha and Sagadeva's or Viśakhadeva's *Vinayakārikā* referred that [the number of umbrellas for the *Arhat* to *Śrotāpanna* have to be made] more than one measurement of fruition which is probably an error.
30. *Byi bo* means "without adornment" or "bald", which signifies the absence of the axle-pole, and thus implies not having the wheels or umbrellas as well.
31. The text cited is *Vinaya-kṣudraka-vastu,* Kanjur, Vinaya, Derge, Vol. THA, fol. 244b3-247a7.
32. There is no doubt that the passages cited by Buston in his text are found to be identical in every respect with those of the commentary on *Vimaloṣṇīṣa* whose author was known as Sahajavilāsa, and *Mchod rten gyi cha rnam par dbye ba* text, of unspecified author and translator, and whose Sanskrit title is also not given. Both the texts substantiate to being basic constructional manuals of the Buddhist Stūpa Architecture and deal specifically with the Proportional Manual of the Stūpa of Enlightenment available in Tanjur. Thus, it is evident that Buston's Proportional Manual of the Stūpa of Enlightenment, based on the commentary on *Vimaloṣṇīṣa* (as claimed by him) is irrefutable. However, on which text did he base his work? Concerning this, we must discover the original source of the work, yet this has nowhere been mentioned by Buston in his works. For details see pp. 8-10.

If the foundation support exists[33], it would be better for it to be as high as possible, but it does not count in the proportion. If the foundation support does not exist, then the measurement of the foundation has to be two large units in height. Its width is not actually stated, although it should be somewhat wider than the "base of ten-virtues". The staircase below and the dome etc. above are to be made as attractive as possible.

As it is said: [34]

> "If a receptacle of remains exists,
> it would be better to have the foundation support as high as possible.
> If the foundation support does not exist,
> the size should be one-third the [length] of the first step."

Upon [the foundation], the base of ten-virtues is one small unit in height and twelve and a half small units in width in each direction right and left, totalling twentyfive.

As it is said:

> Upon that, the base of ten-virtues juts out,
> its thickness half of the first step's thickness.

Next, the first (bottom) step is two small units in height and three large units in width to both the right and left, totalling six. Above that the remaining three steps should have an equal height of two small units each. As for the width, one small unit should be detracted from each side. The flight of four steps' thickness is one large unit, and half its size is the height of a step.

As it is said :

> The flight of four steps have to be made equal in height,
> and a half of the steps' thickness is the height of a step.

---

33. This description contradicts his source work in which it is stated: "If the receptacle of remains exists."
34. Buston had extracted the whole constructional manual of the Indian basic text and elucidated them thoroughly in confirmation with the basic text and thus, displayed them in the style of "As it is said (*Ji skad du*)" in his text. So, in my translation the same pattern will be seen specially in respect of its presentation, categorization and meaning as it is in his text.

The "vase-base" *(bum rten)* is one small unit in height, and eight and a half small units in width to both the right and left, totalling seventeen. Upon this, the "vase-root" *(bum rtsa)* is four large units in straight, (two large units each at the right and left) gradually widening up to the "upper-waist of the vase" *(bum stod kyi rked)* which is five large units wide, (two and a half small units each at the right and left). From this point onwards, the structure is round and solemnly beautiful. Its width is equal to that of the vase-root, and its [the vase's] height, is three large units and one-third part of a small unit.[35]

Upon this rests the "*harmikā*-base" which measures nine one-fifth parts of a small unit at both the right and left, and one small unit in height. The "*harmikā*" is two small units and a quarter part of a small unit to both the right and left—totalling one and a half small units, and one small unit and two-thirds part of a small unit in height.

As it is said:

> The vase-base is half the height of the step.
> The vase is two-thirds the size of the first step.
> The upper-waist is equal to the third step's [width].
> The width of the *harmikā*-base is one-fifth [the length] of the fourth step.
> The *harmikā* is a quarter [the length] of the fourth step, and the height of both is two-thirds and half of the step's [height].

If [one] constructs [the stūpa] according to these prescriptions, the *harmikā*-base appears higher [than normal]. But, in all the other stūpas the *harmikā*-base is lower in height, pointing to an error in translation. Thus, the width of the first step should be equal to the measurement between the first step and the top of the *harmikā.*

As it is said:

> The height of the lower extremity is
> equal to the length of one side of the [first] step.

---

35. The height of the vase established by Buston does not meet with his source work. According to the quotation cited by Buston: "The vase is two-thirds the size of the first step." To interpret this quotation, two-thirds the size of the first step corresponds to sixteen small units on the basis of twentyfour small units established by Buston for the width size of the first step rather than twelve and one-third part of a small unit, if my judgement is not wrong.

The height of the vase is not actually stated, but its outer measurement can be implicitly understood from the above specification. Windows should be made on the eastern and southern sides of the fourth step measuring one-eighth of the step's length. The base of the axle-pole should touch the fourth step. The four large units, starting from the *harmikā* onwards, should equal the height of the thirteen wheels or umbrellas.

As it is said:

> The windows on the eastern and southern sides of the fourth step should measure one-eighth of the step itself.
>
> The base of the axle-pole should touch the fourth step itself.
>
> The height of the thirteen wheels should be three-quarters the size of the first step.[36]

The first (bottom) wheel has a width of six small units, three small units each to both the right and left, and eighteen in circumference. The thirteenth (topmost) wheel is one and a half small units in width: three-fourths part of a small unit each to both the right and left sides, and four and a half small units in circumference. The eleven wheels between these should gradually taper off as they ascend. As the thirteen wheels are equal in height—the height of each wheel carries one part each of the eighteen small units divided into thirteen.[37] Nevertheless, the "Lotus Supporting-umbrella (*gdugs 'degs pad ma*)" below the first wheel and the "Formula of Compassion" (*thugs rje mdo bzungs*) above the thirteenth wheel are also part of the thirteen wheels. So, the "Lotus Supporting-umbrella" is of one small unit, and the height of the "Formula of Compassion" should be made equal to the smallest wheel, i.e. the thirteenth wheel.

---

36. Last line of the passage is more purposive or meaningful for the next passage.
37. The measurements established by Buston for the structures of Lotus Supporting-umbrella, thirteen wheels and the Formula of Compassion requires thorough elucidation as there is likelihood of incomprehension of their perfect measurements. There must have been some error in computation.

    In fact, Buston should have elucidated that the measurement of eighteen small units above the *harmikā* comprise the total height of the thirteen wheels including the Lotus Supporting-umbrella below the first wheel and the Formula of Compassion above the thirteenth wheel. The eighteen small units should be equally divided into fifteen parts by carrying each part as a height

As it is said:

> The first wheel should reach at the four corners of the *harmikā*, and
> a quarter of its circumference is the size of the thirteenth wheel.
> The remaining eleven should gradually narrow.
> All the constructed structures should be elaborately elegant.
> The height of the "Formula of Compassion" should be made equal to the smallest wheel.

At the lower part of the "Formula of Compassion", three-quarters of its size is polished which slightly flares upward and a quarter of its upper part is the sixteen plaits of coil in a form of *utpala*[38] petal.

As it is said:

> At its lower part, three-quarters of its thickness is polished, and one-fourth of its upper part is in a form of sixteen plaits of coil.

Therefore, from the eighteen small units, one is taken by the "Lotus Supporting-umbrella". The remaining seventeen should be equally divided by allotting each wheel the height of one small unit and one-third part of a small unit.[39] As explained below up to this structure

---

of one small unit and one-fifth part of a small unit each rather than the height of each wheel carrying one part of the eighteen small units divided into thirteen parts. On the other hand, he further explains that, "The Lotus Supporting-umbrella and the Formula of Compassion are also part of the thirteen wheels. So, the Lotus Supporting-umbrella has one small unit in height and the height of the Formula of Compassion should be made equal to the smallest wheel." If one arranges according to this order, the proportion of those structures would be as follows: Out of eighteen small units, one is given to the Lotus Supporting-umbrella and the remaining seventeen should be equally divided into fourteen parts by carrying each part as a height of either one and a quarter part of a small unit each or one and one-fifth part of a small unit each. Thus, in both the divisions of seventeen small units divided into fourteen equal parts, there would be differences of a quarter part of a small unit less and one-fifth part of a small unit in excess in the former and later divisions, respectively.

38. *utpala* is a kind of lotus flower blue in colour.
39. The remaining seventeen small units not only comprise the height of the thirteen wheels, but also the height of the "Formula of Compassion" as being part of the thirteen wheels. So, in that case, seventeen small units should be equally divided into fourteen parts rather than into thirteen.

should be built as fascinating as possible. A chain of designs such as Vajras should be drawn on an intermediate space of one-third [lying] between the two-thirds part of each wheel. Upon the "Formula of Compassion", there should be a wooden (pole) having a thickness of half the height of a wheel and two small units in length. On its right and left sides it should equal in measurement half [the size] of a step. That too flares upward and its top gradually becomes thinner with its basis made cross-wise.

As it is said:

> Upon that the wooden (pole) is a half size of the thirteen wheels, and
> its pointed tip is half of the height of a step.

The tip of the axle-pole is two-thirds a part of a small unit, stands upto the disc hole of the umbrella. On tip of this is a moon whose tip is equal to the umbrella and its tips are stretched wide at the right and left. Upon this, there is a sun which is a bit bigger than the moon, and upon this is a spherical pinnacle which is similar to the crest of a young bud of an *utpala*. The umbrella is equal to seventh wheel. The *za ra tshags* is equal to the height of the *harmikā*. The cover of the umbrella is equal to the sixth.

As it is said:

> The axle-pole is about half of the *harmikā* in height and, on it stands the moon whose stretched tips are equal to the width of the umbrella and surround the axle-pole.
>
> The umbrella is equal to the seventh wheel.
>
> The cover of the umbrella is equal to the sixth wheel.
>
> The *za ra tshags* is equal to the height of the *harmikā*.
>
> Then, upon the axle-pole one-third the height of the *harmikā* stands the sun which is a bit bigger than the moon.
>
> The spherical pinnacle on the sun is similar to the crest of a young bud of an *utpala* (flower).

The umbrella and cover of the umbrella are each half a small unit in height. The moon is one small unit. The sun is two small units and the top is one small unit. These four small units should be raised above the fourteenth large unit. On the corners of the sun, the moon, and the Spherical Pinnacle, sharp iron nails should be placed to keep the birds away from resting there.

The colour of the top should be yellow, the sun red, the moon and the cover of the umbrella white, and the umbrella blue. On the four sides of the umbrella the symbols *(mudrā)* of the "four divine races"[40] should be drawn. The colour of the plaits of "Compassion" should be red, while the "Compassion" itself is yellow, and the "ten-fold knowledge"[41] also yellow. The axle-pole is red and the stūpa is white;[42] the base of ten-virtues should be yellow, while the foundation and its support are green.

The method for constructing the stūpa designated as "Flaming Splendour of Blessing", is composed by Buston. The calligrapher is Bhikshu Dasadpa Rinnam (sGra tshad pa rin rnam).

---

40. They are recorded as *Ratnasambhava* at south, *Amitābha* at west, *Amoghasiddhi* at north and *Akṣobhya* at east in the English translation of the Indo-Tibetica I, p. 125.
41. It perhaps indicates the *za ra tshags.*
42. It comprises the structures from the first step onwards upto the *harmikā.*

APPENDIX D

Transliteration of Desid's Proportional Manual of the Stūpa Architecture[1]

Nyis brgya gsum pa thugs rten ni chos longs sprul gsum gyi skabs chos sku'i rten de la spyir dbye ba lnga ste / rang bzhin lhun gyis grub pa dang / bla na med pa dang / byin gyis brlabs pa dang / dngos grub 'byung pa dang / theg pa so so'i mchod rten du bshad pa'i rang bzhin lhun grub ni phyi nang sbyar ba'i snod bcud du bshad de //

Dang po lung mchog bla ma zhes grags pa las /
bling bzhi rmang gser ri rab dang bcas pa bang rim /
yongs 'du'i ljon shing bum par bshad pa phyi snod dang /
kun bzhi rmang / rnam shes tshogs brgyad ka ba /
dbang po gzugs can bang rim / yid dbang bum pa ste
nang bcud mchod rten du bshad pa dang //

rdo rje bkod pa'i brgyud las /
'dod khams bang gi ri bo la /
gzugs khams bang rim khri 'phang can /
gzugs med bum rten bum par bcas /
sku gdung chen po rgyun du gnas / zhes dang //

Smṛti'i (Smṛtijñānakīrti) de kho na nyid drug par /
sa yi khri 'phang zur bcu gnyis /

---

1. Desid Sangyas Gyatso, *Vaidurya dkar po las 'phros pa'i snyen sgron dang dri len gy.a' sel bzhugs so,* Vol. 2, Rpd. from original texts from the collection of Tsepon W.D. Shakapa by T. Tsepal Taikhang, New Delhi, 1971.

gling bzhi gling phran brgyad yin te[2]/
bang rim bdun du brtsegs[3] *pa ni* /
gser gyi ri bdun shes par bya /
dril bu'i dbyibs kyi bum pa ni /
lha gnas ri rab yin ces grags[4]/
bum rten 'khor lo[5] *gdu bu'i dbyibs* /
klu yi rgyal po nor rgyas yin /
kha khyer rim pa drug ldan pa /
'dod khams lha rigs drug du grags[6] /
dbus su srog shing yar bsgrengs pa /
chos dbyings zag med spros bral yin[7] /
'khor lo bcu bdun gyis brgyen pa /
gzugs khams gnas rigs bcu bdun rtags[8] /
char khebs gzugs med khams yin te /
chos dbyings tog tu shes par bya /
zhes snod bcud spyi mchod rten du bshad /
ces zer zhing //

Dus 'khor du /
dkyil 'khor bzhi po bang rim dang /
ri rab bum pa dang /
ri rab gyi mgrin pa dang mdong man chod bre dang /
de yan skra chos 'khor char khebs kyi rnam par gsal bar bshad pa lta bu'o //

Gnyis pa ni / tshad med bsam 'das las 'byung 'bras /
shar du byams pa rdo rje brtegs /
lho ru snying rje rin chen brtegs /

2. In the Tantric section of the Narthang edition, Vol. A, fol. 190a1 stated as "*'dgu pa'i phogs brgyad gling yin te.*"
3. *bsam*, Ibid.
4. *bsgom bya ste*, Ibid.
5. *Khor ba*, Ibid.
6. *'dod lha gnas drug tu btags*, Ibid.
7. *bdag med chos nyid zag med bsgom*, Ibid.
8. From this passage onwards explained in the Narthang edition as follows:
"gzugs khams gnas bcu bdun du btags /
chos kyi dbyid pa yar 'phag pa /
gzugs med khams bzhir shes par bya //

nub tu dga' ba pad ma brtegs /
byang du btang snyoms rgya gram brtegs /
rang byung rin chen snang ba'o //

zhes pa / shar du byams pa tshad med rdo rje du ma brtegs pa la sogs pa bzhir thig le dbang gi rgyud ces bya ba las bshad do zhes grags so //

Gsum pa ni / 'khor lo 'byung ba'i rgyud du grags pa las /
byin rlabs sku gdung cha rgyad gling bzhir snang / zhes pa'i 'grel bar /
shar lus 'phags na byin ldan snyom gter dang mthar legs gyung drung tog gnyis //
lho dzam bu gling na thugs rje sprul pa dang yid bzhin lhun grub gnyis //
nub ba glang spyod na dpe med bsam 'das dang rmad grags chos dbyings gnyis //
byang sgra mi snyan na yon tan rin chen brtegs dang khams gsum bde rgyas sgron me'i mchod rten gnyis bzhugs par shad do //

Bzhi pa ni bdud rtsi mchog gi rgyud las /
ro yi srung ma chen mo ni /
ma mo chen mo brgyad bzhag go /
mchod rten brgyad du rnam par bzhag /
de dag rten gnas chen mo yang /
mchod rten brgyad du rnam par bzhag //

ces pa'i 'grel par / sngon he ru kas drag po btul ba'i tse yul brgyad kyi dur khrod du / ma mo brgyad kyi rten dngos grub 'byung ba'i mchod rten brgyad byung ba ni / ma ga dhar bde byed / sing ga lar ri bo ta la / bal por bya khri kha shor / sing ge gling du ge'u do na / li yul du go ma sa la ghan dha / kha cher ka na ka / za hor du bde spyod gzhon nu'i mchod rten no //

lnga pa la / nyan rang theg chen gyi [mchod rten] gsum mo //
dang po ni chos gos bzhi stab kyi steng du lhung bzed shubs pa la 'khar bsil btsugs pa lta bu'o //
gnyis pa ni rmang gru bzhi'i steng du ngos grub bzhi bang rim

zlum po bang rim bcu gnyis pa 'khor lo rtibs brgyad pa can no //

gsum pa ni slob dpon 'phags pa klu sgrub kyis / lhung bzed sbub pa lta bu bim pa'i zlum po dang / khang bu lta bu dang / rgyal mtshan lta bu'i mchod rten brgyad la sogs pa'o //

'dul ba lung las ni / chos khor la gudgs dang gdugs la char khebs su btags nas so skyes gdugs med pa'i byi bo'o // nyan thos kyi 'bras bu'i grangs kyi gdugs / rang rgyal gyi gdugs bdun / sans rgyas kyi gdugs bcu sgum / char khebs tog dang bcas pa rnam pa thams cad par gsungs so // rgyud sde so so'i dbang du byas nas bya spyod kyi mchod rten bang rim nang du bcag cing phyir 'bur ba'am / dbus 'bur la mtha' gnyis nang du bcum pa 'khor lo bcu gnyis la sogs pa'ang shad par grags / rnal 'byor rgyud kyi sngar bshad pa'i rdo rje brtegs pa sogs bla med kyi dus 'khor nas gsungs pa sogs so //

khyad par las kyi mtha' brjod pa'i mdo las /
sprul pa'i mdzad pa sngon bstan phyir /
mchod rten brgyad du sku gdung bzhag //

ces par ltar / dpal mgon klu sgrub kyis yongs grags dang mthun pa gnas chen po rgyad kyi mchod rten bstod pa dang mdzes pa rgyad pa rgya bzo / ka ma ru dang klu 'jim las byung ba dang mthun par gnas brgyad kyi mchod rten bstod pa zhes mi mthun tsam gnyis byung ba gang ltar ston pa 'di'i mdzad pa khyad par can la brten nas yul ljongs de dang de'i skye bo spro ba skyes ste / dus ston bya ba'i phyir du brtsigs pa sha kya thub pa' mchod rten brgyad du drags pa ni / de la mchod rten gyi mtshan gyi rnam grangs grong khyer ser skyar sku bstams tshe bkra shis sgo mang nas thog ma dang / pad ma spungs pa nas thog mar bzhed pa sogs ji snyed cig mchis shing / stag lo dang smon 'gro pan chen sogs bkra shis sgo mang nas thog mar bzhed cing / rje bla ma phyag na pad ma'i skar rtsis kyi dri lan du'ang bkra shis sgo mang dang / gzungs 'bul gyi lag len du pad ma spungs pa snang bas don gnyis ka 'gal ba mi 'dug rung //

kho bo'i 'dir dang po sku bstams pa'i tshe gter lnga brgya sogs dge mtshan du ma byung bas bkra shis 'byung ba'am zhabs kyi gom pa bdun bor bar pad ma byung ba sogs dang 'brel bar pad spung dbyibs zlum po pad ma'i rnam pa can bang rim bzhi pa'am bdun du'ang bshad pa padma dang 'khor los spras pa / ser skyar lum bi'i tshal du zas gtsang sogs kyi bzhengs pa'i pad spungs mchod rten //

bnyis pa rgyal po'i khab tu mngon par byang chub pa'i dus dbyibs gru bzhi pa gzugs can snying po sogs kyis bzhengs pa'i byang chen mchod rten //

gsum pa va ra na sir chos 'khor bskor ba'i tshe gru bzhi bang rim bzhi blo 'bur dang bcas pa sgo rab brgya rtsa brgyad / 'bring nga drug / tha ma bcu drug par yongs grags bzhed kyang phyogs rer sgo bzhi re byed pa bden pa bzhi / brgyad re byed pa rnam thar brgyad / bcu gnyis su byed pa rten 'brel bcu gnyis / bcu drug tu byed pa stong nyid bcu drug mtshon pa lnga sde bzang pos bzhengs pa'i bkra shis sgo mang mchod rten //

bzhi pa nyan yod du cho 'phrul bstan pa'i tshe gru bzhi bang rim bzhi pa phyogs rer glo 'bur dang bcas pa li tsa bi sogs kyi dze ta'i tshal du bzhengs pa'i mu stegs pham byed dam cho 'phrul mchod rten //

lnga pa gnas yangs pa can gsal ldan du lha'i dbyar gnas mdzad yum la chos gsungs snga dro dgag dbye mdzad phyi dro nam mkha' las babs nas phebs dus bang rim bzhi pa'am brgyad pa ngos rer blo 'bur dang bcas pa'i glo 'bur gyi dbus na them skas yod pa gsal ldan pa dad pa can rnams kyis bzhengs pa'i lha babs sam / yang na sum cu rtsa gsum lha'i mchod rten du grags pa'o //

drug pa rgyal po'i khab tu lhas byin gyi dge 'dun dbyen byas pa mchog zung gis bsdums pa'i dus bang rim bzhi pa zur bzhi mnyam par bcad pa'o / rgyal byed sogs ma ga dha pas bzhengs pa'i 'od zer can nam byams ngos kyang zhes dbyen bsdums mchod rten //

bdun pa yangs pa can du sku tshe zla ba gsum byin gyis brlabs pa'i tshe zlum po bang rim gsum pa de'i grong khyer rnams kyis brtsigs pa'am yang na 'ga' zhig tu lhas brtsigs par bzhed pa'i byin brlabs sam rnam rgyal mchod rten //

rgyad pa rtsa mchog gi grong du mya ngan las 'das pa'i tshe bang rim med pa gdan khri'i steng du bum rten yan chad bzhugs pa rtsa can gyi gyad rnams kyis brtsigs pa'i myang 'das mchod rten //

de la sku gdung cha brgyad du bgos pa'i mchod rten chen po brgyad ras tshig pa'i mchod rten ma tshig pa'i mchod rten sol ba'i mchod rten te bcu gcig // tshems sam mche ba lha dang srin pos khyer ba' i mchod rten / phyis chos rgyal mya ngan med kyis de bzhin gshegs pa'i ring bsrel bzhugs pa mchod rten bye ba dus gcig la bzhengs pa'i mchod rten sogs dang / mya ngan ma 'das gong du dbu skra dang/ sen mo'i mchod rten sogs dpag tu med de / gtso bo sngon ma brgyad du ci rigs par 'dus la / deng sang yang de bzhin bshegs pa'i ring bsrel bzhugs na ni gang zag su'i ched du bzheng yang brgyad po gang rung gi rnam pa thams cad pa bya dgos so // de la'ang dus 'khor sogs nas 'byung ba'i mgul ba thung ba'am / dri med 'grel pa nas bshad pa'i mgrin ring ngam / rgyu dang bzo bo sogs kyis ji bzhin ma thon na / ji ltar 'tsham zhing mdzes pa'ang bya / bu ston rin po che dang stag lo sprul sku 'phrang khab sogs kyis mdzad par yang cung zad skyon re mthong bas kho bo ni 'di ltar 'thad de / dper na pad spung lta bu mtshon na thams cad ba gam man mdzes par dpyad / de yan bcu gnyis su phye ba cha chen / de rer bzhir phye ba cha chung gi tha snyad byas la dge bcu la cha chung gcig //

Bang rim bzhi la bad chung cha chung phyed re khongs su gtogs pa'i rer cha chung gnyis gnyis dang bum rten pad ma can la cha chung gcig bum dpangs cha chen gcig dang gcig gi sum cha gcig / bre gdan gyi rmang la cha chung gcig gi sum cha gcig dang ngo bo sum cha gnyis te gril bas cha chung gcig / bre la cha chung gcig dang gcig gi sum gnyis / gdugs 'degs pa'i pad ma'i dpangs la cha chung gcig / chos 'khor bcu gsum la rer cha chung rer dang de'i bcu gsum cha re / de la sum char phye ba'i cha gnyis gdugs sam pho 'khor dang / sum cha gcig mo 'khor khyon dpangs su cha chen gsum dang cha chung gnyis / thugs rje mdo gzungs dpangs su cha chung gcig / dgugs cha chung phyed dang gdugs khebs cha chung phyed gnyis yin / de steng zla ba la cha chung gcig dang/ nyi ma'i dkyil 'khor cha chung gnyis/ tog la cha chung gcig //

zheng du tshangs thig nas rgyas gyon du dge bcu cha chung bcu bzhi re bsdoms pas cha chung nyi shu rtsa brgyad / bang rim dang po la ni gyas gyon du cha chung bcu gsum re bsdoms pas cha chung nyi shu rtsa drug / bang rim lhag ma gsum rgyar gyas gyon du cha chung re re rim bzhin chung / bang rim bzhi ga'i bad chung rnams cha chung gi bzhi cha re thol la 'don / de steng bum rten rgyar gyas gyon du cha chung dgu re bsdoms pas bco brgyad / bum pa'i rtsa ba'i rgyar gyas gyon du cha chung brgyad re de nas yar je 'phel gyi stod cha brgyad pa nas bcu pa'i bar thad kyi rgyar gyas gyon bsdoms pas cha chung nyi shu rtsa gnyis / de lhag bum stod cha chung gsum dang sum cha gcig bcas pa'i dpangs rim gyis zlum pas rtsa ba'i rgya dang rtse mnyam pa / de ltar bang rim dang po'i rgya khyon dang bang rim de'i mas de nas gdugs 'degs kyi yas man chad mnyam ste cha chen drug cha chung gnyis / nang khong sang gi dbang btang na bang rim bzhi pa'i phyogs shar dang lho ngos la mun pa bsal ba'i gsal khung ni bang rim de ga'i brgyad cha bya //

srog shing bang rim bzhi par zug pa 'thad / bre stan rmang la trsa thig nas phyogs rer cha chung gnyis dang bcu cha dgu de steng bre stan la cha chung gnyis / bre la rtsa thig nas phyogs rer cha chung gnyis dang gcig gi sum cha gnyis re / gdugs 'degs pad ma'i rtsa bar cha chung phyed gnyis steng gi rgya gyas gyon cha chung gnyis gnyis / 'khor lo dang po'i rgya la gyas gyon du cha chung phyed dang gsum ste bsgril bas lnga / gdugs dang po'i rgya la cha chung gnyis dang sum cha gnyis te bsdoms pas cha chung lnga dang sum cha gcig / 'khor lo bcu gsum pa gyas gyon du cha chung phyed dang cha chung gi brgyad cha gcig/ bsgril bas thad kar cha chung gcig dang bzhi cha gcig / mtha' bskor du cha chung gsum dang bzhi cha gsum / de gnyis bar gyi 'khor lo bcu gcig po rim gyis je phrar gyur pa de yang 'khor lo bcu gsum pa'i yas mtha' nas ['khor lo] dang po'i mas thar thig skud bzung ba'i thig btab pas rtogs rtse mo'i gdugs tshangs thig gi gyas gyon du cha chung gcig gi gsum cha gnyis re / gdugs bcu gsum pa'i steng tshad de nas gdugs dang po'i mas mthar sne bzung thig btab pas gdugs gzhan rnams kyi tshad rtogs /

de steng thugs rje mdo gzungs rtsa ba'i rgya 'khor lo bcu gsum pa dang mnyam / dpangs ni 'jam po nyid cung zad gyel ba'i steng rtsa thig nas cha phran re sul bcu drug / gdugs kyi rgya tshangs thig gi gyas gyon du cha phran phyed gnyis dang rgyad cha gsum / gdugs khebs kyi rtsa ba tshangs thig nas gyas gyon du cha phran phyed do dang bzhi cha gcig / rtse mo'i rgya tshangs thig nas gyas gyon du cha phran gnyis re / za ra tshags kyi dpangs cha phran phyed gsum las zheng tshangs thig nas gyas gyon cha phran gsum re stod gdugs dang mnyam / zla ba'i rtse gnyis bsgrad pa tshangs thig nas cha phran gnyis re rtsa ba dpangs zheng 'dra ba cha phran re / nyi ma tshangs thig nas gyas gyon steng 'og tu cha chung gcig gis zlum por bskor / tog gi rgya gyas gyon du cha phran phyed phyed / nyi ma dang tog gi zur sa la sogs pa'i dus bya bsrung ba'i lcags kyi thur ma rnon po mang po gzer //

mdog tog ser po nyi ma dmar po / zla ba dang gdugs khebs rnams dkar po / gdugs sngon po / de'i phyogs bzhir rang rang rigs bzhi'i phyag rgya 'dri bar bshad / thugs rje'i sul ni kha dog dmar po thugs rje ser po chos 'khor gyi pho 'khor ser po / mo 'khor dang srog shing dmar po / mchod rten dkar po / gdugs 'degs sngon po dge bcu ser po sa 'dzin ljang gu / them skas gsum mas nas dmar sngo ser / sreng khri dkar po / dgung sne sngon po / bad chung dmar po / bad chen ljang gur bya //

de nas sa 'dzin gyi dpangs su cha chung gsum / them skas gsum la cha chung re re / gdong chen la cha chen gcig dang cha chung gnyis / gzung sne dang bad chung la cha phran re / bad chen la cha chung gnyis /

rgya tshad sa 'dzin gyas gyon cha chung phyed bcas bcu dgu re dang them skas dang por gyas gyon du phyed bcas bcu bdun / gnyis pa'i gyas gyon du bcu drug / gsum pa'i gyas gyon du phyed bcas bcu bzhir bshad / gdong chen gyi gyas gyon du cha chung bcu gsum / gzung sne bad chung bad chen gsum la mas rim gyas gyon du cha chung bcu bzhi bco lnga bcu drug //

rags pa'i rnam bzhag bre zhal khyim dang bre gdan mgul bum pa sku gzugs bang rim bzhi sku smad skyil krung chos 'khor yan gtsug tor mtshon kyang sgra ji bzhin gyi tshad mi 'byung zhing / dge bcu man sku gzugs kyi cha byad du brtsi bar mi bya //

bum pa'i rtsa ba nas cha chung brgyad kyi bar gzhal ba sgo khyim gyi nang gi dpangs dang rtsa ba'i nang zheng rtsa thig nas gyas gyon du cha chung do re rtsa ba nas cha chung bzhi gyen du gzhal ba'i gyas gyon du zheng cha chung phyed bzhi re de steng cha chung gcig gzhal ba'i gyas gyon du cha phran gsum gzhal mtshams ske ka'am khug mtshams rtse mo'i zheng rtsa thig nas gyas gyon du cha chung do re / rtsa thig 'dzoms snying thig nas gyas gyon du cha phran gsum re gzhal ba sogs kyis sgo khyim gyi nang skor rtogs shing de'i phyi pa tra nang skor gyi zheng rtse mo che zhing rtsa ba je phrar song ba rtsa thig 'dzoms snying thig nas gyen du cha phran bdun gzhal ba'i pa tra'i rtse mo'i zheng cha chung gcig / de nas rim pas je 'phel gyi che ba'i bzhi, drug, brgyad, bcu, bcu gcig, bcu gnyis, bcu gsum, bcu gsum, bcu gsum, bcu gnyis, bcu gcig, rtsa ba bum rtsar zug pa bcu tham pa rnams gzhal ba'i zheng tshad mi 'khyogs pa'i rags thig yin pa rin po che'i rigs kyi sku rten bzhugs pa'i bzhugs khang gi pa tra'i rgya khyon gyi tshad rtogs so //

de la gzhi byas gzhan bdun po'i bsgyur kha bshad par bya ste / de'i bang rim bzhi po'i pad ma med pa de byang chen mchod rten bang rim bzhi po'i logs bzhi dang bre ba gam nas sa 'dzin bar rang rang gi sum cha sum cha 'bur dod byas pa bang rim la sgo brgya dang brgyad pa nga drug pa bcu drug sgo'i cha chung sogs gang 'os byas pa bkra shis sgo mang / bang rim bzhi bre dang ba gam nas sa 'dzin bar rnams gru bzhi rang rang sum cha dbus su 'bur dod pa de'i dbus steng skas gsum bsgrigs nas ba gam steng btsugs pa lha babs mchod rten / skas med pa gzhan de ji lta ba cho 'phrul mchod rten nam mu stegs pham byed / gong du brjod pa'i pad ma spungs pa'i pad ma med cing bang rim bzhi'i zur bzhi bcad de ngos rgyad mnyam par dbyen zlums mchod rten / bang rim bzhi po cha gsum du bsdus pa'i bang rim gsum dang dge bcu bcas pa zlum po ste rnam rgyal mchod rten / bang rim bzhi med pa'i dge bcu'i steng rnam mdzes khyad kyi ma pad cha chung phyed bzhi dang / ya pad bad chung bsdoms par cha chung gsum / pad 'dzoms rked rgyan gyi dpangs la cha chung phyed gnyis dang gyas gyon gyi rgyar cha chung dgu re yod pa myang 'das mchod rten du bzhed de brgyad //

de dag gis sa 'dzin gyi zur bzhir rdo ring bzhi bya ste re re'i zheng la cha chung gnyis gnyis dang dkyus la cha chen bzhi bya / de steng rdo seng kha phyir bltas pa'i mgul pa la gdugs 'og nas drangs pa'i me tog phreng ba btags pas sa 'dzin gyi phyogs bzhir them skas bzhi bya ba dang gdugs dang rgyal mtshan ba dan la sogs gser dril gy.er kha sogs pa rnams che ba dang chung ba rin po ch'i rigs kyi rgyan dang dra phyed sogs ci 'byor par bya'o //

'grel chen dri med 'od nas mchod rten tshad bshad pa kun gyi mgo dka' zhing kun mkyen bus gtan 'bebs mdzad pa la gzhi byas brag nag pa sogs mkhas pa ji snyed kyis rang rang gi bzhed pa'i rigs mi 'dra zhing deng sang shas che ba sprul sku nga la gzigs dang stag tshang lo sta ba'i thig tsa bebs pa mang na'ang mdzes btsal ba las bshad khungs dang sbyor rgyu rang dka' gshis stag lo'i der bre stan zheng chung la chos khor bcu gsum dpangs dmas zhing ches pa dang bad chen dpangs mtho zhing dkyus thungs pa dang / bad chung de bas kyang thungs shing / dge ba bcu dang bang rim thungs pa'i krong pa 'dra ba / 'phrang kha ba'i der chos 'khor bcu gsum zheng che zhing dpangs mthos pa dge bcu nas bang rim gsum zheng chung shing sa 'dzin rgya ches pa nas cung zad bskum pa bcas skyon kun spangs pa'i khul gyi 'di bzhin du btab la //

ENGLISH VERSION OF DESID'S PROPORTIONAL MANUAL OF THE STŪPA ARCHITECTURE[9]

The two hundredth and third (section deals) with "the receptacle of thought (*thugs kyi rten*)'', which symbolises the three *kāyas* (*Dharmakāya, Sambhogakāya* and *Nirmāṇakāya*). The truth body (*Dharmakāya*) in structural form is a "receptacle of offerings (*mchod rten*)". In general, the *mchod rten* has five divisions, viz.:

1. Spontaneous Existence by Nature (*svabhāvasahajasiddha*),
2. Unsurpassable (*anuttara*),
3. Blessed (*adhiṣṭhāna*),
4. Accomplishment of *siddhi* (*siddhi-utpanna*), and
5. Ṣtūpas of different classes of Buddhist saints.

First: The Spontaneous Existence by Nature

The Spontaneous Existence by Nature refers to the animate and inanimate existence (*bhājana-sattva*) of external and internal phenomena.

According to the so called *Lung mchog bla ma:*[10]

The four continents (*catvāri-dvīpāni*) are the foundation, golden mountains and the mount Sumeru are the steps. The wishful-filling tree (*kalpa-druma*) is referred to as the vase. These are the external inanimate phenomena. The basis of all (*ālaya*) is the foundation, the eight consciousnesses (*aṣṭa-vijñāna*) are the columns, the physical sense-organs are the steps, and the mental sense-organs are the vase. This explains the internal animate phenomena as the stūpa.

According to the *Vajravyūhatantra:*[11]

On the foundation of Sumeru of the Desire-realm (*kāmadhātu*) having the Form-realm (*rūpadhātu*) as the steps, and the Form-

9. *Vaiḍūrya dkar po las 'phros pa'i snyan sgron dang dri lan g.ya' sel bzhugs so,* Vol. II, pp. 711-26.
10. Could not access it.
11. *Sarvatathāgata cittajñāna guhyārthargarbhavyūha vajratantra siddhiyogā gamasamājasarva vidyāsūtra mahāyānabhisamaya dharma paryāvyūha nāma sūtra,* Kagyur, Nying Gyud, Derge, Vol. KA, Toh. 829, fol. 280a4-5; Narthang, Vol. DZA, 406b6-407a2.

less-ream (*arūpadhātu*) as the vase-base and the vase. The great remains shall exist at all times.

In the *Saṭtattvavyavasthāna* of *Smṛtijñānakīrti*:[12]

The twelve corners of the earth's step,
are the four continents (*catvāri-dvīpāni*) and the eight sub-continents (*aṣṭa-kṣudradvīpāni*).
The arrangement of seven steps,
are known to be the seven golden mountains (*saptakanaka-parvata*).
The bell-shape of the vase,
is known as the mount Sumeru—the place of *devas.*
The bangle-shaped wheel of the vase-base,
is known to be the *Nāga* king Vāsuki.
The six stages of the altars,
are known as the six classes of the Desire-realm gods.
The axle-pole raised at the centre,
is the uncontaminated (*anāsrava*) absolute reality (*dharmadhātu*) devoid of all elaborations.
The adornment of seventeen wheels,
are the characteristics of the seventeen classes of the Desire-realm.
The umbrella-cover is the Formless-realm, and
the absolute reality should be known as the Spherical Pinnacle.
Thus, the animate and inanimate phenomena are collectively referred to as the stūpa.

In the *Kālacakra-tantra* it is said that:[13]

The four *maṇḍalas* are the steps.
The mount Sumeru is the vase.
The neck and face of the Sumeru below that are the *harmikā* and the areas from the hair upward are clearly explained as the aspect of the Dharma-wheels and the cover of umbrella.

The second [unsurpassable] is, the result which came forth from

---

12. *Sattattvavyavasthāna* (*De kho na nyid drug rnam par bzhag pa*), Tangyur, Gyud, Narthang, Vol. A, fol. 187a7-190a6; Derge, Vol. YA, Toh. 1621, fol. 167a1-170a5.
13. Could not access it.

the unthinkable immeasurable i.e.

In the East the erected *Vajra* is [immeasurable] love (*maitrīyapramāṇa*).

In the West the erected jewel is [immeasurable] compassion (*karuṇāpramāṇa*).

In the South the erected lotus is [immeasurable] joy (*muditāpramāṇa*).

In the North the erected *Svastika* is [immeasurable] equanimity (*upekṣāpramāṇa*).

A gem of self-evolve shall appear [there].

Thus, it is said that the four types of immeasurable (*catvārapramāṇa*), such as love in the east, erected many *Vajras* etc. as explained in the *Tilakābhiśaktantra* (*Thig le dbang gi rgyud*).[14]

The third [Blessed] one is, according to the *'khor lo 'byung ba'i rgyud*:[15] the eight parts of the blessed remains appear in the four continents. Thus, according to its commentary [elucidated the following eight stūpas] viz.,

In the eastern continent (*Pūrvavedeha*), there are two stūpas, i.e. *Jindan Nyomter* and *Tharlek Yungdrung Tok,*

In the southern continent (*Jambudvīpa*), there are two stūpas, i.e. *Thugje Tulpa* and *Yeshin Lhundrup,* in the western continent (*Aparagodanīya*), there are two stūpas, i.e. *Padme Samdas* and *Medak Chosjin,* and

In the northern continent (*Uttarakuru*), there are two stūpas, i.e. *Rinchen Tseg* and *Khamsum Degyay Donme.* Thus, these are said to have existed.

The fourth [accomplishment of *siddhi*] is, according to the *Bdud rtsi mchog gi rgyud*:[16]

A chief guardian of the corpse,
employed as the eight female-guardians (*mātṛkā*).
Even the permanent residence of these [great corpses],

14. Could not access it.
15. Could not access it.
16. Could not access it.

employed as the eight female-guardians,
were comfortably posited in the eight stūpas.

Thus, it is said in its commentary that:

Earlier when, *Heruka* had subdued the *Rudra* there arose eight stūpas of accomplishment as the receptacle of the eight female-guardians at the cemeteries of the eight countries. They were *Bde byed* at Magadha, *Ri bo ta la* at Śrilanka, *Bya khri kha shor* in Nepal, *Ge'u do na* at *Singhadvīpa, Go ma sa la ghan da* at Liyul [probably Khotan], *Ka na ka* at Kashmir, and the stūpa of *Bde cod zhon nu* at Sahor [Zahor].

Fifth, stūpas of the three different classes of Buddhist saints, i.e. *Śrāvaka, Pratyekabuddha* and *Mahāyāna.* The first one resembles the resting of a mendicant's staff (*khakkhara*) upon an inverted alms-bowl, with a robe folded four times underneath. The second has a quadrangular foundation upon which a square surface stands with twelve circular steps and the eight spokes of a wheel. The third, according to Nāgārjuna, (a) is like an inverted alms-bowl which is circular like *Bimba* (a kind of fruit having a red colour), (b) like a little house, and (c) the eight types of stūpas like the victory-banner (*dhvaja*).

According to the *Vinayapiṭaka,*[17] the Dharma-wheel is termed as the umbrella and the umbrella as the cover of the umbrella. An ordinary person's stūpa is bald, that is, it has no umbrella. The *Śrāvaka's* stūpa has umbrellas equal to the number of fruition. The *Pratyekabuddha's* stūpa has seven umbrellas. The Buddha's stūpa has thirteen umbrellas, and all the other parts together with the cover of the umbrella and the spherical pinnacle. Regarding the individual *tantric* classes, it is said that for the stūpas of *Kriyā* and *Caryā tantrics,* their steps narrow from inside and bulge out from exterior or the centre bulges out with contracted inwardly from both ends, and with twelve wheels etc. As for the *Yogatantra*, it is the same as mentioned earlier in the *Kālacakra anuttarayoga* section, with an erection of *Vajras*, etc.

In particular, according to the *Las kyi mtha' brjod pa'i mdo*:[18] "Due to the prior exhibition of the events by the *Nirmāṇakāya*, the relics were deposited in the eight stūpas." Thus it has been said.

17. Could not access it.
18. Could not access it.

According to Nāgārjuna, there were two different versions of the praise for the stūpa—"Praise to the stūpas of the eight great sacred places", which is popularly known in accordance with Indian workmanship of the eight deeds, and "Praise to the stūpas of eight sacred places", which is known as made from marbles and Nāga's clay. Nevertheless, inhabitants of their respective countries were enraptured in consequence of the noble deeds of this teacher and built the eight stūpas of Śākyamuni to commemorate the special occasions.

Regarding the enumeration of the names of the stūpas, there are different ideas such as accepting the "Multiple Auspicious Doors", as the beginning, and accepting the "Heaped Lotuses", as the beginning when the Buddha took birth at Kapilavastu. Taglo and Mendo Panchen etc., have accepted the "Multiple Auspicious Doors", as the first. Also, in the text entitled, *"sKar rtsis kyi dri len"*,[19] of Je Lama Chagna Pema (*rJe bla ma phyag na pad ma*), the "Multiple Auspicious Doors", has been accepted (as first). But, in the *"Gzung 'bul gyi lag len* text",[20] the "Heaped Lotuses", has been accepted (as first). Both versions do not agree.

Here, I (Desid) prefer the stūpa of "Heaped Lotuses", which was constructed by Śudhodhana etc. in the grove of Lumbini in Kapilavastu, for commemorating a manifestation of various auspicious signs like the appearance of five hundred treasures and lotuses in between the pacing of seven steps when the Buddha was born, etc. It has four or seven circular steps in the form of lotuses. Even it has been enunciated of having eight steps, these are adorned with lotus designs and wheels.

The second is the "Stūpa of Enlightenment", which was constructed by Bimbisara etc. at Rājagṛha when the Buddha attained enlightenment. It has four steps which are square in shape.

The third is the stūpa of "Multiple Auspicious Doors", which was constructed by the five disciples[21] [of the Buddha] to commemorate his turning of the wheel of law (*Dharmacakrapravartana*) at Varanasi. It consists of four square steps which project out at the centre. It is generally accepted that this stūpa has 108 doors at the maximum, 56 in

19. Could not access it.
20. Could not access it.
21. See Chapter I, footnote 46, p. 18.

the medium and 16 in the minimum. Four doors each in every direction symbolise the Four Noble Truths (*catvāri-āryasatya*), eight doors each symbolise the eight doors of liberations (*aṣṭa-vimokṣa*), twelve doors each symbolise the twelve links of dependent origination (*dvādaśaṅgapratītyasamutpāda*), and sixteen doors each symbolise the sixteen emptinesses (*Śoḍaṣa-śūnyatā*).

The fourth is the "stūpa of Miracles", or "Conquest of *Tīrthikā* (non-believers)", which consists of four square steps with projections in each direction. This was constructed at Śrāvastī in the Jeta Grove where the Buddha performed the great miracle.

The fifth is the stūpa of "Descent from Heaven", or "the Heaven of thirtythree (*Trāyastriṃśāḥ*)". It was constructed at Śaṅkāśya by the devotees of Śaṅkāśya to commemorate the Buddha's descent from heaven in the evening after lifting the restriction (*Parimāṇa*) in morning, preceded by an annual summer retreat and teaching Dharma to his mother. It has four or eight steps and projects outwardly in the centre of each side, with a staircase at the centre of the projected area.

The sixth is the "stūpa of Reconciliation", which is also called the stūpa "of rays", or "of affection". It was built by Jeta etc. of Magadha when the two chief disciples[22] reconciled the discord created in the *Saṃgha* by Devadatta at Rājagṛha. It has four square steps, whose corners are cut off evenly forming an octagon.

The seventh is the "stupa of Victory", or "of Blessing", which was constructed in Vaiśālī either by the inhabitants of that town or by the Deva according to other sources, when the Buddha prolongated his life span for three months at Vaiśālī. Regarding its shape, it has three circular steps.

The eighth is the "stūpa of Nirvāṇa", which was constructed in Kuśinagara by the Mallas of Kuśinagara during the Parinirvāṇa. This has no steps, and the structure above the vase-base is standing directly upon the Throne.

In addition to these, there are eight great stūpas containing relics divided into eight parts, the stūpas which were built from burnt and unburnt clothes and the stūpa of charcoal, listed totalling eleven stūpas. There is also a stūpa containing the canine teeth which were carried

---

22. They are Śāriputra and Maudgalyayānaputra.

away by *Devas* and demons. Later, Aśoka the Dharma King constructed at the same time ten million stūpas[23] containing the relics of the Tathāgata. Also, uncountable stūpas containing (the Buddha's) hairs and nails etc. were built before his passing into Parinirvāṇa. In general, all stūpas can be classified under the eight categories of stūpas. Even today, a stūpa must be built in the complete form in any one of the eight stūpas, if it contains the relics of the Tathāgata, irrespective of the person for whom the stūpa is built. The stūpa may have a short neck as mentioned in the *Kālacakra* text, etc. or it may have a long neck as described in the commentary on *Vimaloṣṇīṣa*. If the stūpa cannot be built accordingly (due to inferior quality) of materials and craftsmanship etc., one may build an attractive and appropriate one. In the works of Buston, Tag Tsang Lotsaba, and Tulku Phreng kheb etc., I noticed slight defects in the structure of beauty.

I prefer that, with the stūpa of "Heaped Lotuses", all parts below the cap (*ba gam*) are done attractively. Above that, it is divided into twelve parts, which are termed as a large unit, each of these are subdivided into four parts, which are termed as a small unit. (Measured in this way), the "base of ten-virtues" is a small unit in height. For the flight of four steps have two small units each in height including a half small unit each for the small edge of the four steps. The lotus-shape of the "vase-base" is one small unit and the "vase" is three large units plus one small unit and one-third part of a small unit in height. The lower part of the "*harmikā*-base" is one-third part of a small unit, while the actual "*harmikā*-base" is two-thirds part of a small unit — thus one small unit when combined. The *harmikā* is one and two-thirds part of a small unit. The "Lotus Supporting-umbrella" is one small unit in height. Each of the thirteen wheels are one small unit and one-thirteenth part of a small unit in size. By dividing each one of these into three parts: the two-thirds of its part is the umbrella or male-wheel, and one third of its part is the female-wheel. In total, this makes three large units and two small units in height [equivalent to fourteen small units]. The "Formula of Compassion" should be one small unit in height. The "umbrella" is a half small unit and the "cover of umbrella" is one and a half small units. Upon that,

23. The number of stūpas mentioned by the author seems a bit of an exaggeration.

sit the "moon", of one small unit, and the "disc of the sun" of two small units. The "spherical pinnacle" is one small unit.

[Regarding breadth], the "base of ten-virtues" is fourteen small units wide, each at the right and left of the central axis, twentyeight small units in total. The first step is thirteen small units in both the right and left sides, totalling twentysix. The width of the remaining three steps should shorten gradually by a small unit each from both the right and left sides. The upper edges of all the four steps should project out a quarter part of a small unit. Upon that, the vase-base is eight small units in width in both the right and left sides, eighteen in total. The "vase-root" is eight small units in width in the right and in the left, then it gradually flares upward to the area between the eighth and tenth at its widest range of twentytwo[24] small units is the total width of both the right and left [of the shoulder part of vase]. The remaining three small units and one-third part of a small unit in size is the height of the upper part of the vase which should gradually be curved round until its top becomes equal as the width size of the vase-root. In this way, the extent of the first step and the area between the lower part of this very step and the upper part of the Supporting-umbrella[25] should be equal in measurement, corresponding to six and a half large units.

If the interior [of the stūpa] is treated as a hollow,[26] windows should be made on the eastern and southern sides of the fourth step measuring an eighth size of that very step [in order] to clear away the darkness.

The axle-pole which is touched on the fourth step must be authentic. The lower part of the *harmikā*-base is two small units and nine-tenths part of a small unit on each side from the axis. Upon that stands the *harmikā*-base which is of two small units; the *harmikā* is two small units and two-thirds part of a small unit on each side from the axis.

---

24. In the English translation of Indo-Tibetica I, the measurement of the widest extent of the shoulder part of the vase is wrongly translated as ''twentyone quarters'', p. 130.
25. Translated it as ''umbrella'' which may lead to misinformation, op. cit., p. 130.
26. Translated as "To perform the consecration of the interior", for the Tibetan version of '*Nang khong sang gi dbang btang na*', which is nowhere near the exact content of the Tibetan meaning, op. cit., p. 130.

The basis of the Lotus Supporting-umbrella is one and a half small unit, while the width of its upper part is two small units each from the right and left of the axis. The width of the first (bottom) wheel (intermediate space between the two-thirds part) is two and a half small unit each at the right and left, totalling five. The width of the first umbrella is two small units and two-thirds part of a small unit on each side, five small units and one-third part of a small unit in total. The thirteenth (topmost) wheel is a half plus an eighth part of a small unit at both the right and left, one and a quarter part of a small unit straight, and three small units and three-fourths part of a small unit in circumference. Between these two wheels [i.e. the bottom and the topmost] the eleven intermediary wheels should gradually shorten [their width]. These proportions can be determined by drawing a line with the help of a measuring tap from the top extremity of the thirteenth wheel down to the bottom ends of the first wheel. The topmost umbrella is two-thirds part of a small unit at both the right and left of the axis. The measurement of the remaining umbrellas can be determined by drawing a line, while holding a cord or measuring tap from the top of the thirteenth umbrella down to the bottom of the first umbrella.

The base of the "Formula of Compassion" is equal in width to the thirteenth wheel, and its height slightly flares outwardly from its smooth base upward, and above that is the sixteen plaits of coil one small unit on each side from the axis. The width of the umbrella[27] is one and a half small units plus three-eighths part of a small unit at both the right and left of the central axis. The base of the umbrella cover is one and a half small units plus a quarter part of a small unit on both the right and left of the axis, while the width of [its] upper part, to the right and left of the axis, is two small units. The *za ra tshags* is two and a half small units in height and the width is three small units at both the right and left of the axis, and [its] top [should be made] equal to the umbrella.[28] The moon's two points are stretched out by two small units on each side from the axis, while the width as well as the height of its base are equal

27. It has been misinterpreted as "The width of the point of union of the sixteen foldings", op. cit., p. 131.
28. Interpreted as "equal to the top umbrella", instead of "equal to the umbrella", op. cit., p. 131.

having one small unit each. The disc of the sun has a radius of one small unit in measurement. The width of the spherical pinnacle is half a small unit each at both the right and left sides.

Many pointed rods of iron have to be inserted on the corners of the sun, the moon and on the spherical pinnacle to guard against birds.

Colour of the Stūpa

[The colour of the various structural components of the stūpa are as follows:] The spherical pinnacle is yellow, the sun is red, the moon and the cover of the umbrella are white, and the umbrella is blue. It is said that on the four directions of the umbrella the symbols of the four divine races are to be drawn. The plaits of the compassion is red, while the "Formula of Compassion" itself and the male-wheels are yellow, and the female wheels and the axle-pole[29] are red. The stūpa is white, the "Supporting-umbrella"[30] is blue, the base of ten-virtues is yellow, and the foundation is green. The three staircases starting from down upward are red, blue and yellow, respectively. The Lion Throne[31] is white, the cornice is blue, the small edge is red, and the big edge is green in colour.

Proportion of the Lion Throne

Thereafter, the foundation is three small units in height. For the three staircases one small unit each. The cornice and the small edge are one small unit each, while the big edge is two small units.

In breadth, the basement or plinth is nineteen and a half small units each on both the right and left sides. The first or bottom staircase is seventeen and a half small units each at the right and left. The second or middle staircase, on both the right and left sides, sixteen small units each, and the third or topmost one carries on both the right and left side, fourteen and a half small units each. The "main facade" is thirteen small units each at the right and left. Starting from down upward the cornice, the small edge and the big edge, on both the right and left of the axis, fourteen, fifteen and sixteen small units each, respectively.

29. Axle-pole and its colour is not given, op. cit., p. 132.
30. Interpreted only as "umbrella", op. cit., p. 132.
31. Instead, it has been misinterpreted as "the face of the lion", op. cit., 132.

To be given a rough account, the *harmikā* is the face, the *harmikā*-base is the neck, the vase is the body, the flight of four steps representing the lower part of the body in a cross-legged posture, and the area above Dharma-wheels symbolise the protrusion of the head (*uṣṇīṣa*). However, an exact measurement does not occur. The base of ten-virtues and below that are not to be counted as the proportion of the body.

The area at the distance of eight small units from the basis of vase is an interior height of the portal (*sgo khyim*) and its interior extent is two small units each on both the right and left of the axis. The measurement of three and a half small units each on both the right and left are the ending area of four small units, which should dilate upwardly from its (vase) base. The area which is one small above this has three small units each on both the right and left of the axis. At this point of intersection, there forms a nook whose bending point is two small units each at the right and left of the central axis.

One may understand the inner circle of portal (*sgo khyim*) by measuring, for instance, three small units each at the right and left of the axis where central axes are met. Behind that is the width of the scroll-pattern (*pa ta*) which is encircled inwardly, the tip is wide and the basis becomes thinner. Then, from here, it gradually increases and measures as follows—four, six, eight, ten, eleven, twelve, thirteen, thirteen, thirteen, twelve, eleven, and finally, the basis touches to the vase-base. This is rough proportion of the width so that the measurement of the width does not become unstraight. By this way one may understand the measurement of the width of the scroll-patterns at the place where the precious image resides.

Based on this, I (Desid) will explain the implied measurements of the other seven stūpas. The stūpa in which the flight of four steps are not adorned with lotuses is the stūpa ''of Enlightenment".

In the stūpa of ''Multiple Auspicious Doors'', the four sides of the flight of four steps, the *harmikā* and the area from the cap to the basement project out by one-third part of their own sizes. The number of doors on the steps is one hundred eight, fiftysix and sixteen, and the size of the doors should be made in accordance with the requirements.

The stūpa of ''Descent from Heaven'', is the one where the flight of four steps, the *harmikā* and the area from the cap down to the basement are quadrangular or square projected by one-third part of their own sizes. [In addition], in the centre three ladders are arranged which are placed just above the cap.

The stūpa where there is no ladder and rest of the parts are exactly same as above, the stūpa of "Miracle" or "Conquest of *Tīrthīkās* (non-believers)."

The stūpa of "Reconciliation", is like the stūpa of "Heaped Lotuses", mentioned earlier, but not adorned with lotuses and the four corners of the flight of four steps cut off to form eight even sides (like an octagon).

The stūpa of "Victory", is the one where the flight of four steps are subsumed into a flight of three steps which are circular, as is the base of ten-virtues.

The stūpa of "Nirvāṇa", is the one where there are no four steps, but upon the base of ten-virtues, as a matter of beauty, the lower lotus is of three and a half small units and the upper lotuses, together with a small edge is three small units. The waist-ornaments at the meeting point of one and a half small unit in height and nine small units each at the right and left of the axis.

At the four corners of these basement, four pillars should be erected, each measuring two small units in width and four large units in length. Upon the necks of the stone-lions facing outwards, flower garlands should be hung from below the umbrella. The four staircases should be erected at the four corners of the basement and should be decorated with as many ornaments as available, such as bigger ones like umbrella, victory-banner, flags, golden bells, string of small bells etc. and smaller ones, such as ornaments made out of precious materials and half hanging ornaments etc.

The proportion of the stūpa described in the great commentary of Vimala-Prabhā is hard to be understood by all. Many eminent scholars like Dagnak (Brag nag) etc. based their work on the Buston's work, expressed ideas different from each other. These days most people emphasise the proportions established by Tulku Ngala zig and Tagtsang Lotsawa, but other than looking attractive these are hard to prove with reference to their sources.

In the Taglo's system, the width of the *harmikā*-base is a small unit in width and the thirteen Dharma-wheels are lower in height and broader in breadth. The big edge is higher in height and shorter in length. The small edge is even shorter than that [of the big edge]. The base of ten-virtues and the steps are also shorter looking stiff. In the Phreng kha pa's one, the thirteen Dharma-wheels are broader in breadth and higher in height. From the base of ten-virtues to the three steps are smaller in breadth and the basement, too, wide and slightly contracted. Thus, by avoiding all these defects one should build the stūpa in accordance with this measurement.

Bibliography

Kagyur texts are listed alphabetically by Tibetan title in the primary sources of section I and Tangyur texts are listed alphabetically by author in the primary sources of section II; Tibetan treatises along with later works are listed in English alphabetically by author in the secondary sources followed by unknown authorship works, journals and dictionaries.

(I) Primary Sources (Kagyur Section)

Kun nas sgor 'jug pa'i 'od zer gtsug tor dri ma med par snang ba de bzhin gshegs pa thams cad kyi snying po dang dam tshig la rnam par lta ba zhes bya ba'i gzungs (Samanta mukha praveśa raśmivimaloṣṇīṣa prabhāsa sarvatathāgata hṛdya samayavilokita nāma dhāraṇī)

Gyudbum, Derge, Vol. PHA, Toh. 599; Zungdus, Vol. WAM, Toh. 983.

Tr = Jinamitra, Śilendrabodhi and Yeshes sde.

Dkyil 'khor thams cad kyi spyi'i cho ga gsang ba'i rgyud (Sarva-maṇḍala-sāmānyavidhīnām-guhya-tantra)

Gyud, Derge, Vol. WA, 806; Tantra, Narthang, Vol. NA; Derge, Vol. PHA, Toh. 599; Zungdus, Derge, Vol. WAM, Toh. 983.

Tr = Jinamitra, Śilendrabodhi and Yeshes sde.

Rgyud kyi rgyal po chen po dpal rdo rje mkha' 'gro zhes bya ba (Srivajraḍāka-nāma-mahātantrarāja)

Gyud, Derge, Vol. KHA, Toh. 370.

Tr = Gayadhara, 'gos lhas btas.

Mchod rten gcig gdab pa'i cho ga

Gyud, Narthang, Vol. TU; Derge, Vol. PU, Toh. 3071.

Mchod rten gcig btab na bye ba btab par 'gyur ba'i gzungs

Gyud, Derge, Vol. PHA, Toh. 602; Zungdus, Narthang, Vol. NA; Derge, Vol. E, Toh. 921.

De bzhin gshegs pa thams cad kyi thugs gsang ba'i ye shes don gyi snying po rdo rje bkod pa'i rgyud rnal 'byor grub pa'i lung kun 'dus rig pa'i mdo theg pa chen po mngon rtags pa chos kyi rnam grags rnam par bkod pa zhes bya ba'i mdo (Sarva tathāgata cittajñāna guhyārthagarbhavyūha vajratantra siddhi yogā gama samāja sarva vidyā sūtra mahāyānābhisamaya dharmaparyāvyūha nāma sūtra)

Nying Gyud, Narthang, Vol. DZA; Derge, Vol. KA, Toh. 829.

Tr = Dharmabodhi, Dānarakṣita, Che bstan skyes.

'dul ba phran tshegs kyi bzhi (Vinaya Kṣudraka-vastu)

Vinaya, Derge, Vol. DA, Toh. 6; Narthang, Vol. DA.

Tr = Vidyakaraprabhā, Dharmaśribhadra, and Bande Dpal 'byor.

'dul ba gzhung dam pa (Vinaya-uttaragrantha)

Vinaya, Derge, Vol. PA, Toh. 7A.

Dpal bde mchog 'byung ba shes bya ba'i rgyud kyi rgyal po chen po (Śrī Mahāsambarodaya tantrarāja nāma)

Gyud, Narthang, Vol. GA; Derge, Vol. KHA, Toh. 373.

Tr = Gzhan phan mtha' yas and Smon lam grags

Re = Gzhon nu dpal.

'phags pa 'od zer dri ma med pa rnam par dag pa'i 'od ces bya ba'i gzungs (Ārya Raśmivimalaviśuddhaprabhā nāma dhāraṇī)

Gyud, Narthang, Vol. NA; Derge, Vol. NA, Toh. 510; Zungdus, Derge, WAM, Toh. 982.

Tr = Vidyākarasiṁha, Dpal gyi lhun po'i sde

Re = Atiśa and 'brom ston.

'phags pa yongs su mya ngan las 'das pa chen po'i mdo (Ārya Mahāparinirvāṇa sūtra)

Dho. Derge, Vol. TA, Toh. 119

Tr = Wang phan shun, Dge ba'i blo gros and Rgya mtsho'i sde.

'phags pa lag na rdo rje dbang bskur ba'i rgyud chen po (Ārya Vajrāpaṇi-abhiṣeka-mahā-tantra)

Gyud, Derge, Vol. DA, Toh. 496.

Tr = Śilendrabodhi and Ye shes sde.

Shes pa thams cad mthar phyin par grub pa'i mchod rten zhes bya ba'i gzungs (Sarvaprajñāntapāramitāsiddha caitya nāma dhāraṇī)

Gyudbum, Narthang, Vol. NA; Derge, Vol. PHA, Toh. 601; Zungdus, Derge, Vol. E, Toh. 884.

Rab tu gnas pa mdor bsdus pa'i rgyud (Supratiṣtha-tantra-saṁgraha)

Kagyur, Gyudbum, Derge, Vol. TA, Toh. 486.

Tr = Jñānavajra, 'bro shes rab grags pa.

(II) Primary Sources (Tangyur Section)

Abhyākara Gupta

dkyil 'khor gyi cho ga rdo rje phreng ba zhes bya ba (Vajrāvali-nāma-maṇḍala-vidhi), Gyud, Derge, Vol. PHU, Toh. 3140.

Tr = Abhayākaragupta, 'khor lo grags

R[1] = Śes rab dpal

R[2] = Ratnarakṣita, Rāhulśribhadra and Chag chos rje dpal

R[3] = Blo rtan.

Anonymous

Mchod rten brgya rtsa brgyad bya ba, Gyud, Derge, Vol. PU, Toh. 3070.

Anonymous

Mchod rten dgu gdab pa'i cho ga, Gyud, Derge, Vol. PU, Toh. 3075.

Anonymous

Mchod rten lnga gdab pa'i cho ga, Gytud, Derge, Vol. PU, Toh. 3074.

Anonymous

Mchod rten gcig gdab pa'i cho ga, Gyud, Derge, Vol. PU, Toh. 3071.

Anonymous

Mchod rten gdab pa'i cho ga, Gyud, Derge, Vol. PU, Toh. 3076.

Anonymous

Mchod rten gnyis gdab pa'i cho ga, Gyud, Derge, Vol. PU, Toh. 3072.

Anonymous

Mchod rten gsum gdab pa'i cho ga, Gyud, Derge, Vol. PU, Toh. 3073.

Avadhūtī

Mchod rten sgrub pa'i cho ga mdor bsdus pa (Caitya sādhana vidhi piṇḍita), Gyud, Derge, Vol. CU, Toh. 2605.

Bodhisattva

'phags pa kun nas sgor 'jug pa'i 'od zer gtsug tor dri ma med par snang ba'i gzungs bklag cing mchod rten brgya rtsa brgyad dam mchod rten lnga gdab pa'i cho ga mdo sde las btus pa, Gyud, Derge, Vol. PU, Toh. 3069; Narthang, Vol. TU.

Dharmamitra (Chos kyi bshes gnyen)

'dul ba mdo'i rgya cher 'grel pa (Vinayasūtratika), Vinaya, Derge, Vol. U, Toh. 4120; Narthang, Vol. LU.

Tr = Jinamitra, Klu'i rgyal mtshan.

Dipaṅkara (Mar med mdzad ye shes)

Gtsug tor dri med kyi gzungs cho ga, Gyud, Derge, Vol. PU, Toh. 3081 and 3082.

Guṇaprabha

'dul ba mdo'i 'grel ba (Vinaya sūtravṛtti), Vinaya, Derge, Vol. LU, Toh. 4122.

Guṇaprabha

'dul ba mdo [rtsa ba] (Vinayasūtra), Dho, Narthang, Vol. ZU; Derge, Vol. WU, Toh. 4117.

Tr = Jinamitra, Klu'i rgyal mtshan.

Guṇaprabha

'dul ba mdo'i 'grel pa mngon par brjod pa rang gi rnam par bshad pa zhes bya ba (Vinaya-sūtra-vṛttyabhi-dhāna-sva vyākhyāna nāma), Vinaya, Derge, Vol. ZU, Toh. 4119.

Tr = Alamkaradeva, Ga rod tshul khrims 'byung gnas shas pa.

Lalitavajra

Mchod rten grub pa'i cho ga mdor bsdus (Caitya siddhi vidhipiṇḍikṛta), Gyud, Derge, Vol. MI, Toh. 1927; Narthang, Vol. PI.

Tr = 'gos Lhas btsas.

Nāgārjuna

Gnas chen po brgyad kyi mchod rten la bstod pa (Aṣṭamahāsthāna caityastotra), Todtsok, Derge, Vol. KA, Toh. 1133 and 1134; Narthang, Vol. KA.

Tr = Tilaka, Pa tshab Nyima grags.

Prajñākara

'dul ba mdo'i rnam par bshad pa (Vinaya sūtra vyākhayāna), Vinaya, Derge, Vol. RU, Toh. 4121; Narthang, Vol. SU.

Rigs kyis byin

Bya ba bsdus pa zhes bya ba (Kriyasaṁgṛaha-nāma), Gyud, Derge, Vol. KU, Toh. 2531.

Tr = Kīrticandra, Yarlungs pa Grags pa rgyal mtshan.

Sahajavilāsa

Kun nas sgor 'jug pa'i 'od zer gtsug tor dri ma med par snang ba de bzhin gshegs pa thams cad kyi snying po dang dam tshig la rnam par lta ba zhes bya ba'i gzungs kyi rnam par bshad pa (Samanta mukha praveśa raśmi vimaloṣṇīṣa prabhāsa sarva tathāgata hṛdaya samaya vilokita nāma dhāraṇīvṛtti), Gyud, Derge, Vol. THU, Toh. 2688; Narthang, CHU.

Tr = Jayadeva, Tshul khrims brtsegs

Śāntigarbha (Zhi ba'i snying po)

Mchod rten grub pa'i cho ga (Caityasādhana vidhi), Gyud, Derge, Vol. JU, Toh. 2652; Narthang, Vol. GU.

Śāntigarbha (Zhi ba'i snying po)

Mchod rten gyi cha dbye ba 'dul ba las 'byung ba'i mdo (Caitya vibhaṅga vinayoddhṛta sūtra), Gyud, Derge, Vol. PU, Toh. 3078; Narthang, Vol. TU.

Smṛtijñānakīrti

De kho na nyid drug rnam par gzhag pa (Sattattva vyava sthāna), Gyud, Derge, Vol. YA, Toh. 1621; Narthang, Vol. A.

Tr= Smṛtijñānakīrti.

Viśākhadeva or Sagadeva (Sa gā'i lha)

'dul ba tshig le'ur byas pa (Vinaya kārika), Vinaya, Narthang, Vol. HU; Derge, Vol. SHU, Toh. 4123.

Tr = Jayākara, Prajñākīrti

Re =Rong ston shes bya kun rig.

Secondary Sources

Bodong Panchen Choglas Namgyal (Bo dong pan chen phyogs las rnam rgyal)

rten gsum bzheng tshul bstan bcos lugs bshad pa bzhugs so, Collected Works of Bodong, Vol. KHA (2), Ed. by S.T. Kazi, Repd. by Tibet House, New Delhi, 1969.

Buston Rinchendup (Buston rin chen grub)

byang chub chen po'i mchod rten gyi tshad bzhugs so, Collected Works of Buston, Vol. PHA (14), Ed. by Dr. Lokesh Chandra, Pub. by IAIC, New Delhi, 1969.

Buston Rinchen Dup (Bu ston rin chen grup)

dpal dus kyi'khor lo'i cho ga yon tan kun 'byung, Collected Works of Buston, Vol. CA (5), Ed. by Dr. Lokesh Chandra, Pub. by IAIC, New Delhi,1969.

Chenga Lodos Gyaltsen Pal Sangpo (sPyen lnga blo gros rgyal mtshan dpal bzang po) *mchod rten gyi tshad ston pa legs bshad gser gyi phreng ba,* Vol. CA.

Desid Sangyas Gyatso (sde srid sang rgyas rgya mtsho circa 1653-1705 A.D.)

Vaidurya dkar po las 'phros pa'i snyen sgron dang dri len gy.a' sel bzhugs so, Vol. 2, Rpd. from original texts from the collection of Tsepon W. D. Shakapa by Tsepal Taikhang, New Delhi, 1971.

Francke, A. H.

Antiquities of Indian Tibet, Part I, Pub. by S. Chand and Co. (Pvt.) Ltd., New Delhi.

Jackson, David P. and Janice A.

Tibetan Thangka Painting: Methods and Materials, Sarinda Publications, London, 1984.

Jamyang Zhaypa Ngawang Dorjee ('jams dbyangs bzhad pa'i ngag dbang rdo rje circa 1648-1721 A.D.)

mchod rten brgyad kyi thig rtsa mdor bsdus, Collected Works of Jamyang Zhaypa, Vol. 1, New Delhi, 1974.

Jan Pieper

Stūpa Architecture of the Upper Indus Valley, Anna Libera Dallapiccola (ed. et al.), The Stupa: Its Religious, Historical and Architectural Significance, Franz Steiner Verlag, Weisbaden, 1980.

Je Tsong Khapa Lobsang Dakpa (rje tsong kha pa blo bzang grags pa)

lam gyi rim pa gsang ba kun gi gnad rnam par phye ba sngags rim chen po, Collected Works of Je Tsong Khapa, Vol. GA.

Khenchen Ngawang Chodak

Sdom gsum kha skong gi rnam par bshad pa legs shad rgyan gyi me tog, Ven. T. G. Dhongthog Rinpoche (Ed. and Pub.), New Delhi, 1978.

Kongtul Karma Ngawang Yontan Gyatso (Kong sprul karma ngag dbang yon tan rgya mtsho)

shes bya kun khyab mdzod, Vol. E(1).

Kunkhen Pema Karpo (Kun mkhyen pad ma dkar po circa 1527-29 A.D.)

mchod rten brgyad kyi thig rtsa bzhugs so, Vol. 1, Rpd. from the Gnam 'brug se ba byang chub gling blocks by Kargyud Sungrab Nyamso Khang, Darjeeling, W.B., 1973.

Lodos Sangpo (Blo gros bzang po)

bde bar gshegs pa'i sku gzugs kyi tshad kyi rab tu byed pa yid bzhin nor bu, See Indo-Tibetica I, English Translation.

Minling Lochen Dharmasri (smin gling blo chen dharmasri)

dri med rnam gnyis kyi gzungs la brten te mchod rten bzhengs pa la nye bar mkho ba'i cho ga bklags pas grub pa, Collected Works of Minling, Vol. PA (XIII), Pub. by Ven. D. G. Khochhen Tulku, Nyingmapa Lama'i College, Clement Town, Dehra Dun, 1976.

Namkha Sengye (Nam mkha seng ge)

mchod rten gyi rnam bzhag phan bde'i gsos gyur ces bya ba zhugs so, Vol. CHA (2), Gedan Sungrab Minyam Gyunphel Series, Pub. by Ngawang Gelek Demo, New Delhi, 1982.

Phrengkhaba Lodos Sangpo (Phreng kha pa blo gros bzang po circa 16th centruy A.D.)

Bzo rig pa'i bstan bcos mdo rgyud gsal ba'i me long.

Rongtha Lobsang Damchos Gyatso (Rong tha Blo bzang dam chos rgya mtsho)

Thig gi lag len du ma gsal bar bshad par bzo rig mdzes pa'i kha rgyen zhes bya ba bzhugs so

Sumpa Khenpo Yeshes Paljor (Sum pa khen po ye shes dpal 'byor)

sku gsung thugs rten gyi thig rtsa mchan 'grel can me tog 'phrin mdzes zhes bya ba, Collected Works of Sumpa Khenpo, Vol. NGA (IV), Rpd. by Dr. Lokesh Chandra, IAIC, New Delhi, 1979.

Sumpa Khenpo Yeshes Paljor (Sum pa khen po ye shes dpal 'byor)

sku gsung thugs rten rab gnas bya tshul rgyas 'bring bdus pa'i lag len cha lag dang bcas pa dge legs byin zhes bya ba, Collected Works of Sumpa Khenpo, Vol. NGA (IV), Rpd. by Dr. Lokesh

Chandra, IAIC, New Delhi, 1979.

Sumpa Khenpo Yeshes Paljor (Sum pa khen po ye shes dpal 'byor) *sa brtag blang ba spyad pa bum gter dang bcas pa'i lag len mdor bsdus utpal tshun bu,* Collected Works of Sumpa Khenpo, Vol. NGA (IV), Rpd. by Dr. Lokesh Chandra, IAIC, New Delhi, 1979.

Thupten Legshay Gyatso
The Gateway of the Temple: Manual of Tibetan Monastic Customs, Jackson, David P. (Tr.), Pub. by Ratna Pustak Bhandar, Nepal, 1979.

Tucci, Giuseppe
Stupa : Art, Architectonics and Symbolism (Indo-Tibetica I), Dr. Lokesh Chandra (ed.), Uma Marina Veski (Tr.), Aditya Publication, New Delhi, 1988.

Zhuchen Tsultim Rinchen
Gzungs 'bul gyi lag len nyung gsal bzhugs so, Collected Writings of Zuchen Tsultim Rinchen, Vol. CA (3), Rpd. from the Ven. Luding Rinpoche's Examples of Sde dge edition of the Gsung 'bum by ca Jamyang Norbu, New Dehi, 1973.

Dri med rnam gyis kyi mchod rten dkyil 'khor du bzhug pa'i cho ga dang mchod rten gyi thig yig, Nyingma Kama Gyaspa, Vol. 2 (KHA), Pub. by Dupjung Lama, Kalimpong, West Bengal, 1982.

Dri med rnam gnyis kyi mchod rten bzhengs bskabs nyer mkho'i zin bris gzhan phan zla snang, Nyingma Kama Gyaspa, Vol. 2 (KHA), Pub. by Dupjung Lama, Kalimpong, West Bengal, 1982.

Ten suttas from Dīgha Nikāya, Bibliotheca Indo-Tibetica Series No. XII, Rpt., of Burma Pitaka Association Publication, Pub. by Central Institute of Higher Tibetan Studies, Varanasi, 1987.

Journals

Hajime Nakamura, The *Aṣṭamahāsthānacaityastotra* and the Tibetan versions of a text similar to it, Indianisme Et Bouddhisme, Me'langes offers a' Mgr E'tienne Lamotte, Universite Catholique De Louvan Institut Orientaliste, Louvain-La-Neuve, 1980.

Sharpa Tulku and Michael Perrott (Tr. and Prep). "The Ritual of

Consecration'' *Tibet Journal,* Library of Tibetan Works and Archives, Vol. X, 1985.

Dictionaries

Chandra, Lokesh, *Tibetan-Sanskrit Dictionary* (Rpt.), Rinsen Book Co., Kyoto, 1982.

Das, Sarat Chandra, *A Tibetan-English Dictionary* (Rpt.), Gaurav Publishing House, New Delhi, 1985.

Krang dbyi sun, *Bod rgya tshig mdzod chen mo, Mi rigs dpe skrun kang,* 1984.

Tsepak Rigzin, *Tibetan-English Dictionary of Buddhist Terminology*, LTWA, Dharamsala, 1986.

Index